Lost and Found

In *Lost and Found*, Dr. D'Souza has diagnosed the most significant problems currently plaguing individuals and our society. He prescribes simple, well-founded approaches to bolster our sense of meaning, and, in turn, make life worth living.

—**Gregory H. Borschel, MD,** James Joseph Harbaugh, Jr. Professor of Surgery,
Indiana University and Chief of Plastic Surgery,
Riley Children's Hospital, Indianapolis, Indiana, USA

Lost and Found is a jewel of a thought-provoking and elegantly written book with which we may or may not entirely agree. I call it a piece of art, which is deep and clever yet a pure joy to read. Although I read it in one sitting, the beauty of Dr. D'Souza's book is that each of its chapters stands on its own, despite his underlying key takeaway message. The latter made me think of philosophers across history, society, science, complex social and health problems, like intellectual intolerance or drug addiction, with practical, educational, and therapeutic solutions. It is an invitation to learn by thinking of people and especially of oneself. As the title of the book indicates, and as highlighted by psychiatrist and writer Dr. Victor Frankl, sometimes you must lose yourself in order to better find yourself. Thank you, Dr. D'Souza for reminding us of the importance of and hope through meaning in one's life!

–**Rima Azar, PhD**, Associate Professor of Health Psychology,
Psychobiology of Stress & Health Lab
Psychology Department, Mount Allison University
Sackville, New Brunswick, Canada

LOST AND FOUND

How Meaningless Living is Destroying Us and Three Keys to Fix It

Mark D'Souza, MD

NEW YORK

LONDON • NASHVILLE • MELBOURNE • VANCOUVER

Lost and Found

How Meaningless Living is Destroying Us and Three Keys to Fix It

Published in New York, New York, by Morgan James Publishing. Morgan James is a trademark of Morgan James, LLC. www.MorganJamesPublishing.com

Proudly distributed by Publishers Group West®

A **FREE** ebook edition is available for you or a friend with the purchase of this print book.

CLEARLY SIGN YOUR NAME ABOVE

Instructions to claim your free ebook edition:

1. Visit MorganJamesBOGO.com
2. Sign your name CLEARLY in the space above
3. Complete the form and submit a photo of this entire page
4. You or your friend can download the ebook to your preferred device

ISBN 9781636983837 paperback
ISBN 9781636983844 ebook
Library of Congress Control Number: 20239500229

Cover Design by:
Chris Treccani
www.3dogcreative.net

Interior Design by:
Christopher Kirk
www.GFSstudio.com

Morgan James is a proud partner of Habitat for Humanity Peninsula and Greater Williamsburg. Partners in building since 2006.

Get involved today! Visit: www.morgan-james-publishing.com/giving-back

Dedicated to my incredible wife, Natalie, and our loving dog, Luna. You are my dreams that came true, and without you, this book, another mere fantasy, would have never been realized.

TABLE OF CONTENTS

ACKNOWLEDGMENTS

The journey of writing and publishing a book is seldom traveled alone, and I have been fortunate to have the companionship and expertise of many along this adventure.

First and foremost, my deepest gratitude goes to my ever-supportive wife, Natalie D'Souza, who has been a constant source of encouragement and a pillar of strength every step of the way. Your belief in this endeavor has been my driving force.

I extend heartfelt appreciation to my meticulous developmental editor, Melissa Wuske, whose insights and suggestions significantly enriched the narrative. Your expertise was invaluable and helped shape the manuscript into its final form.

A huge thank you to Jessica Filippi, my proficient copyeditor, for the keen eye and dedication in polishing the text, ensuring clarity and precision in every sentence. Your attention to detail brought a high level of excellence to this book.

Many thanks are also due to Catherine Turner, my exceptional proofreader, who diligently and expertly refined the manuscript. Your exhaustive commitment to every last letter and punctuation mark has significantly enhanced the book's precision and fluidity.

I am immensely thankful to Terry Whalin, my acquisitions editor, for seeing the potential in this work. Your foresight and confidence in my ideas have been fundamental to the delivery of this project.

I am deeply grateful to Gayle West, my author relations manager, for her crucial role. The journey from a nearly complete manuscript to a published book is deceptively long, and you have carefully guided me every step of the way to finally bring this vision to fruition.

A special acknowledgment goes to Morgan James Publishing, for their belief in this project and for providing the platform for its publication. Your professionalism and support have made this journey a rewarding experience.

Profound thanks are directed to my parents, mother-in-law, and brother. Without your inspiration, this book truly would not be possible.

Lastly, I am indebted to the great thinkers, past and present, from Socrates to Jordan Peterson, and everyone in between. My work stands on the shoulders of giants. Their relentless pursuit of truth, expression of courage in the face of adversity, and unyielding service to the cultivation of a discerning society have laid the foundations upon which I dare to tread. Their legacy is a constant reminder of the potential that resides within every endeavor to unravel the complex tapestry of human existence.

With a heart full of gratitude, I share this work, hoping to contribute, even if minutely, to the endless dialogue that propels humanity forward.

Introduction:

THE STATE OF THE WORLD

Things Have Never Been Better

One could easily argue that these are the best of times; that things have never been better. Since 1800, around the start of the Industrial Revolution, there has been an explosion in wealth. Gross Domestic Product (GDP) barely grew from AD 1 to 1800 before skyrocketing. In 1900, the average person lived on $1.90/day in today's money (Hasell and Roser 2019).

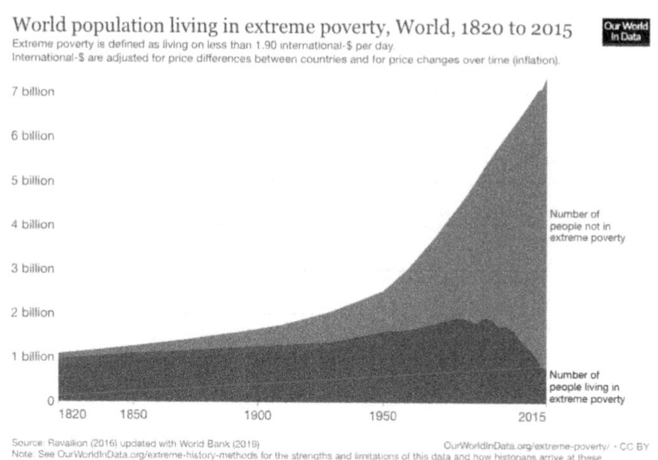

Hasell and Roser (2019) created this graph based on information compiled from the following sources: Ravallion (2016), Bourguignon and Morrison (2002), and World Bank (2019). Image courtesy of Hasell and Roser (2019), Creative Commons License CC BY 4.0: https://creativecommons.org/licenses/by/4.0/.

The difference between now and then is the rise of capitalism. No economic system is impervious to exploitation, but world-renowned psychologist and author Jordan Peterson says this of capitalism: "Although it produces inequality, it also produces wealth, and all the other systems don't, they just produce inequality" (Peterson and Zizek 2019). The rich are getting richer, but what about the poor? Every day from 1990 to 2015, 128,223 people were lifted out of poverty (Roser and Ortiz-Ospina 2019a). This kind of progress isn't often featured in today's news.

With the growth of capitalism and the decline of Communist economies following the fall of the Soviet Union, global wealth has seen a significant increase. This shift reflects a growing understanding among countries of the perils associated with excessive central planning.

One of the UN millennial goals set in 2000 was to reduce the rate of absolute poverty in the world by 50 percent by 2015. Poverty is defined as $1.90/day in American dollars. We beat that deadline by three years (UN News 2012), and higher targets of poverty fell at the same rate.

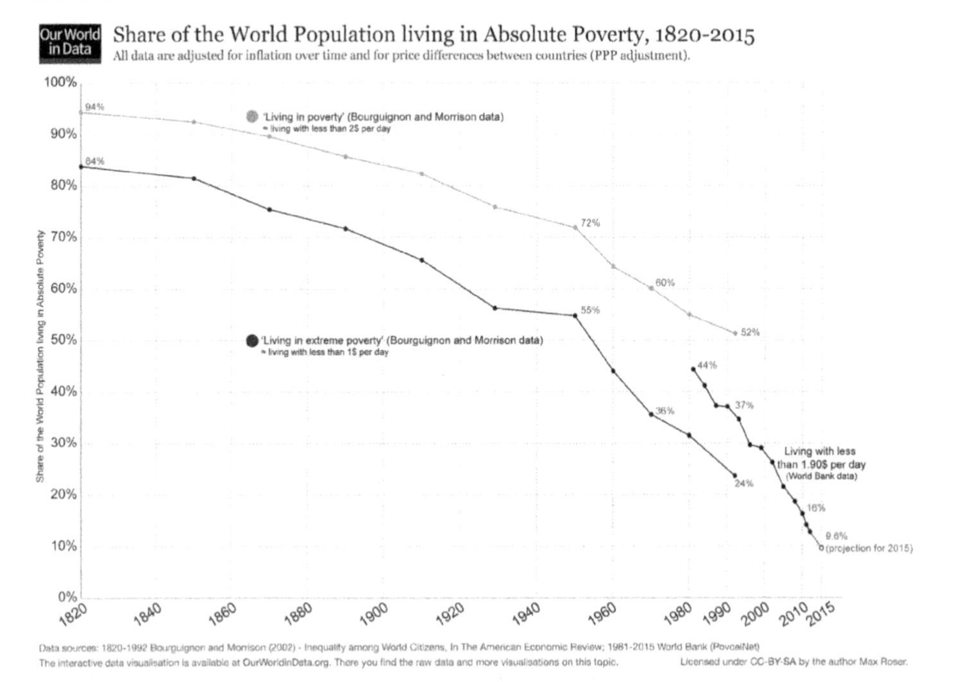

Roser and Ortiz-Ospina (2019b) created this graph based on information compiled from the following sources: Bourguignon and Morrison (2002) and World Bank (2019). Image courtesy of Roser and Ortiz-Ospina (2019b), Creative Commons License CC BY-SA 4.0: https://creativecommons.org/licenses/by-sa/4.0/.

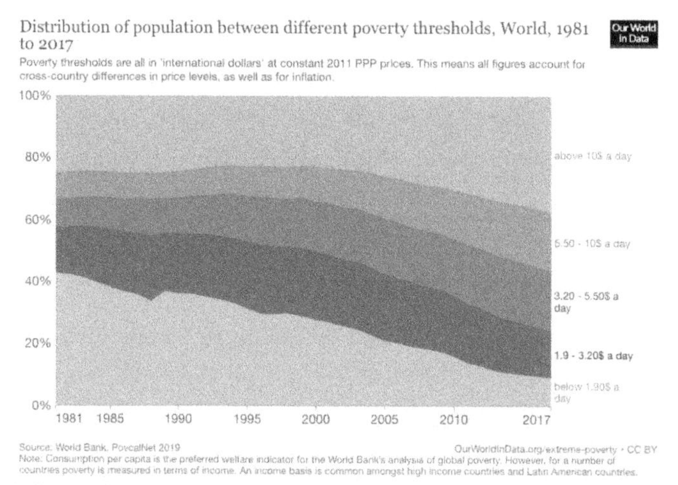

Roser and Ortiz-Ospina (2021) created this graph based on information compiled from the following sources: Bourguignon and Morrison (2002) and World Bank (2019). Image courtesy of Roser and Ortiz-Ospina (2021), Creative Commons License CC BY 4.0: https://creativecommons.org/licenses/by/4.0/.

The UN estimates that all people will be out of absolute poverty by 2030. Already developed nations have robust safety nets for the poorest. They don't provide much compared to what is available to people of median wealth, but the social safety nets of fifty, one hundred, or one thousand years ago didn't include free healthcare, shelters, and food banks.

Wealth is not a zero-sum game. Just because someone gains wealth doesn't mean someone else must lose it. Its overall quantity can grow. Wealth can also trickle down from the wealthiest to the poorest. There is, of course, unjust inequality when people cheat—but there's also inequality achieved justly, when people get ahead with hard work and skill. The only way to be completely equal in outcome is for us all to be on the bottom of the distribution. As nineteenth-century philosopher Alexis de Tocqueville is often credited with warning, some are so enamored of equality that they would rather be equal in slavery than unequal in freedom. Not everyone can have the first marked-up iPhone, the buyers of which subsidize the hefty development cost. If we didn't have business-class flights, which effectively act as subsidies, economy-class fees would increase. In a forcibly equal world, we would have limited technological progress, as there would be no incentive to innovate. But in our current meritocratic system that rewards innovation, standards of living for everyone improve. While it's a disproportionate improvement for the wealthy, it's still an improvement for everyone.

Some worry that the world cannot afford to have more people—that the population is too large—but every additional person born on the planet has made things cheaper for us. For example, as the population of the world has increased by 70 percent, the price of natural resources has declined by 70 percent. Counterintuitively, more people means more wealth (J. Peterson and Tupy 2021).[1]

While the world is still far from perfect, in a material sense, things have truly never been better.

Things Have Never Been Worse

But it is also the worst of times. Despite our riches, depression is a leading cause of disability worldwide according to the World Health Organization (WHO) (WHO n.d.). Luxuries such as central heating, Netflix, and antibiotics are widely available—things not even royalty had a thousand years ago. Yet people have never been so miserable and unfulfilled.

Today is an on-demand era. People believe—perhaps unconsciously—that no one should be uncomfortable for any length of time and that there are products to alleviate all discomfort. I call it "magic pill syndrome": a cultural phenomenon whereby there's a singular cure for all that ails you.

Examples of literal or metaphorical magic pills include CBD (a form of cannabis), marketed as treatment for an ever-multiplying number of diseases with little evidence (Allan et al. 2018; Busse et al. 2021; Kahan, Srivastava, and Clarke 2019), or solar and wind power, the panacea for climate change. The entire fitness and supplement industry is predicated on this notion. Marketers take full advantage of the fact that nutritional supplements are not regulated with the same scrutiny as pharmaceuticals by the Food and Drug Administration (FDA), even though many contain ingredients with biological effects (FDA 2021). They use black truths like "natural," "organic," "holistic," and "integrated" to sell their products to people eager for solutions. This is the shadow side of capitalism.

World-famous motivational speaker Tony Robbins puts it well: "We are driven to suffering. If you don't have physical pain, you create emotional pain. If you have neither, you create existential pain" (Robbins 2016). One of his deeper principles is that our society has created a culture of expectation to replace one of appreciation. People are rarely grateful for how good they have it. To a certain extent, this is understandable. People are wired biologically not to notice their emotional responses if everything is going too well. People are programmed to pay attention to the things that aren't working. This is partly because it's not efficient to constantly be grateful for things that are predictable, as it takes too much mental energy (J. Peterson and Murray

2021). A singular focus on gratitude is not balanced either. People need balance to create perspective.

But suffering rather than balance prevails, despite people's best efforts. Later in the book we'll look more at how Kierkegaard and Dostoevsky theorized that humans need purpose and a mission to thrive. But without these, people don't just wither away; we self-harm proportionally to the degree we are aimless.

We are miserable, in immense pain, and spiritually bankrupt.

Seeing the Way Through

In my medical career, particularly in the fields of addiction and chronic pain, I see people with existential angst to varying degrees. A good proportion of physical chronic pain is magnified by how much the person is suffering emotionally, though no study could ever quantify this. When people say "my back hurts," it often means "my life hurts," though they seldom recognize the connection. There is a spectrum of varying degree to which existential suffering manifests as physical pain and a corresponding degree to which people numb themselves with harmful things. But at the far end of the spectrum of self-harm from having no purpose is IV opioids. Heroin used to be the main opioid of abuse, but that later changed to the more powerful opioid fentanyl, and now the even more potent carfentanyl (used clinically in animals only). This crisis is worsening. I propose that the opioid crisis is driven by society sinking deeper and deeper into nihilism, the belief that life is meaningless.

But people don't have to be wrestling with addiction to feel the deep effects of our descent into meaninglessness. Opioids are at the extreme end of the numbing behaviors we use to avoid pain, but for many people, the search for meaning leads us to seemingly more benign interests and affiliations, which I call replacement religions. We'll explore some of those in part 2 of the book, but first, in part 1, we'll look at the historical and ideological shifts that have led to the dire situation we're in. Finally, in part 3, we'll look at the keys to getting ourselves back on track. While it won't be easy to reverse course, there are key ideas that people and society can implement to restore the greatness of humanity, which is the key to stopping the damage we're doing to ourselves, including the opioid epidemic.

While the problem is deep, there's no need for despair. Delving into understanding how we got here and the many faces of nihilism will shed light on the keys to moving toward a new future—back where we belong.

Notes on Viewpoint

First, while society faces problems that take many forms, my profession as a physician specializing in addiction gives me a unique vantage point on the depth and destruction that these problems cause. Throughout the book, I'll share my experience—but don't think that just because you or your community aren't entrenched in addiction that you've escaped the harm of nihilism. It takes many forms, as we'll see throughout the book, particularly in part 2.

Second, even though this book has highlighted the flaws of the radical left, much of it applies to the radical right, who are also enthralled in ideology, thought suppression, and the idea that the ends justify the means. The book's focus on the radical left is, however, because they hold the levers of power in the West. They are culturally dominant despite being only 6–8 percent of the population (Pew Research Center 2021; S. Hawkins, Míriam, and Dixon 2018). According to a 2023 Angus Reid poll, which categorized Canadians across the political spectrum, over half of respondents in all categories except the most left-leaning admitted to self-censoring at least weekly (Angus Reid Institute 2023). This suggests that if you find yourself holding your tongue, you likely do not align with the views of the elite, whereas those who can speak freely are probably in the most left-leaning demographic. The mainstream (and legacy) media is predominantly left-leaning, as is Big Tech. People lose their jobs for having right-leaning views, not left-leaning ones. Further, the radical left has control of language; hence, it is the bigger threat. Ideally we can all be centrists, believing in free speech to sort out our differences, although peace and prosperity is a far less compelling story to sell than righteous discrimination from the political extremes.[2]

Third, since I come from a Christian background, I am not deeply familiar with other traditional faiths. Nonetheless, I believe that they likely offer a similar package of essential benefits found only in traditional systems of meaning.

PART 1:
How We Got Here

Chapter 1:
THE DEATH OF GOD

Belief in God, in something greater than us, has declined steadily over the last two hundred years. This is not surprising, given the great technological progress we have made with our own hands. Besides noting this trajectory, various philosophers have commented on the negative consequences of this change in societal bedrock. While there's disagreement on how this will play out, it is clear that without God, people will look for something else to be their guiding light.

Nietzsche's Great Proclamation

In 1882, Friedrich Nietzsche proclaimed, "God is dead. God remains dead. And we have killed him. How shall we comfort ourselves, the murderers of all murderers? What was holiest and mightiest of all that the world has yet owned has bled to death under our knives: who will wipe this blood off us? What water is there for us to clean ourselves?" (1882).

All prophets speak in some sort of code. Nietzsche's parable of the madman is no different. Nietzsche had witnessed the Industrial Revolution in full force. Science, objectivism, rationalism, and empiricism had taken primacy in people's lives. People could witness with their own senses the amazing inventions of humanity. More than ever before, the world looked very different from the time a person was born to the time they died.

Before the Industrial Revolution, this pace of technological progress did not exist. Worship of an ineffable, superordinate principle—in the West, codified as God—allowed one to live without needing to question the multitude of inexplicable events in one's life such as natural disasters, suffering, which direction the sun rises, and so on. Many people accepted the way things were as God's will. But by Nietzsche's time, the engine of technological evolution had accelerated in an unstoppable manner. In the face of seemingly limitless human ingenuity, people began to question what had seldom been questioned: If humans could explain all these phenomena and create all of these things, then was the concept of God made up to ease the suffering of not understanding—and has the concept outlived its usefulness?

Nietzsche believed that the collapse of the Judeo-Christian structure would be absolutely catastrophic for the West. If people no longer believed that God gives meaning and purpose to their lives—and even to their suffering—he worried that society would slide deeper into nihilism, lacking strong, positive goals. Describing the bloody murder of God by human hands was Nietzsche's way of prophesizing the downstream consequence of people's abandonment of God: millions of deaths. World wars and mass murders under ideological umbrellas in the twentieth century and beyond showed the truth of his prediction.

Nietzsche's great proclamation was a cultural observation that our idea of God was no longer strong enough to serve as the foundation for truth and morality. We've lost our anchor to a common understanding of reality and hierarchy of values. Further, the transcendent morality that underlined Western culture collapsed. This could be interpreted as a set of dogmatic beliefs (e.g., as simple as the Ten Commandments). Now we could do whatever we wanted.

Put another way, life cannot be meaningful without the concept of God at the highest and most abstract levels. Life has proximal meanings such as family, career, and hobbies. Some meanings are deeper than others, but there is definitely a hierarchy. And something undefinable used to be at the top, the value around which all other values were organized.[3] Alternatively, this ultimate principle at the pinnacle of our value hierarchy could be seen as the enduring legacy of human experience, a collective insight transcending individual existence and extending through time.

I believe that the death of God is a dynamic process that has deepened over the decades. World events cause it to go forward and backward. For example, global events such as the Cold War may have pushed the process back slightly as the West sought refuge in its unifying structure again. But the biggest driver of our sojourn into nihilism is technological change. The experience of people in any given location did not greatly change between AD 100 and AD 200 or between 1400 and 1500. But someone from 1900 transported to the year 2000 would be paralyzed by the shock of all the magical things we can do. Into the twenty-first century, our rate of technological change has become a near vertical slope.

The expansion of human magic—human abilities and their preeminence—only deepens the knife into God's wound, reaffirming that he is dead.

"What festivals of atonement, what sacred games shall we have to invent . . . Must we ourselves not become gods simply to appear worthy of it?" continued Nietzsche in his 1882 seminal revelation. The collapse of the West's highest unifying value left a black hole. I use the term black hole because meaning (or values or goals) abhors a vacuum, and the void will suck in something else to fill it whether people want to or not. People can't existentially have no values (see the section on Bazarov in chapter 2). In a sense, people have to become their own deities—their own supreme value—or they must place something else other than God on the top rung. They invent their own values or succumb to an ideology (e.g., communism or fascism).

Humans without God

In the absence of God, in 1883 Nietzsche foretold the coming of the superman, or, literally translated from German (Übermensch) "over-man." In a world without a default metaphysical principle, the superman is the person who creates his own values and meaning rather than becoming nihilistic. He is free from any outside influence or prejudice. Regular people need to put their faith in something, be it God, science, or another replacement religion. The superman, however, puts all his faith in himself, relying on nothing else. This next-level man is an over-man because he has overcome himself: his own whims, influences, and biological nature. I believe the superman is someone who has their own moral code and acts according to their will, completely impervious to any life experience or outside influence. Before Nietzsche could further develop this concept of creating one's own values, he became mad and died.

Carl Jung tried to answer Nietzsche's psychological question of the death of God. To him, each person's god was whatever resided at the top of their moral hierarchy. Their god was what they believed most deeply in, which was revealed by their acts, not their words (J. Peterson 2018). Jung disagreed with Nietzsche's idea of the superman, saying that people can't simply invent their values and impose them on their actions (J. Peterson 2017a).

Jung's idea plays out rather sensibly. People can supersede their biological drives, but they can only do so to a limited extent. How successful are New Year's resolutions? Why does the snooze button exist on the alarm clock? Why do many addicts say they're going to quit but are completely unable to do so? A person might believe they can fly, but they will hit the pavement known as reality. People can't act as if they are the fundamental source of their own values independent of some more deeply held (usually unconscious) belief (J. Peterson 2019a).

Rodion Raskolnikov in Fyodor Dostoevsky's *Crime and Punishment* puts the superman idea to the test. This novel was published in 1866, so it is not a chronological retort to Nietzsche's idea; it's evidence that these great minds were grappling with the same profound questions (J. Peterson 2019a). Raskolnikov commits the perfect murder, rationally justified by reasoning out how many people will benefit from the death of an old pawn broker who contributed nothing good to the world. He believed that money could liberate him from poverty and then he could help many others. He carries this rationale out to its completion, along with the axiom *exitus acta probat*, the ends justify the means. By shunning transcendent morality, Raskolnikov believes at first that he has overcome the moral failings of human nature and Judeo-Christian rules. But by the end of the novel, he finds himself mentally wrecked. Rife with guilt, his justifications no longer uphold him psychologically. In the spirit of "the truth shall set you free," Raskolnikov ultimately confesses and is sent to jail (Dostoevsky [1866] 2019). In the matter of whether or not you can create your own values, Dostoevsky clearly sides with Jung: Nietzsche's superman idea is not viable.[4]

Jordan Peterson calls those in the mold of Raskolnikov "solipsistic identitarians" and posits that they are technically two-year-olds:

> Two-year-olds are very governed by emotions, completely incapable of negotiation, egotistical in that their worldview dominates, they have no notion whatsoever of negotiated play, and their belief is their identity is 100 percent generated by them dependent on what they feel moment-to-moment . . . so generate your own values, what . . . are you going to do with your wife or your husband or your friend? They're just going to live by your values all of a sudden? (J. Peterson and Pageau 2022)

So you can kill God, but it doesn't rectify the hunger for a highest, orienting principle. The black hole–like vacuum will fill up with something. But what?

Chapter 2: THE RISE OF NIHILISM AND RATIONALITY

Nihilism is the void, the belief in nothing that occurs once faith in the transcendent collapses. Reason itself is always part of this void, the idea that all there is to be known can be reasoned out, that you can be the highest source of knowledge. Dostoevsky explores the consequences of the death of God in his literary works, and his findings are depressing; he uncovers a natural link between this belief in nothing, atheism, and poor mental health.

Bazarov, the Prototypical Nihilist

Yevgeny Bazarov is a most fascinating character in Ivan Turgenev's *Fathers and Sons*, published in 1862. He is a young medical student who believes in absolutely nothing; he is a nihilist. He believes in not believing in anything, least of all in tradition. His goal is the teardown of society. "We break things down because we are a force," he says. His friend's father counters, "One must construct too!" Yet Bazarov replies, "That is not our affair, the ground must be cleared first." Bazarov was the world's first social justice warrior, which is someone who justifies tearing down, even by violent means, for a cause they deem moral and virtuous.

Bazarov finds fault with everything—every value, authority, music, emotion, and principle—and wants to destroy it all. To him, there is room only for rationalism. He even ridicules love, calling it an "unforgivable stupidity." The problem is, he develops a love interest himself, committing a performative contradiction. His love interest ironically likes him in part because he "has the courage not to believe in anything." Yet, he lacked the ability to leave her. One day, the man who believes in nothing declares his love. "He was gasping; his whole body was visibly trembling . . . It was passion struggling inside him, strong and tragic" (Turgenev [1862] 2008).

To be a pure nihilist, the ultimate conclusion is self-destruction. When you have torn everything down, there is nothing left but to turn inward and destroy yourself. Bazarov's last effort to prove his adherence to nihilism is in not taking any precautions while performing an autopsy, which causes him to catch typhoid fever. Yet he ends up betraying his nihilism, asking for his love interest to come see him, and telling her how beautiful she is before he dies.

Through the character of Bazarov, Turgenev shows that nihilism is against human nature and leads to a diminished desire to live. *Fathers and Sons* foreshadowed the nihilistic forces that would rip apart Russia decades later when a movement of nihilists started the Russian Revolution in 1917.

For us today, his story embodies the limits of nihilism, the ultimate fallibility of rationalism.

Nihilism

Nihilism is the belief in nothing, that life is meaningless. The root is the Latin word *nihil*, which means "nothing." The word was used sparsely for centuries, then popularized in Turgenev's *Fathers and Sons* ("Nihilism" n.d.). Nihilism is darkness. There is no objective truth, morality, values, or purpose. Taken to its rational conclusion, the ultimate expression of nihilism is that it would be better if being never existed at all.

While this can certainly seem sad or depressing, belief in nihilism is also understandable in our modern culture. Life has never been so materially easy yet spiritually empty. What is the point of it all?

Jordan Peterson calls this Mephistophelean philosophy, inspired by the character Mephistopheles from German folklore (J. Peterson 2017c). Mephistopheles is best captured in *Faust* by poet Johann Wolfgang von Goethe. In this story, Mephistopheles is the devil, and perhaps best encapsulates in all of literature the argument against existence itself: "I am the spirit that negates. And rightly so, for all that comes to be deserves to perish wretchedly; 'twere better nothing would begin. Thus everything that your terms, sin, destruction, evil represent—that is my proper element" (Goethe [1832] 1963).

The spirit of Mephistopheles exists in all of us. We all have moments when life seems pointless, when darkness seems poised to swallow everything. Do you pay attention to this spirit in you? How do you respond to it? Consider daily life, like when someone cuts you off in traffic, and larger situations, like the loss of a job or loved one.

The question is not so much whether darkness exists, but the degree to which it overtakes the light, and the degree to which people make it the center of their lives. Following our darker impulses often seems to be the path of least resistance. Living selfishly is easier than putting others first. And being honest and truthful is far more challenging than having a low threshold to lie.

Rationality

Rationality is the flip side of the coin of nihilism. "I don't believe in anything; there is no source of wisdom higher than me. So I reason things out for myself." There were warnings about the dangers of making rationality supreme in the centuries leading up to the death of God.

In John Milton's *Paradise Lost* (published in 1667), he tells the story of Adam and Eve being tempted by the fallen angel, Satan. Jordan Peterson surmises that Satan represents the spirit of rationality, the intellect. In this great work, Peterson believes that Milton predicts the rise of totalitarianism, born out of the capacity for the intellect to fall in love with itself and then blot out any other influences. This is to say, "What I know is everything that needs to be known, and if it were only manifest in the world, the world would become a Utopia." It is a retelling of the biblical Tower of Babel story (J. Peterson 2017c). Satan believed that everything he knew was sufficient and he could do without the transcendent, without anything greater. Peterson believes that Milton hints that this reason to the exclusion of everything else would produce totalizing systems, then they would immediately turn everything they touched into something indistinguishable from hell. This is what the rational mind produces when it worships itself as if it's absolute (J. Peterson 2017d).

A century after Milton, German philosopher Immanuel Kant took rationalism to the next level. Fellow German Heinrich Heine, a poet, said that Kant was far more deadly than Robespierre, because whereas Robespierre simply decapitated a king, Kant decapitated God (Biggar, Orr, and Peterson 2021). Theologian James Orr believes that Kant's *Critique of Pure Reason* was a critique of reason's tendency to always overreach itself beyond what could possibly be given in experience. But Kant's impact was also the turn to the self and the primacy of reason. Jordan Peterson echoes Heine's quote, that Kant is the Enlightenment figure who elevated reason to the position that God once occupied (Biggar, Orr, and Peterson 2021).

In the same manner as the rationalism of the Enlightenment, now scientism is the view that science is the best or only objective means by which we get knowledge and that empiricism constitutes the most authoritative worldview. Marxism is a great example of rationality taken to its extreme, as Milton predicted. *The Communist Manifesto* is a thought experiment. Authors Karl Marx and Friedrich Engels (1848) designed a totalizing system a priori that would fix the world's problems. But when their principles have been taken to their logical end points, every single instance has produced mass murders. Fascism is no better, and Hitler's totalizing principles are codified in *Mein Kampf*.[5]

You can't be against rational, logical dialogue. This is an adult form of communication and is necessary for highly useful discussions. However, it's crucial that rationality serves us, not the other way around. The idea that reason is all that's necessary in life, that it will produce a solution to all of life's problems, and that it will usher in the Utopia leads only to tyranny, suffering, and ultimately a form of hell—not heaven—on Earth. I believe this is what's meant by the saying, "The fear of the LORD is the beginning of wisdom" (Proverbs 9:10). You can't solve all problems through calculation. In fact, the more complex the problem, the less likely some leader or government can solve it with logic.

The Unholy Trinity of Nihilism, Atheism, and Depression

I believe there is a link between nihilism, atheism, and depression. This connection is illustrated extremely well in Dostoevsky's *Demons* (published in 1872) through a number of characters.

The main character, Nikolai Stavrogin, is "handsome, strong, fearless, intelligent, and refined," but at the same time, according to the narrator, "there is something repellant about him." His rule of life is "that I neither know nor feel good and evil and that I have not only lost any sense of it, but that there is neither good nor evil." This man believes in nothing. He is a pedophile and rapist as well as a revolutionary criminal. He is thoroughly "unfettered by morality."

I suspect that good mental health is tied to having some sort of spiritual foundation, and Stavrogin's spirit tries to break through during his pre-suicide confession to a monk, but he keeps reverting to reason. Ultimately, his nihilism triumphs: he kills himself, logically and efficiently. He leaves a brief, precise note. By no means does he appear deranged in the slightest. Suicide is the logical conclusion of his depression.

Then there is Alexei Kirillov, a young engineer (the most rational of professions!) deeply influenced by Stavrogin toward the logical extreme of atheism, the absolute supremacy of the human will. "If God does not exist, then all will is mine, and I am obliged to proclaim self-will." Kirillov believes that this purposeful act of suicide, by demonstrating the transcendence of this fear, will show that there is no God other than the human will; thus, there is no need to invent God. Like Stavrogin, this is a rational suicide. "God is the pain of fear of death. Whoever conquers pain and fear will himself become God."

Both Kirillov's and Stavrogin's life philosophies are tied to a hyper-rationalism that doesn't leave room for the unknown, the unseen, or God. It's a philosophy that leads them, rather logically, to death.

In contrast, there's Ivan Shatov. He started out in the same mold as Stavrogin and Kirillov. He had socialist convictions at university and was expelled. But by the time frame of the novel, he has completely rejected his former beliefs and defends Russia's Christian heritage. Shatov philosophizes against Stavrogin:

> Not a single nation has ever been founded on the principles of science or reason . . . Socialism is from its very nature bound to be atheism seeing that it has from the very first proclaimed that it is an atheistic organization of society, and that it intends to establish itself exclusively on the elements of science and reason . . . There never has been a nation without a religion, that is without an idea of good and evil.

Shatov is ultimately sacrificed at the altar of rationality when he is murdered by a group of revolutionaries, influenced by the chaotic ethos embodied by Stavrogin. Shatov's character seems to be the voice of Dostoevsky himself, who was in his youth part of a Utopian revolutionary group, the Petrashevsky Circle. He was arrested and even sentenced to death. He and his group were all lined up by the firing squad, but a last-minute letter from the Czar arrived just in time, commuting the sentence. Instead, he spent four years in a Siberian prison camp and later dramatically reformed his views ("Fyodor Dostoevsky" n.d.).

Near execution of Dostoevsky (Pokrovsky 1849).

Over time, Dostoevsky saw atheism as the root cause of Russia's deepening social problems. He wrote to his friend that "a man who loses his people and his national roots also loses the faith of his fathers and his God," speaking mainly of Stavrogin (Frank 2010). In *Demons*, the Russian man has lost his true national identity, which is inextricably linked with the orthodox Christian faith; he tries to fill the void with ideas derived from Western modes of thought (i.e., socialism). This novel clearly tackles the question of the death of God ten years prior to Nietzsche's publication. Moreover, Dostoevsky links socialism to atheism and nihilism, but there is a common pathway of rationality that fills the void. Socialism—not fascism—was building in Russia during Dostoevsky's time, and it could easily have been any other totalitarian ideology filling his pages.

Dostoevsky prophesized the victory of communism:

> Communism will conquer one day, irrespective of whether the Communists are right or wrong. But this triumph will stand very far from the Kingdom of Heaven. All the same, we must accept that this triumph will come one day, even though none of those who at present steer the world's fate have any idea about it at all. ["Demons (Dostoevsky Novel)" n.d.]

He was so prophetic in *Demons* that he described a reader at a gala as ". . . a man of about forty, bald front and back, with a grayish little beard, who . . . keeps raising his fist over his head and bringing it down as if crushing some adversary to dust."

Figure of Vladimir Lenin, founder of the Soviet Union. Image courtesy of openclipart.org.

There is an unholy trinity of nihilism, atheism, and mental illness in Western society today. Since the Industrial Revolution, and increasingly with our advancing material prosperity, the nature and perception of mental health conditions like depression, anxiety, and post-traumatic stress disorder (PTSD) have undergone significant changes. Although these conditions surely existed historically, their understanding and prevalence have evolved alongside societal transformations. People throughout history have undoubtedly experienced what we would today deem massively traumatic: soldiers from another town killing your family, being threatened by a saber-toothed tiger, maternal-infant mortality, and so on. However, these were often viewed as part of the universal human experience. Why didn't people experience these tragedies as crippling? The answer is quite simple: People had immense responsibilities. They had to strive every day just to survive. If something traumatic happened, they had no choice but to carry on.

Conversely, life today is so easy that people are able to be overcome by tragic events and still attend to their basic survival. Most people in the Western world today have never killed a chicken. We can order food from the grocery store with a few clicks of the mouse. We can succumb to grief while facing the overwhelming reality of losing a loved one and still manage not to starve to death. Philosopher Søren Kierkegaard predicted that life might get so materially easy that we would actually try to make things harder ([1846] 1992). Likewise, Orwell believed that Hitler understood that his people would give up creature comforts for a greater collective purpose (Orwell 1940).

Muslim scholar Hamza Yusuf highlights the contrast between our society and that of our ancestors:

> The sense of entitlement that humans have is overwhelming. This idea that we're entitled to health, wealth, for things to work out, it's not the way life is designed, it never was. It's something the ancients really understood. Modern people have a difficult time grappling with this because they're not well spiritually. Pre-modern people were much healthier spiritually. Certainly all these pre-modern civilizations understood that life was trial and tribulation first and foremost. The Quran says it's God who created death and life to try you, to reveal who is the best of you in actions. (Yusuf and Peterson 2022)

The Bible also teaches that there is a purpose beyond this life—reunion with God in heaven, one that makes the inevitable suffering and pain on Earth worthwhile.

But the ease of modern life has diminished our sense of meaning, the accomplishment we feel just to survive the day. In generations past, a belief in God, gods, or at least something beyond the purely objective and rational instilled a sense of meaning beyond self and circumstance. I suspect that most of our ancestors didn't stay awake at night wondering, "What does it all mean?" or "Why am I here?"

I mean this with absolute respect to people today, but our current mental health labels (let alone mental healthcare) are a luxury that our ancestors didn't have. I say this to establish a sense of the unique situation humanity is in today, so we can understand our problems, how they came to be, and how to fix them.

A key to understanding and solving these problems is in the role true religion plays in people's lives. I broadly define a "true religion" as a belief system that is deep and traditional, one that has stood the test of time. It has some element of mystery to it, precluding a full rational description, and a sophistication that orients believers in their conduct and lives in general. As society evolves with technology and new challenges, the day-to-day meanings of the system's teachings need reinterpretation and updating, such as through priests and debate, but the deeper principles hold true.

Chapter 13 explores the differences between true religions and replacement religions and discusses criteria for categorizing belief systems in these terms.

Chapter 3:

FREE WILL WITHOUT PURPOSE LEADS TO DESTRUCTION

In the last ten to fifteen years, we have seen an explosion of zombies in our storytelling. Why are zombies all the rage right now? University of Toronto psychologist John Vervaeke has the best explanation I have found on this idea. He believes the popularity of zombies in storytelling is zeroing in on this specific mythology in an attempt to articulate something that's gone profoundly wrong, and that is the current crisis of meaning. Zombies have lost most of the capacity for meaning—they can't speak, they eat the very organ that creates meaning, and they wander aimlessly in the physical world. This strikes a psychological chord with billions of people today who feel like they're wandering aimlessly in life, just going through the motions (Vervaeke, Mastropietro, and Miscevic 2017).

Zombies actually resemble Nietzsche's description of the "last man." He said the last men will be all alike, resembling herd animals (hence the term "herd mentality"), enjoying simple pleasures and mediocrity. Nietzsche's last men lack positive beliefs (Nietzsche [1885] 1999). In essence, they lack any sense of drive, purpose, mission, values, or goals. I believe that Nietzsche is describing the opposite of his superman.

People generally aim for comfort over challenge. We think we can invent happiness by eliminating every worry in life. Essentially, we are becoming unconscious zombies. Has today's society already manifested Nietzsche's last men? This chapter explores what has gone wrong. The degree to which people are devoid of meaning varies, and this chapter covers a system called the levels of energy that maps out how much meaning any individual has in their life.

In 2018, I co-founded an addictions clinic that soon after became a small chain. In my role as medical director over the following two years, I worked closely with many patients struggling with opioids. Opioid addiction has been growing substantially over the last few years.

Three Waves of Opioid Overdose Deaths

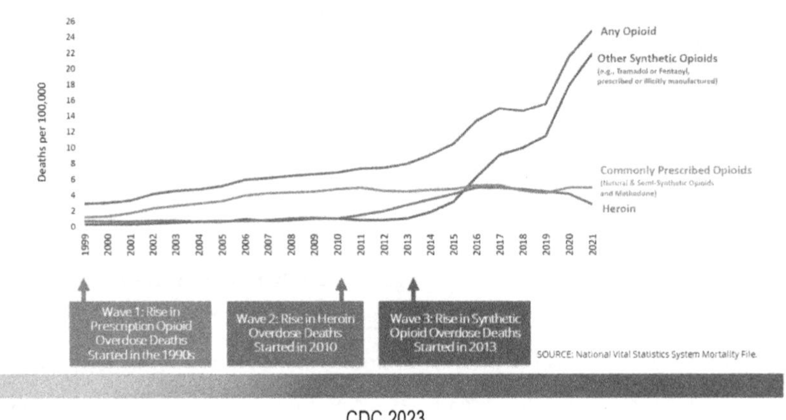

CDC 2023

The number of drug overdose deaths in 2021 was over six times the same statistic in 1999, and over 75 percent of those cases involved an opioid (CDC 2023).[6]

I wondered not only what would cause an individual to adopt such dramatically self-destructive behavior but also why the opioid crisis was becoming an epidemic. Over the next few years when addictions medicine was my primary professional focus, I came up with three broad, psychological reasons.

- First, it is human nature that free will always triumphs over reason. The worse off a person's overall condition, the more objectively self-destructive they will be as they demonstrate this. As is commonly attributed, George Bernard Shaw once remarked, "Alcohol is the anesthesia by which we endure the operation of life." This chapter explores this hypothesis at length.
- Second, humans are built to strive for purpose, but today's material success has deprived us of the innate challenge of existence.
- Third, as a response to existential suffering, people have deepened their desire to be unconscious (hence zombies as a cultural phenomenon).

The Underground Man

What would you do if you won the lottery? It's a common question. Beyond what luxurious things you'd buy, the question is really asking, "If you had enough money that all your material needs were taken care of—food, mortgage, education, leisure, vacations—how would you spend your time?" Think about it for a moment. I actually challenge you now to stop reading and spend a few minutes jotting down what comes to mind.

Maybe you would quit your job, sleep in every day, play golf, live on the beach, or travel for the next five years straight. Maybe you wouldn't change a thing. What if everything was handed to you and you didn't have to lift a finger? Would you just lie down watching Netflix and drinking champagne for the rest of your days?

Taking it further: What if you were deprived of absolutely all adversity from cradle to grave? That would be amazing! Right?

Dostoevsky gives a poetic look at these ideas in *Notes from Underground* ([1864] 2019): "What can be expected of man? . . . Drown him in a sea of happiness, so that nothing but bubbles of bliss can be seen on the surface; give him economic prosperity, such that he should have nothing else to do but sleep, eat cakes and busy himself with the continuation of his species." The main character of the book is a retired civil servant living in Saint Petersburg. Being underground refers to a state of urban alienation. His existence is so mundane (which many modern people can relate to) that it drives him to nihilism: "And even then out of sheer ingratitude, sheer spite, man would play you some nasty trick. He would even risk his cakes and would deliberately desire the most fatal rubbish, the most uneconomical absurdity, simply to introduce into all this positive good sense his fatal fantastic element."

He goes on to say, "It is just his fantastic dreams, his vulgar folly that he will desire to retain, simply in order to prove to himself—as though that were so necessary—that men are still men and not the keys of a piano" (Dostoevsky [1864] 2019).

So, if every single need of yours was taken care of, Dostoevsky says you would mess it up to create some uncertainty and go on an adventure. Would your choice lead to your redemption or your ruin?

Dostoevsky wrote *Notes from Underground* in part as a retort to his contemporary Utopian thinkers—in particular, Nikolai Chernyshevsky. Chernyshevsky's novel *What Is to Be Done?* touts the idea of rational egoism, the principle that an action is rational if it maximizes one's self-interest (Scanlan 1999). Utopian thinkers believed that science and reason could solve all remaining problems and that the end result would be the perfect existence. Interestingly enough, *What Is to Be Done?* was itself written in response to *Fathers and Sons* by Turgenev ("What Is to Be Done? (Novel)" n.d.).

In *What Is to Be Done?*, Chernyshevsky was inspired by the Crystal Palace that was shown in London at the Great Exhibition of 1851. He used this idea to theorize of a Crystal Palace as a metaphor for his Utopian world.

Delamotte 1854

Using only the most modern technology, the Crystal Palace was built with cast iron and glass as clear as crystal. It embodied science and rationality. In Dostoevsky's response novel, the underground man describes the palace as a "chicken coop" posing as a crystal palace. He wants to stick out his tongue at it, symbolizing free will over reason and individuality over collectivism (Dostoevsky [1864] 2019). I imagine the underground man today would do the same at big government omnibus policies that are likewise predicated on the notion of Utopia.

Chernyshevky's philosophy is flawed because it neglects the freedom of human will and grossly misjudges human nature—namely, our inherent predisposition to irrationality. Nevertheless, *What Is to Be Done?* was an immensely impactful book. Literary critic Joseph Frank claims that "Chernyshevsky's novel, far more than Marx's *Capital*, supplied the emotional dynamic that eventually went to make the Russian Revolution" (New World Encyclopedia contributors 2011).

Vladimir Lenin found this work so inspiring that he read it five times in one summer, modeling himself to a certain extent on one of the key characters, Rakhmetov, who was a literary prototype for the ideal Soviet man. He was someone who overcame his own impulses, a true Nietzschean superman who lived selflessly for the good of the collective. Utopian works have always been Trojan horses—they sound so appealing, yet they usher in our downfall because they are inaccurate and incomplete maps of the landscape, and they leave little room for course correction.

Humans are inherently irrational, and we will always try to assert our free will, even if this goes against logic and our own conscientious interest. This is contrasted with the idea embodied by Chernshevsky's Crystal Palace, that, assuming we understood our interests well, we would let rationality be our guide and never do anything against our own causes.

I believe that Chernyshevsky would simply tear up his book if he observed at a drug addictions clinic! From what I've seen, I've learned that we act according to our desires, not in obeisance to reason. People can decide at any time to act in a way that might not be considered in their own self-interest. Some will go to great lengths of self-destruction to simply validate their existence and individuality, that their free will is unpredictable, and that they are truly free.

Utopianism, like Chernyshevsky's rational egoism, is fallacious. It posits that if everyone in the world understood what was really in their best interests, they would never do anything irrational or destructive. But as Dostoevsky understood, human behavior is far more complex.

The underground man leaves his toothache completely untreated. He exclaims, "'Well, even in toothache there is enjoyment'" (Dostoevsky [1864] 2019). Logically, one should see a dentist for a toothache, yet with this action he proverbially sticks out his tongue at the conveniences of modern life. He continues to taunt ideas of truth and reason:

> Twice two makes four seems to me simply a piece of insolence. Twice two makes four is a pert coxcomb who stands with arms akimbo barring your path and spitting. I admit that twice two makes four is an excellent thing, but if we are to give everything its due, twice two makes five is sometimes a very charming thing too. (Dostoevsky [1864] 2019)

I actually think Dostoevsky predicted that humankind would experience a catastrophe like the opioid epidemic, the ultimate victory of free will over reason. This crisis is nested inside our deeper crisis of meaning.

Without a deep religious overarching narrative, reason remains alone in the void. Reason may give us efficient nuclear power and take us to the moon, but then we're left with nothing to do. Faced with advancing science, increasing nihilism, and living such anonymous, figuratively underground lives, opioid abuse is the modern untreated toothache. Yes, people want some degree of certainty—there's no joy in living in abject poverty or in a conflict-ridden area—but having our lives formulaically plotted out deprives us of the adventure of life.

Tony Robbins says that certainty and uncertainty/variety are two of the core human needs,[7] even though they are inherently at odds. By this I believe that he means we need a balance between chaos and order in our lives. He praises uncertainty frequently: "Variety is the spice of life! . . . The quality of your life is directly proportional to the amount of uncertainty you can comfortably have . . . The realm of uncertainty is where all your passions are found" (Robbins 2016).

An opioid-addicted patient once told me that when somebody dies from an overdose, people want to buy from that guy's dealer. "It's like they want to go as close to the edge as possible." Yes, addiction is complex; it's a hijacking of the mesolimbic reward pathway in the brain. There's a genetic component as well. But logically the risk-reward profile is so skewed, which is what led me to this psychological explanation. The opioid crisis is the rebellion of rebellions against reason and the tip of the spear of our societal descent into nihilism. It is a large and growing group of people collectively sticking out their tongues at the Crystal Palace of modern life.

Levels of Energy

The spirit of the underground man is in each of us, but every individual expresses free will differently. Some people's "toothache"—the thing we rely on to help us cope with the feeling of purposelessness and hopelessness—is smoking cigarettes, for others it is watching too many mediocre Netflix series while barely paying attention, and yet others are using dangerous recreational drugs. Let's define "underground complex" as the things you do (or don't do) that are not logically in your best interest, in order to unconsciously and psychologically demonstrate the triumph of your free will over reason.

But what determines how one expresses their underground complex?

I came across the concept of levels of energy through author Frederick Dodson and physician David Hawkins. Both published books on the topic, Dodson in *Levels of Energy* in 2010 and Hawkins in *Power vs. Force* in 2014. The concept is nebulous and pseudoscientific. But I have yet to encounter a framework that better correlates with the degree of self-destructive behavior each of us manifests. Science is not the only route to discovering what is true, and this abstract concept is, like a great story, a meta-fiction; it is something more accurate than any formula.

The concept is that there are clearly definable, perceivable, and achievable levels of energy. Each level corresponds with specific physical, mental, and emotional realities. Depending on whose model you look at, the lexicon differs, but the general progression is the same. From lowest to highest, they are as follows: shame → guilt → apathy → grief → fear → desire → anger → pride → courage → neutrality → willingness → acceptance → reason → love → joy → peace → enlightenment (Dodson 2010). I believe the degree of irrational, self-destructive behavior to which one's underground complex manifests is inversely proportional to one's energy level.

The levels of energy scale can be simplified into high, mid, and low. One summary is via the having-doing-being paradigm. For low levels of energy, the focus is on having. Those in this category focus on material possessions—what they can get. They are almost exclusively at the mercy of the native energy field of their environment. They generally seek to gain, not give, from others. They don't profoundly influence but are easily influenced themselves. For mid levels of energy, the focus is on doing. They take action to acquire what they want. These people are highly engaged in taking practical steps for tangible, external results. For high levels of energy, the focus is on being. For people at this level, it's not important what they have, own, or do for work, but rather who one is via personality, attitude, and energy field. The focus is on contribution to others and society (Dodson 2010).

	Categories of high levels of energy	**Categories of mid levels of energy**	**Categories of low levels of energy**
1	infinity or divinity	intelligence; knowledge; reason	pride; superiority; arrogance
2	oneness; non-duality; vast awareness	acceptance; interest; attention; neutrality	antagonism; criticism; discontent; complaint; blame
3	bliss; peace; serenity; lightness	willingness; kindness; optimism; activity	anger; domination; aggression; coldness
4	ecstasy; exaltation	courage; relaxation; eagerness; fun	craving; need; compulsion; unfulfilled desire
5	unconditional love	contentment; routine; functionality; boredom	fear; worry; shyness; inferiority; paranoia
6	humor; happiness		grief; sorrow; self-pity
7	love; intuition; appreciation		apathy; despair; depression; hopelessness
8	power; initiative; integrity		guilt; shame; psychosis; humiliation; hatred
9	beauty; creativity; imagination		
10	joy; creativity		

Source: Dodson 2010.

Each person has a unique experience of life, their basic vibe. It's their habitual emotion, chronic state, or basic energy level. This is the state you're in most often, the one you vibrate out. We all know people who are usually grumpy and others who generally conduct themselves with a big authentic smile. Their basic vibes are grumpy and joyful, respectively.

From this midpoint, you have a range. For example, with someone whose basic vibe is pride (in the higher end of the low-vibration category), a few weeks of good circumstance could vault them into reason (which is high vibration), where others can have logical conversations with them. A few bad weeks could also make them descend into self-pity, which is in the lower end of the low-vibration category. But unless there is some deep internal change (e.g., the alcoholic who takes Alcoholics Anonymous sessions seriously and is dry for the rest of his or her life), these changes are temporary and they will ultimately revert to their basic vibe set point of pride. Like oil and water, they are inherently incompatible with joyful, happy people, activities, and circumstances. There is no science behind this, but I believe people's native level of energy is based on a combination of nature and nurture. For example, there is a genetic component to depression. But you can also work on yourself to improve your basic vibe. Just because you usually emote apathy does not mean you can't progress to a higher set point through determination and hard work.

Delving further into the low-vibration category, the focus is on wanting things but not putting effort into earning them. The hallmark of someone in low vibration is living life according to the whims of others and circumstance, rather than what's truly important to them. An example of this is car accident "victims" who exaggerate or fake an injury to get unwarranted compensation. I have significant experience with this in my medical work and can usually tell on the balance of probabilities who is faking and who is not.

Those with higher vibrations are able to temporarily dive lower (Dodson 2010). The emotions on the lower end of the scale are most definitely useful at times in life (for example, being fair but firm when negotiating a price to repair your sink with a plumber who is trying to take advantage of you), but that's when you control the emotions, not the other way around. Controlling these kinds of emotions occurs when a higher-vibration person has integrated their shadow self. According to Carl Jung, the shadow represents the dark, more primitive animal instincts inherent in humanity (Rogan and Peterson 2017).

I believe the existence of the shadow and what to do about it was first hinted at in Genesis 4:7: "But if you do not do what is right, sin is crouching at your door; it desires to have you, but you must rule over it." Anger, aggression, and force are naturally low-vibration traits. There is a context for using those traits in high vibration properly, but those who are in low vibration are often ruled by these darker forces. Think of an unhappy McDonald's customer shouting at the staff for putting the wrong condiment on their burger. It's easier to do this than to have a firm but calibrated conversation with the staff to fix the error. Naturally there is a gray area in this context, but I believe this biblical line suggests you must master these low-vibration forces rather than let them consume you.

The shadow is well conceptualized in the film *Star Wars: Episode V, The Empire Strikes Back*, where Luke goes into the cave in Dagobah and has a vision of himself being Darth Vader. Before he enters, he asks his teacher, Master Yoda, what is in the cave. The answer is simply, "Only what you take with you." A generation later, Rey has a similar vision on Ahch-To in *Star Wars: Episode IX, The Rise of Skywalker*. In these scenes, both characters recognize their capability for being consumed by their shadow selves, rather than being in control of these dark but necessary human emotions.

My absolute favorite example of the shadow is the biblical scene of Jesus in the temple where he gets mad and sets a colossal boundary:

> When it was almost time for the Jewish Passover, Jesus went up to Jerusalem. In the temple courts he found people selling cattle, sheep and doves, and others sitting at tables exchanging money. So he made a whip out of cords, and drove all from the temple courts, both sheep and cattle; he scattered the coins of the money changers and overturned their tables. To those who sold doves, he said, "Get these out of here! Stop turning my Father's house into a market!" (John 2:13–16)

In this case, Jesus was always in control, his shadow fully integrated. He consciously descended to anger—a lower level of energy—in a calibrated manner to assert his beliefs, before returning to his basic vibe of enlightenment.

Deliberately going low is very different than inadvertently falling into it, though you must be careful of staying in that state too long. Nietzsche warns, "Whoever fights monsters should see to it that in the process he does not become a monster. And when you look long into an abyss, the abyss also looks into you" ([1886] 2017).

Those whose set point is in low vibration almost certainly haven't integrated their shadow selves. It's a spectrum, but the lower the vibration level one resides at, the smaller the chance that they have an awareness of the shadow. I believe that shadow integration is required to attain higher levels of vibration. Consciously setting boundaries and using force in a calibrated manner is a precondition for fulfilling one's potential and living a complete life. Being kind but not naive, able to scare off those who wish to take advantage of you (e.g., an overbearing boss or a greedy car salesman); these are necessary skills to navigate the world well. As a metaphorical illustration of the importance of the integrated shadow, Carl Jung believed that no tree can grow to heaven unless its roots reach down to hell (Jung 1969).

If you are depressed, your set point is in the realm of low vibration. The glass is effectively empty. Simple chores like taking the dog out, washing dishes, or even brushing your teeth can feel incredibly burdensome. When you are depressed and something good happens, you are vibrationally unable to receive it, and you'll still see and experience it from a pessimistic point of view.

Vibrating in Groups

Have you ever noticed why petty people tend to stick together and why loving people do the same? Like energy attracts like energy. This also explains why people don't leave abusive relationships. If a person keeps attracting abusive partners, even if they could have learned from previous experiences, they are not themselves vibrating at a high enough level to truly want to be with someone who treats them well. To change the kind of person they attract, a person needs to change their own vibrational energy.

Countries and societies also have vibrational levels. I believe that the Western world was at the highest vibration any society had ever been until sometime in the 2010s when the penetration of the darker sides of internet technology started dragging us down. Mass media has always tried to keep us in fear, but over the last decade it has become polarized and hyperfixated on clickbait. The internet has fostered blogs and forums where confirmation bias spirals you downward. X, the social media platform formerly known as Twitter, can easily turn the average person into a virtual mobster, allowing for all that low-vibration energy to come out without any consequence as the user hides behind their anonymous account. An example of where a countrywide vibrational level is apparent is North Korea; Dodson speaks about North Korea being in low vibration. According to him, North Korea is aggressive, cold, and angry, having no real power except that inherent in weapons (2010).

Dodson does not have a favorable view of Marxism's vibrational level, and neither do I. Marxism's general level of energy is very low to low vibration. *The Communist Manifesto* (which I encourage everyone to read), the doctrinal document of socialism, is a call to violent revolution, explicitly rejecting peaceful methods and asserting that such a transformation "cannot be effected except by means of despotic inroads." Almost as if Marx was speaking about the social justice riots today, he says that the proletariat "smash to pieces machinery, they set factories ablaze" (Marx and Engels [1848] 2004).

Dodson's take on *The Communist Manifesto* from an energy level perspective is that it projects hatred, fear, revenge, and apathy on every page, and that this philosophy itself is responsible for the poverty, mass starvation, and violence in all countries founded on it. This is contrary to popular claims that communism is actually founded on high ideals and has been distorted and abused by those in control. Perhaps Marx's most famous proclamation was "The proletarians have nothing to lose but their chains. They have a world to win. Working men of all countries, unite!" (1848). This implies that workers are victims of exploitation, rather than regular people who applied for and accepted the job of their own free will (Dodson 2010). In reality, however, the dynamic between employer and employee can be mutually beneficial.

Dodson points out the hypocrisy of modern-day Marxists. The Marxist corporation-hater is wearing clothes produced by business, walking on pavement produced by business, using medicine produced by business, and using online tools produced by business. Almost everything we're surrounded by was produced by business, otherwise we'd still be in caves. Rather than giving business and industriousness the gratitude and respect it deserves, large parts of society vilify them. Dodson decries the low-energy-level denizens of the far left as experts in reality distortion. They take a small segment of society and inflate it to appear as if the majority of a certain group is evil. They then exaggerate and sensationalize those evils until the view is that any successful businessperson is an evil capitalist (Dodson 2010).

Eros and Thanatos

Similar to the levels of energy, the Freudian concepts of Eros and Thanatos can help explain the same phenomenon of vibration along a spectrum, from higher to lower, from peace to hatred. According to Freud, people have a life instinct (Eros) and a death drive (Thanatos) (1922). In my adaptation of these Freudian concepts, Thanatos describes the compulsion to engage in risky, self-destructive acts. Eros describes life-affirming conduct, a by-product of a high will to live. Those in high vibration are high on the Eros-Thanatos spectrum, while those in low vibration are lower on this spectrum. Someone who is actively suicidal is fully in Thanatos, while someone whose life is brimming with meaning is fully in Eros. Most people are somewhere in between, and they move along this spectrum throughout their lives. Turgenev's character Bazarov, for example, was high in Thanatos while he dangerously performed an autopsy without precautions. He caught typhoid fever from this careless act and died.

Examples to Highlight Features of Low Vibration

As an example of manifestations of low vibration, or fully in Thanatos, consider the waiting room in a medical office or emergency room. It is very different from context to context. The stress of those unexpectedly needing to go to the emergency room depresses their vibrational levels. I often found impatience and short-term thinking to be a hallmark of emergency room patients (compared with patients in other contexts), as well as a solipsistic inability to realize there are other people also in need. The only nonemergency waiting room that had similar levels of short-term thinking was the addictions clinic. Understanding that a clinic without wait times doesn't exist (a contextual Utopia), even though my addictions patients were minutes away from relief (particularly if they were in withdrawal), they would frequently rather leave the clinic and not get treated if it meant waiting twenty minutes more, even though many of them did not have jobs.

Another feature of low vibration is having a strong impulse to scapegoat. I call the scapegoating impulse the strength of your desire to externalize a specific enemy. The stronger the impulse, the more focused and intense the blame on the enemy. If you label an oppressor, you can see yourself as the oppressed. If someone else is the villain, you can be the hero. People are psychologically driven to identify a chief villain in their lives. This is paired with a cause that gives their lives meaning.

In the narrative of your life, be very wary of turning someone into your great Satan. Are you sure you're not the problem? Donald Trump is a great example of a societal scapegoat. He became a cartoon version of all that is evil for the mainstream media, someone incapable of a single good or competent deed. While no one can defend the manner in which he often speaks, I'm in awe that so few people have heard of the Abraham Accords, an achievement that I believe would get any other president a Nobel Peace Prize. Have you ever heard of these accords?[8]

One way you gauge someone's level of energy is to view them in situations where there exists a diffusion of responsibility. Diffusion of responsibility, also known as the bystander effect, was coined in the 1960s by psychologists John Darley and Bibb Latané. They documented that the greater number of people present, the less likely any individual will help someone in need since it's easier to rationalize that someone else will (Latané and Darley 1968).

The diffusion of responsibility scenarios that I am exposed to most regularly are driving, public healthcare, and social media. Tailgating, driving far over the speed limit, aggressively changing lanes in rush hour, and road rage are all features of drivers stuck in short-term thinking. I noticed during the pandemic, which has pushed almost all people down a few notches in their levels of vibration, how much more anger there was on my home city of Toronto's roads.[9] Sometimes I even wondered whether these people had a death wish. Maybe they didn't, but maybe 10 percent of them wanted to die, or at least because of their Thanatos drive believed that it would be better if they weren't alive. Given that only a fraction will be caught by police for dangerous driving, the responsibility level is low.

Public healthcare is another common scenario of a diffusion of responsibly on behalf of the patient. This was especially true in the ER, but not exclusively. In what other workplace can the "customer" (using a more general term) shout at the staff, threaten them, and still get care?

Again, how do people behave with anonymous accounts on X, formerly known as Twitter?

When it comes to the debate between preventative medicine and pharmacotherapy, it's absolutely not a one-size-fits-all solution. Different levels of vibration determine how actively people can engage in their own healing. Of course, I would much rather my patients diet and exercise, or meditate and pray when in pain, but I understand that many are not vibrationally able to do the preventative therapies, and only pills can help mitigate the damage. Tell someone at the higher levels of vibration to quit smoking or to start going to the gym, and they'll do it. But advise someone in the throes of depression to do this, and it's like you're speaking Greek; instead, it's antidepressants for mood disorders or bariatric surgery for weight loss.

Struggling for Something Better

You aren't stuck at your low level of vibration. You aren't trapped in Thanatos, partially wishing you were dead. But you do have an inherent set point, and you have to work to change it. Developing yourself personally, becoming more conscious, can move you upward, and your life will become far more satisfying.

People harm themselves in proportion to their vibrational level, or where they are on the Eros-Thanatos spectrum. We numb ourselves from the pain of existence. For those in higher states of energy, it can be as innocuous as watching too many mediocre Netflix shows and barely paying attention. For those lower down, it could be smoking cigarettes or excessively drinking alcohol. For those at the end-spectrum of Thanatos, it's IV opioids. But change is possible at all levels.

One of the more remarkable cases of my drug addiction patients left a deep impression on me. For confidentiality, let's call him John. John was a young man who had trouble maintaining a job. In opioid addiction care, patients ideally get on methadone or buprenorphine as replacement opioids that give less of a high but prevent withdrawal symptoms. Patients give urine samples, often at weekly intervals, that are tested for the presence or absence of drugs. John kept testing positive for illicit drug use, week after week. I was dismayed at how such a young person that I believed to have far more potential could just go through the motions of life and let his promise slip away. This pattern continued week after week, month after month.

Suddenly, one day his urine test was negative for anything but what I prescribed. I believed it must be an aberration, and the next week he would be back to testing positive for recreational drugs. Yet the next week he was also clean. He was clean the week after that, and the week after that. What had changed?

He told me that growing up he had a dream of getting his pilot's license. More recently, he investigated this process and found out that to do so, he cannot be on any opioid, including the one I prescribed to keep him away from illicit drugs. He also said he needed to have records on his medical file showing that for a long period of time his urine samples were clean. John never tested positive again with me. Months later, I tapered him off buprenorphine, and then he only had periodic visits with me. Still, all his urine tests were clean. I was not only impressed but inspired. The last time I saw him, he had started his pilot's license training. In those last few months, he seemed happy and motivated. I realized what he was missing all this time that made the entire difference was purpose, a life mission. John and other cases like his have been my inspiration for writing this book. People like John have illuminated a crucial insight: Western society is increasingly losing touch with a sense of purpose. To counteract existential malaise and restore meaning to our lives, it is imperative that we embrace and pursue clear goals and values.

PART 2:
Searching for Meaning

Chapter 4:

INTRODUCTION TO REPLACEMENT RELIGIONS

When people and societies abandon deep, sophisticated, ineffable faith in something transcendent (let's call it God), what fills the void besides absolute reason? Turgenev illustrated with his character Bazarov that something has to fill that void, whether you want it to or not. Saint Augustine believed there's a perennial temptation to replace God with something else (Augustine, n.d.). But worshipping anything but God will lead to ruin.

This idea is crystallized explicitly in the golden calf conundrum in the story of Exodus. While wandering the desert, the Israelites created a golden calf, and it replaced God as the recipient of their highest worship.

Poussin 1633

Moses was absent during this time, having a private tête-à-tête with God and receiving the Ten Commandments, the fundamental principles that would guide Judeo-Christian morality for millennia. Moses was enraged when he saw the golden calf on his return, and he had it burned. God initially threatened to annihilate the entire nation but relented following Moses's intercession. Instead, God commanded the execution of three thousand Israelites and subsequently sent a plague as punishment. The golden calf symbolized a tangible but ultimately hollow replacement for God, representing a convenient but superficial object of worship. This story serves as a literary example of the disaster that befalls when God is not held as the highest value.

Later in the Bible, Jesus speaks of replacement religions as such:

> No one can serve two masters. Either you will hate the one and love the other, or you will be devoted to the one and despise the other. You cannot serve both God and money. Therefore I tell you, do not worry about your life, what you will eat or drink; or about your body, what you will wear . . . (Matthew 6:24–25)

What do you worship? What you worship is what you value as the highest worth to you, and your life will be organized around this priority.

A replacement religion is an incomplete belief system or prime value elevated above others, designed to give meaning to the world in lieu of a deep, sophisticated religion. But these replacements do little to quench people's thirst for meaning. They are, in essence, golden calves.

All replacement religions are akin to the Buddhist idea of the hungry ghost. These are creatures with large empty bellies, small scrawny necks and, importantly, tiny little mouths. No matter how much they eat, these substitutes for religious notions are never enough to fill the emptiness on the inside. Replacement religions do not satiate. Instead, they will eventually lead you to ruin in some form or other, in terms of life satisfaction, but definitely in regard to an unquenched sense of meaning. Replacement religions are like Trojan horses—they are attractive on the surface, but once you fully buy in, they lead to disaster.

Moral hegemony also accompanies a replacement religion, allowing the worshipper to fall into oppressor-oppressed binary thinking. For example, in Putin's Russian nationalist ideology, it is morally upright to castigate and scapegoat the West (namely, America), while absolving Russia of all blame. Attacking someone's foundational belief, their replacement religion, can provoke them to fight to the death. This response is partly due to an underlying insecurity about their beliefs, as deep scrutiny through debate might expose their weaknesses. While this can also apply to adherents of traditional religions, in such cases, the religion is functioning more as an ideology, akin to Pharisee faith, as explained in chapter 5. Innumerable jokes are made about Jesus and Christianity on TV without inciting violent backlash, yet an ill-considered remark on a contentious social justice issue today might necessitate increased vigilance. There are even brain changes seen on neuroimaging when people are willing to fight and die for a cause. These studies show diminished activities in areas of the brain previously implicated in calculating costs and consequences (Hamid et al. 2019; Pretus et al. 2019). Essentially for the right cause, people throw out reason and logic.

You can have several possible replacement religions, but to truly attempt to replace God with one, it has to be alone at the top of your value structure; you must personally and deeply identify with it. Having good finances is universally important, but it is not a replacement religion if that top rung is occupied by an actual religion (and you embody that religion's deep principles) or if it is not your guiding light to the exclusion of other things. In these cases, having good finances is just an important value; it is not a replacement religion for you. A good litmus test of whether something is your replacement religion is how strongly you react when it is criticized. The closer to a core belief it is for you, the more emotionally and irrationally you will react to its critique. Many other beliefs depend on this deeper belief, the replacement religion, so people are very quick to defend it. An example is the climate activist who, when questioned about the cost-benefit analysis of electric vehicle subsidies, screams at and labels the questioner a hateful climate denier.

Pride is a popular golden calf. It's popular because it makes you feel good; it's no wonder it's one of the seven deadly sins. At the top rung of your hierarchy of values, pride gives you the belief that you can do no wrong. In this position, pride supersedes money. How often do businesspeople make decisions that are silly from a financial perspective but serve the ego well? A prideful person doesn't take any criticism, even from a loved one. Sometimes the choice is a dichotomous one—you can have your pride or your pants, but not both. By this I mean, choose either your pride or sound financial decision-making. But pride in this position comes with specific costs—namely money, truth, and long-term benefit. Pride knows no limits, and it might take everything from you. "Pride goes before destruction, a haughty spirit before a fall" (Proverbs 16:18).

Some other examples of replacement religions include science, nationalism (which also rose tremendously in the nineteenth century), communism, fascism, substance abuse, some forms of love and relationships (such as the toxic or codependent variety) and, more recently, elements of pop culture. This section of the book explores these examples in more detail. Chapter 5 specifically illustrates how ideologies can serve as such faulty belief systems.

The Search for Meaning

The presence or perception of meaning halts the search for meaning. In other words, the more you believe your life is full of meaning, the less you need to look for new meaning—and vice versa.

Jung believed that UFO sightings were replacements for religious revelations ([1959] 2002). Research by psychologist Clay Routledge found that the more secular people were, the less they believed in God. This led to a greater search for meaning, which then predicted their likelihood of belief in aliens and UFOs (Routledge, Abeyta, and Roylance 2017). There was also preceding research suggesting those who believed in UFOs had low religiosity. Effectively, UFOs have become deities for some atheists. Routledge also found that new age religion thrives in the parts of the United States that tend to be least religious, as measured by variables such as low church attendance (Routledge and Peterson 2021).[10]

Turgenev's character Bazarov showed that the quest for believing in something—for having values, for having deeper ideals or meaning—cannot be extinguished. Put another way, you can pretend you don't have a religious instinct, but it just goes into hiding and tricks you by substituting something that doesn't seem religious but you still treat as holy. The religious instinct needs to be given proper attention and focused on something abstract and transcendent that fills you up with meaning. Otherwise, you paint your world inappropriately with a cheap substitute for religious meaning. Simply put, even atheists and nihilists display behaviors that suggest an underlying pursuit of greater significance. Bazarov's acknowledgment of the beauty in his love interest, for instance, exemplifies an inherent yearning for something profound beyond the surface. Similarly, many professed atheists behave as if guided by a moral code. This mirrors Clay Routledge's research, which connects secularism with an intensified search for meaning, manifesting in beliefs like UFOs as quasi-religious concepts (Routledge, Abeyta, and Roylance 2017). This suggests that the human pursuit of something transcendent or meaningful persists, even in the absence of conventional religious faith.

One of the most popular types of replacement gods we have in our current culture is superheroes. Instead of the Nietzschean superman, we have DC comics Superman. In the last decade, Marvel in particular has done an incredible job retelling the hero myth via their vast array of characters, and these stories need retelling as the world we live in is constantly changing. Neither of these comic publishers would have been successful in 1700, but they are now filling the void left by the death of God. Superheroes are replete with qualities and powers that seem to reflect mystical and religious aspects. They inspire us to imitate them as they navigate the moral quagmires of today's world. They are one level up from the athletes whose posters adorn the walls of sports fans.

Similarly, *Star Wars* fans demonstrate a religious instinct. The mythology of *Star Wars* is incredibly intricate. Viewers like me, who are big fans of the franchise, are drawn to this richness of storytelling as a way of searching for more meaning in their lives. But despite its popularity and increasingly layered narrative, pop culture lacks the profound substance of a real religion. This is true not only for Christianity, which I often reference due to my background, but likely true for all traditional religions. While *Star Wars* transcends mere entertainment, offering more nuance than a basic belief system, it doesn't achieve the expansive complexity inherent in traditional religions. Unlike these ancient faiths, it isn't supported by centuries or millennia of evolving literature that reinterprets its narrative to reflect different eras. No civilization has been built upon its ethos and mythos. Moreover, it falls short of directly addressing fundamental moral and societal principles, such as the sanctity of traditional marriage, the reverence for one's parents, or the ethics of life and death. Essentially, *Star Wars* can be seen as a streamlined version of Christianity, replete with superior marketing but missing the rich, multifaceted teachings and cultural impact of established religions. Like a fast-food meal that at least offers calories, *Star Wars* provides some overarching pattern of how to live a good and moral life. However, a full course meal of whole food will be nutritiously superior in the way that traditional religions are more morally enriching.

Religious or atheist, your value structure is either organized in a hierarchy, or it isn't organized at all. Someone who knows you well will be able to identify whether your value structure is organized or not, and they probably will be able to point out some of your top values. Ideally, your search for meaning is satisfied by having a deep religion occupying the top rank, but there are worse options than not having religion in your hierarchy. Those without any organization with their value structure are plagued by volatility, anxiety, stress, and high delay discounting (effectively short-term thinking). These are people who live in chaos. They are more than slightly different every time you see them. You can probably intimate some of their higher values, but the order is completely jumbled. They need to organize themselves internally in order to better face the world (and themselves).

The Risks of Replacement Religions

I believe the most vulnerable to more malignant types of replacement religions are teens and young adults. Psychologist Jean Piaget is most famous for his theory of cognitive development of children. Stage four is the formal operational stage, that of adolescent egocentrism. It has been labeled by subsequent psychologists as a messianic stage, in which many young people "are prone to adopt idealistic and utopian social and political ideas which they reassert with an almost zealous vigor. Yet, at the same time, and probably due to a lack of experience and an egocentric tendency, they tend to underestimate the difficulties and the ramifications of attempts to implement their ideals in complex, real-world settings" (Rogmann 2021).

Psychologist Jens Rogmann elaborates on the three substages of the adolescent stage, the last of which being when they start to comprehend the practical limitations of reality and integrate into adult roles in the best-case scenarios (2021). Young adults are in a difficult situation. They are now fully conscious of the world, yet in general they lack the life experience and skill to meaningfully contribute. Many replacement religions offer shortcuts to feeling like they are contributing. For example, activism is the express lane to feeling like you're doing something noble, even if the consequence of your advocacy harms the people you claim to be helping. Instead, I believe that developing critical thinking—how to think and reason—is more important than any particular set of instruction. As the Islamic prophet Mohammed says, as paraphrased by Hamza Yusuf, "Master yourself so that you don't become 'yes' people, that when people do good, you do good, and when they do bad, you do bad. But be so that when people do good, you're with them, and when they do bad, you refrain from their evil" (Yusuf and Peterson 2022).

To summarize the idea of replacement religions, I defer to Saint Augustine. In *City of God*, he delineates two types of loves: the love of God (*caritas*) and love of anything else, something earthly (*cupiditas*). If God isn't your ultimate love, you're going to love something else and place it as your highest value (Saint Augustine, n.d.). Consider, for instance, the response of many governments during the pandemic, where the paramount values became safety and control. This focus made it challenging to balance the pros and cons of public policies, leading to the neglect and subjugation of critical aspects like children's education and mental health, among other societal goods. Safety and control, while important, represent *cupiditas*, not *caritas*. Like all false idols, they have the potential to warp reality, facts, and data to fit their narrative (Pageau 2023). Hence, the true meta-goal cannot be found in the material world. Instead, it must be something transcendent (Kaczor and Petrusek 2021). Choosing a replacement religion will ultimately distort not only you but also your relationships and society, as the Israelites found out during their golden calf worship.

So, what is your highest value?

Chapter 5:

IDEOLOGY AS A REPLACEMENT RELIGION

Ideology is a manner or the content of thinking characteristic of an individual, group, or culture; a systematic body of concepts ("Ideology" n.d.). An ideology is a low-resolution universal explanation. That is to say, it is a belief that many things, if not everything, can be totally explained by a set of ideas. Thus, in practicality, nuance and granularity are lost.

This does not make anyone with any claim an ideologue. An assertion is ideological in nature if it is overly reductive and devoid of deeper arguments: "COVID-19 vaccines are very risky." A well-articulated argument is not ideological: "There is some risk to the COVID-19 vaccine, though there is no zero-risk proposition. There are pros and cons, and we can use the existing data for individuals to make decisions and jurisdictions to make recommendations."

Ideologies are perhaps the most common form of replacement religion, though not every ideology adopted becomes someone's highest value or foundational belief. To clarify, if you don't identify with the ideology, if when challenged you don't react viscerally, it is not a replacement religion for you.

Ideology is appealing, especially to those steeped in the search for meaning who are looking for a replacement religion. First, it gives you a universal explanation for the deep complexity of life—suddenly you can explain the multitude of complex global problems and have a simple answer about how to solve them. You feel entitled to suspend reason in service of this shorthand. Second, you now wear the mantle of virtuousness and have a convenient villain to oppose.

Here are some features that can indicate pathologized ideologies:

1. All subscribers to an ideology essentially have a uniformity of views on various topics. For example, the reductive credo of many environmental organizations is something like "Humanity is killing the planet, and we can save it by stopping all fossil fuels immediately."
2. Complete certainty; there's no debate or negotiation, and there is censorship of counterpoints. For example, "Canada is the best country in hockey, I don't care what you say. And if you disagree, you'd better watch it!"[11]
3. Subscribers start with their conclusions, then seek confirmation bias. For example, "One doctor on social media said that the vaccine is dangerous, and he had a lot of likes. Then I googled this and found a lot of hits saying the same thing. So it must be true."
4. Strong scapegoating impulse with ad hominem attacks. For example, "Donald Trump is so awful. If it wasn't for him, we wouldn't have any social issues whatsoever." This ties into the idea of collective guilt, such as the Jews for the Nazis, or those with some degree of wealth for the Communists. The scapegoating impulse produces a devil effect, whereby the scapegoat can do no right, but it dangerously and inaccurately produces a corresponding halo effect whereby the scapegoat's opponent can do no wrong (Cook, Marsh, and Hicks 2003).

The most popular ideologies come with a very clear villain, the othering of which allows people to paint themselves as the hero. If the villain fades for some reason, the subscribing person becomes existentially uneasy and is compelled to quickly identify another villain so they can maintain their place as the hero.

I believe that scapegoating is the eighth deadly sin; it is a subset of pride. The act of scapegoating means you're assigning someone the label of evil, which makes you automatically good. The scapegoating impulse is convenient, and it feels good. Assigning blame first without deep introspection to see where your responsibility lies is childish; it's part of a relationship with fantasy instead of objective reality. Like Jesus said, only he who is without sin can throw the first stone.

Sometimes this narrative is accompanied by the false dichotomy: "You're either with us or against us."[12]

Even more profound, Aleksandr Solzhenitsyn writes in the *Gulag Archipelago*:

> Ideology—that is what gives evildoing its long-sought justification and gives the evildoer the necessary steadfastness and determination. That is a social theory which helps to make his acts seem good instead of bad in his own and others' eyes, so that he won't hear reproaches and curses but will receive praise and honors.

Solzhenitsyn spent eight years in a Soviet gulag. Though we may not be mass murderers like the ideologues who imprisoned him, we must realize we're all vulnerable to false ideologies. He believed the only prerequisite for doing evil was being human, that "the line between good and evil runs down every human heart" (1974).

Ideologies require self-deception. The distortions in perspective can be subtle enough to pass unnoticed, despite their potential for generating pathology. At some point the discrepancy between reality and fantasy is so wide that you have to be willfully blind to continue on. But those most ardently possessed by their ideology can continue to believe as long as they don't receive feedback from the environment that is powerful enough to force them to reexamine their belief system (J. B. Peterson and Djikic 2017).

What about all the historical and present wrongs done under the guise of traditional religion? Traditional religions can actually function as an ideology for some people. I call this Pharisee faith, in honor of a parable from the New Testament where Jesus criticized a self-righteous Pharisee who was loudly praying to display his virtue, though his actions did not line up with his words. Jesus says,

> And when you pray, do not be like the hypocrites, for they love to pray standing in the synagogues and on the street corners to be seen by others. Truly I tell you, they have received their reward in full. But when you pray, go into your room, close the door and pray to your Father, who is unseen. Then your Father, who sees what is done in secret, will reward you. (Matthew 6:5–6)

In the conversions by the sword during colonization, or in today's world where some clergy have sexually abused children, there is a great mismatch between word and deed.

These people likely believed they were righteous, but they had a simplistic understanding of the religion at the level of an ideology with all the benefits. They did not embody the deeper, authentic meaning. Worse, some furthered their own self-interest under the guise of religion, which breaks one of the Ten Commandments, taking the name of God in vain. In Matthew 23:33, Jesus even alludes to Pharisees being condemned to hell.

Be wary of those who virtue signal. Are they good in deed, or are they Pharisees?

We all fall prey to ideologies, though not all are pathologized. Every fall I believe that my favorite hockey team, the Toronto Maple Leafs, will finally win the Stanley Cup. They have not won since 1967. (The internet is rife with memes mocking this drought, but I could not bring myself to include one!) Try telling me otherwise, and I will snap back at you. That is, until the spring arrives, when they invariably get eliminated, and I eat my humble pie. This illustrates another of the payoffs of ideology—it gives you a tribe. You immediately have a group of people to call your own, those who "get" you.

Another example of an ideology is the belief that Canadian healthcare is the best in the world, and that all healthcare should be free and unlimited. I believe it's hard for people to appreciate something when they have no skin in the game, like free healthcare. Even Tommy Douglas, the founder of Canada's famed universal healthcare system and winner of the "greatest Canadian" poll, understood this. He said, "I think there is a value in having every family and every individual make some individual contribution. I think it has psychological value. I think it keeps the public aware of the cost and gives the people a sense of personal responsibility" (Frontier Centre For Public Policy 2004).

This is an ideological debate I am deeply familiar with. While Chair of the Ontario Medical Association's Toronto district in 2017, I sent out a survey to all Toronto doctors asking a series of questions on what our priorities should be in the next round of negotiations with the government. Two of the sixteen questions were about the possibility of patient accountability (copayments and no-show fees). Suddenly this was in the local news. The socialist doctor groups were outraged. "To bring up health care privatization . . . is simply inappropriate," wrote Doctors for Responsible Healthcare. By this, they meant there should be no debate. Truly, if this were the case, then no one would select these options, and the results would reveal that the survey had been two questions longer than necessary. I was also inundated with emails from doctors who thought this way, aghast that we had dared include these questions. The strange thing was that each email had the same talking points, manifesting the ideology. They said the evidence was conclusive, but the evidence they sent me, as well as the survey itself, showed clear room for debate.[13]

It is nearly impossible to break ideologues out of whatever hold with which their demonic spirit possesses them. If you have ever tried to argue (logically reason) with someone in the depths of ideological possession, if demons truly existed, it would be indistinguishable from this experience. I am not at all saying that demonic spirits exist. We've all seen TV shows where a character becomes inhabited by a spirit or even an alien, and their personality changes dramatically (e.g., Venom from Marvel Comics). During the possession, you can barely get glimpses of the native personality, no matter your methods. But once the spirit leaves, the person returns to normal. It is in this manner that you may find yourself engaging with someone gripped with their ideology, when on a relevant topic. For example, your friend you've known for decades may suddenly shift into ideology mode when you speak with them about climate change, then return to the familiar person you know once you shift out of the topic.

Using more secular terminology, it's like a software is running them; they're not really there themselves. Conversation breaks down rapidly, assuming it begins at all. The meta-goal of this demon or software is to stay in power, which often means not to be exposed (hence the central tendency to censorship). To that end, the proximal goal is to win the argument, often by silencing.

Ideology just tells you what to think about everything so you're always right and someone else is always wrong. Moreover, the other side is always evil. As you feed your Utopian and authoritarian impulses, more power to you.

One example of ideology being unable to stand up to deeper examination is the massive problem with the way we discuss climate policy in the West: If it truly means the end of the world, then how can we justify spending money on any other problem? Aren't we morally obliged to commit every last tax dollar to fixing it? Shouldn't we gut healthcare and social services to pay for the proposed solutions? However, if there is more nuance to the issue, then we should be debating and prioritizing our goals, climate action being only one of them, and then also debating the proposed solutions.

What about the apocalypse of an asteroid hitting Earth? Nuclear war? An even more deadly pandemic? Maybe climate alarmists might find the idea of an alien invasion a more fulfilling replacement religion!

Finally, even if this truly is an existential crisis beyond any doubt, is mass panic and depression the best overarching strategy?

Understandably we cannot have nuanced knowledge in everything, so having a shorthand understanding of things can sometimes be useful. But recognize that the cost of using shorthand is that it moves you away from the truth. Acknowledge its limitations.

The Importance of Language to Ideology

> If thought corrupts language, language can also corrupt thought. A bad usage can spread by tradition and imitation, even among people who should and do know better . . . This invasion of one's mind by ready-made phrases (*lay the foundations, achieve a radical transformation*) can only be prevented if one is constantly on guard against them, and every such phrase anaesthetizes a portion of one's brain.
>
> —Orwell 1946

While free speech is the kryptonite of the radical left, they most certainly have a superpower—that is, linguistic hegemony. They are very particular on language. Think about how many new words have been introduced into our vocabulary or gained a different connotation in the last five years alone (e.g., lived experience, Latinx, cis, microaggression, colonial, ally, racialized, etc.). Even their commonly used moniker of "progressive" sounds great, yet their core policies are incredibly regressive. For a historical example, Mao's "Great Leap Forward" led to millions of deaths. Under the guise of flowery yet vacuous words and holding the mantle of protector of the oppressed, those wielding the linguistic hammer become unassailable.

Do you believe the world is going to end soon because of climate change? Do you believe that our society is systemically racist? Do you believe in diversity, equity, and inclusivity? If you answered yes, you have signaled that you're on the side of the morally right. But if you didn't answer yes, or even questioned what some of these terms mean, then you failed and are linguistically defaulted as an oppressor. Today, this can be accompanied by job insecurity.

Out of principle, don't allow any ideology—right or left—to perform linguistic sleights of hand. But also fight to preserve choice of language because of the negative downstream effects it will have on you. Try saying aloud or writing down "[your name] is a horrible person." Do it repeatedly. Set an alarm for every hour, and say it ten times once an hour while you're awake. Do this for a few days. How do you feel?

I received my first formal patient complaint in 2013. The medical regulatory body, the College of Physicians and Surgeons of Ontario, activated its investigative process. The problem was that it is well known (and advised by my lawyer) that I should not try to actively defend myself. The best way to get through it at the time was to adopt an attitude of "mea culpa" with a 100 percent conciliatory tone. The complaint was processed over the course of the next four years, with interviews and many letters in between. This was my own Maoist struggle session.[14] The more apologetic, and even pathetic, I portrayed myself, the more chance I would be granted leniency. I was left in limbo, wondering when it would ever end, meanwhile trying to deliver good care. Though this particular patient case wasn't a shining moment for me, there was no bad patient outcome. Is one complaint enough to wreck a doctor's career?

I found myself through that process writing, saying, and rehearsing for the entirety of the proceedings how bad I was and how much I had learned from the inquiry. There is of course a kernel of truth in every perspective (and frankly, there is no limit for improving for anyone), but I found it extremely challenging to live the idea in temporary bursts that I'm a horrible doctor, without believing it. I found it just as challenging to provide as good care as possible as my medical practice continued unhindered. For this, I needed to get good at doublethink, the ability to hold two contradictory ideas in your mind at the same time ("Doublethink" n.d.). Maybe 20 percent of me believed I was a horrible doctor at times, maybe more. I recall there was a time when I thought patients would be better off if I didn't practice medicine. I also seriously considered leaving medical practice in 2015. Though I was ultimately cleared, the duress and length of the ordeal left an indelible impression on me. In 2018 I left emergency medicine, my true professional passion, for good. My main motivation for working in other medical fields was a lower likelihood of litigation.

The point is that you will believe things that you say and write down repeatedly; speech, thought, writing, and action are intrinsically interconnected. "Two plus two equals five," said the interrogator to the thought criminal Winston Smith in George Orwell's *1984*. (Was Orwell referencing Nietzsche's underground man, who used the same phrasing?) He tortured Winston until he said it back to him. The interrogator explained to Smith that control over physical reality is unimportant to the Party, provided that the citizens of Oceania subordinate their real-world perceptions to the political will of the Party (Orwell 1949).

An Example of Ideological Language in Education

I recalled Orwell's prophecy in 2021 when multiple North American school boards began to propose making math subjective to reduce discrimination. For example, "The Ontario

Grade 9 mathematics curriculum emphasizes the need to recognize and challenge systems of power and privilege" (Ministry of Education 2021).

The original Ontario curriculum change included this statement: "Mathematics has been used to normalize racism and marginalization of non-Eurocentric mathematical knowledges, and a decolonial, anti-racist approach to mathematics education makes visible its historical roots and social constructions." After a backlash, the government dropped the words *racist, Eurocentric, subjective,* and *decolonial* within two days. But their virtue signaling intent had already been betrayed.

Math was developed by incredible people from India, China, Greece, and Babylon, and by Jews, Christians, Muslims, and people of so many other faiths. That's quite culturally diverse.

The stated goal is "achieving equitable outcomes in mathematics for all students . . ." (Ministry of Education 2021). It is far easier to say this than to try to tackle the multiple nuanced causes of unequal opportunity such as poverty, crime, and fatherless homes.

"A mathematics curriculum is most effective when it values and honors the diversity that exists among students and within communities" (Ministry of Education 2021). If this means that some people are more adept at math naturally than others, then students should and will get different grades.

The new curriculum will be called "culturally responsive and relevant pedagogy (CRRP)" (Ministry of Education 2021). This is doublespeak, which is language that obscures, disguises, distorts, or reverses the meaning of words ("Doublespeak" n.d.). It may take the form of euphemisms, in which case it's mainly meant to make the truth sound more palatable. There's intentional ambiguity in language. For example, in an attempt to minimize the controversy of euthanasia, the Canadian government called it "medical assistance in dying" just so the acronym could be MAiD (D'Souza 2022). As Orwell says, "Political language . . . is designed to make lies sound truthful and murder respectable" (1946). With Canadian MAiD, something that was controversial and illegal until only a few years ago suddenly sounded at least palatable, if not charming.[15] Doublespeak is similar to "Newspeak" language in *1984.* Orwell warned that Newspeak's goal was to narrow the range of thought, as there would be no words to commit a "thoughtcrime" (1949). Speaking of thoughtcrime, the best way to never offend someone is to never think offensive thoughts. The best way to get through a politically correct world unruffled is simply not to think. Otherwise, the Thought Police that Orwell conceived of will come after you. To guard against doublespeak, recognize that words and phrases can have multiple meanings, and try to determine the intended and sometimes hidden meaning with such language.

"In an anti-racist and anti-discriminatory environment, teachers know that there is more than one way to develop a solution" (Ministry of Education 2021). So, can two plus two equal five? I am concerned the downstream effect of this new curriculum will be that the basic structural functions of our society that we take for granted, such as bridges and airplanes, will be jeopardized in a generation. The focus appears to be on teaching our kids what to think—not how—and policing their hearts and souls instead of prioritizing reading, writing, and arithmetic. The pressure to conform to radical left morality is so strong, this curriculum change was brought about by the conservative party of Ontario.

Words are important. "What's the harm [of saying it the way we want]?" Words affect your thoughts, which in turn affect your beliefs. And then it's a slippery slope on the way to a postmodern abyss. Don't let anyone compel your words. Don't repeat things you do not believe to be true.

Conclusion

What ideologies do you subscribe to? As an exercise, take a moment to write down all the causes you are passionate about. Reflect on where your spare time and perhaps even donations go. What Facebook groups do you belong to? What are the common conversational topics with your friends? What artwork or posters adorn your walls? What are the common issues that trigger you? Refer to the table of contents of this book for a list of popular ideologies. Do any of them strike a chord? With your full list, move on to the next step.

Next, try to write down a detailed argument for each belief. Even simpler, try to think of a single downside of your position. For example, can you conceive of a point after which your movement has gone too far? If you can't do either of these, then this is an ideology for you. This is even more true if you can identify the oppressor and the oppressed in each reductive belief system.

Self-awareness is a great first remedy. As a second step, try to articulate the opposing view's argument (a technique called steelmanning). If you are able to articulate the other side of the argument, you can strengthen your position, or at least see its flaws. Then you can revise your position with a more sophisticated argument, and then it is no longer an ideology.

Relinquish all ideologies. Be an enemy to the dogmatic. Engaging in civil debate with those with differing views is the best way to expose the biases in your blind spots, which everyone has. In this manner, we hope that the best ideas will win out.

The next few chapters will discuss examples of a few ideologies that are prevalent in today's society. While each is different, they're all ways people fill the void of real religion, and their emptiness can lead to destruction.

Chapter 6:

SOCIAL JUSTICE WARRIOR REPLACEMENT RELIGION

Social justice is great, but social justice warriors are of the low-vibration mold. Their activism is just an excuse for their unintegrated shadow to manifest. There is perhaps Freudian projection of their own violent nature onto the oppressor of the day. In the words commonly attributed to Freud's best student, Carl Jung, "The most dangerous psychological mistake is the projection of the shadow on to others; this is the root of almost all conflicts." I believe that psychological projection is similar in practice to what's known today as gaslighting.

It isn't wrong to feel bad for the downtrodden. In fact, these sentiments are quite noble and demonstrate the size of your heart, at least in isolation. But they sell a simplistic oppressor-oppressed binary narrative. If a good cause is justification for you to vandalize and beat people up, that's deplorable. The social justice warrior movement has its roots in *The Communist Manifesto*. The foundational document of socialism strives for equal outcome (equity) by violent means explicitly. "Peaceful means [are] necessarily doomed to failure" (Marx and Engels [1848] 2004). *Exitus acta probat*: the ends justify the means.[16]

Author Thomas Sowell believes that envy has been successfully rebranded as "social justice" (Sowell 2002). Social justice warriors are powered by both a sense of fairness and envy, skillfully marketing the former while concealing the latter. They stoke resentment in their converts. For example, Democratic Representative Alexandria Ocasio-Cortez attended the Met Gala event in 2021 wearing a dress emblazoned with the slogan "Tax the

Rich." Social justice warriors have a strong scapegoating impulse, projecting evil onto the rich, while overlooking their own wealth. "The rich" are frequently ambiguously defined as anyone possessing more than oneself. It's notable that individual tickets for the Met Gala event were priced at $35,000 (Fleming 2021).

This leitmotif of the ends justifying the means plays itself out in modernity, just as it did with Marx. The father of postmodernism, Michel Foucault, provided the doctrinal connection explicitly in a debate with Noam Chomsky in 1971: "When the proletariat takes power, it may be quite possible that the proletariat will exert towards the classes over which it has just triumphed, a violent, dictatorial, and even bloody power. I can't see what objection one could make to this" (Chomsky and Foucault 2006). Postmodernism is an anti-grand-narrative philosophy that emerged in the twentieth century. That is to say that it is skeptical of any explanation, ideology, or system of belief. This includes challenging objective reality and the scientific method of the Enlightenment. Every view is just someone's perspective. Truth and morality are relative, so facts don't really matter (Rogan and Peterson 2017; "Postmodernism" n.d.). That being said, postmodernism seems to permit Marxism, itself a grand narrative, viewing hierarchies as unjust manifestations of power, and dividing the world into oppressor and oppressed (Peterson and Zizek 2019; Rogan, Peterson, and Weinstein 2017).

As a modern example, when New York City mayor-elect Eric Adams declared in 2021 that he was ready to take a tougher approach on crime, Black Lives Matter New York leader Hawk Newsome threatened violence. "There will be riots. There will be fire, and there will be bloodshed" (O'Neill and Marsh 2021). Eric Adams rightly did not cower. Again, *exitus acta probat*; the ends justify the means.

Nikole Hannah-Jones, founder of the 1619 Project,[17] claims that "destroying property, which can be replaced, is not violence . . . you can't say that regular citizens should play by all the rules when agents of the state clearly are not [referring to George Floyd's death]" (Wulfsohn 2020). To social justice warriors, it seems two wrongs make a right.

Contrast this with the words of Martin Luther King Jr.:

> Nonviolent resistance does not seek to defeat or humiliate the opponent, but to win friendship and understanding . . . The nonviolent resister must often express his protest through noncooperation or boycotts, but he realizes that noncooperation and boycotts are not ends themselves; they are merely means to awaken a sense of moral shame in the opponent . . . The

> aftermath of nonviolence is the creation of the beloved community, while the aftermath of violence is tragic bitterness. (King Jr. 1957)

King also says:

> If you have weapons, take them home; if you do not have them, please do not seek to get them. We cannot solve this problem through retaliatory violence. We must meet violence with nonviolence. Remember the words of Jesus: "He who lives by the sword will perish by the sword." (King Jr. [1958] 2011)

Martin Luther King Jr. had six principles of nonviolence that we as a society would be wise to listen to (King Jr. [1958] 2011):

1. Nonviolence is not for the faint of heart.
2. Nonviolence seeks to defeat injustice, not people.
3. The goal of nonviolence is reconciliation.
4. Redemptive suffering holds transformational power.
5. Nonviolence pertains to physical acts and internal thoughts.
6. The universe is on the side of justice.

Marks of Cain

In the last decade, several words have cropped up that have the power of the mark of Cain.[18] That is to say, anyone painted with these words is societally shunned. Here is a list of the most common ones:

- racist
- sexist
- transphobic
- climate denier
- Nazi
- fascist
- colonial
- hateful
- arrogant

These "mark of Cain" words are so powerful that they even affect people's employment. They are immensely imbued with reputational damage. In years past, the applications of these words were truer to their definitions. Now, however, the criteria to attain these labels is so wide, anyone can accrue them. Disagree with someone who identifies as a victim (which again is entirely subjective), and suddenly you are labeled with one of these terms. Marks of Cain are convenient narratives when you don't want to confront your own insecurities.

"The word 'racism' is like ketchup," says Thomas Sowell. "It can be put on practically anything—and demanding evidence makes you a 'racist'" (Sowell n.d.). Sowell alludes to the Kafkatrap nature of this and all the other "mark of Cain" words.[19] By using these terms so liberally, it has become far more challenging to identify those who have truly earned them.

These words can often be used by the radical left to denote those they are most afraid of. Jordan Peterson has not only been called all the words I have identified but even has the distinction of being labeled a "super Nazi" (Flood 2021).[20]

His detractors greatly struggle to debate with him, and hence they resort to such ad hominem slurs.[21] One of my most influential medical professors once told a group of students, "If they can't come after your medicine, they'll come after you personally." This was in the context of patient care and the complex interplay of hospital dynamics. It took me years to understand the full profundity of this wisdom. In a more generalizable context, if you are earning ad hominem attacks, let alone marks of Cain—well done. You are doing a good job. And if it's in the context of a debate, you must have made some great arguments. You are probably triggering their insecurities. Their deep, foundational beliefs are shaking. If they can't come after your points, they will come after you personally. So the next time you hear someone smearing another with a mark of Cain, ask them what exactly that person did to earn that, then judge for yourself. For example, "What exactly did this person say that is racist?" Don't let your propensity for a short attention span, or for Nietzschean herd mentality, mar someone's good name via reputational damage.

Social justice movements are the offspring of Marxism. This is at least true of the movements that are more extreme with their demands. When activists display an inherent hatred toward Enlightenment (Western) values and a desire for tearing the system down through revolution, it's just Marxism repackaged. Like adherents of Marxism, they instinctively claim the moral high ground and slur their opponents with marks of Cain. From forbidden to tolerated to equal to superior goes the slippery slope, because for revolutionaries, the revolution can never end. Social justice activism can be an avenue to find meaning, displace anger and depression, and achieve power. Many activists do not support the spirit of free inquiry, but they condone force and even violence if done for their "just" cause. True to their Nietzschean superman blueprint, they create their own moral code without consideration for or negotiation with others. For them, *exitus acta probat*; the ends justify the means.

Note: This chapter in particular reviews many of the unacceptable features of the radical left, but here we can start to see where the radical left converges with the radical right. They both share authoritarian and "might makes right" philosophies. Violence and censorship are staples of both extremes. The book focuses on the radical left because it is culturally mainstream in large part due to linguistic misdirection, but both political poles are of very low vibration and are to be avoided.

Chapter 7:

DIVERSITY-EQUITY-INCLUSIVITY REPLACEMENT RELIGION OF THE RADICAL LEFT

The diversity-equity-inclusivity mantra is also a replacement religion. Cultural institutions and corporations of the West are effectively mandated to have an officer with this title, or even an entire division. This movement has also infiltrated the medical profession. Medical journals are increasingly replete with publications carrying this slogan. No one is against these words, as they all sound intuitively good. But they are never fully defined, and it is verboten to question them.

Inclusivity

Let's start with inclusivity. Christian icon carver Jonathan Pageau gives a good analogy about a basketball team that illustrates one of the problems with this overlying value. The purpose of the team previously probably was to win games. But if you say the primary purpose is inclusion (which might be true in many leagues, especially in primary school), that knocks winning down to the second rung at best. So you're devouring the main purpose. Now suppose you say inclusion is the primary purpose of every single institution—suddenly the military's main goal isn't to defend a nation or win wars, medical student applicants with the most acumen don't become doctors, and the most talented musicians don't entertain us. And those who refuse to live by this code become scapegoats and oddly enough must be excluded (J. Peterson and Pageau 2021).

Inclusion as the primary value for an elementary school soccer team is laudable. But inclusion rising to among the top organizational values, as it has in many corporate mission statements, can be outright dangerous. On this note, both American and British militaries have been criticized in the last few years for prioritizing inclusion along various intersectional identities over merit (Rubio and Roy 2022). As an example, the Royal Air Force was accused of an "effective pause" on offering jobs to White males (Prestigiacomo 2022). Do we want the most capable people defending our countries, or do we want to first of all ensure that select intersectional identities are represented at the very least proportionally? I suspect that the latter thrust is what the execution of inclusivity in the West truly means.

Diversity

And what does diversity mean? It appears to be diversity in a number of select dimensions, but no more than that. It certainly does not mean diversity of opinion. This results in a quota system, one that is not based on merit or competence, just based on select immutable characteristics. Do you like movies? Hollywood reporters Peter Kiefer and Peter Savodnik interviewed a group of writers and directors, and they found that the directors were all scared of not meeting the diversity requirement. This means that they have to seek out BIPOC people first for casting roles in their films (Kiefer and Savodnik 2022).

This setup in Hollywood is playing itself out in all other Western institutions. Of all people, even Vladimir Putin sees the failings of the woke agenda. In a speech, he connected what is happening now in the West with the Communist rise to power a century ago in his country:

> The advocates of so-called "social progress" believe they are introducing humanity to some kind of a new and better consciousness . . . Russia has been there already. After the 1917 revolution, the Bolsheviks, relying on the dogmas of Marx and Engels, also said that they would change existing ways and customs, and not just political and economic ones, but the very notion of human morality and the foundations of a healthy society. The destruction of age-old values, religion, and relations between people, up to and including the total rejection of family (we had that, too), encouragement

> to inform on loved ones—all this was proclaimed progress and, by the way, was widely supported around the world back then and was quite fashionable, same as today. By the way, the Bolsheviks were absolutely intolerant of opinions other than theirs . . . In Hollywood, memos are distributed about proper storytelling and how many characters of what color or gender should be in a movie. This is even worse than the agitprop department of the Central Committee of the Communist Party of the Soviet Union. (Mahjar-Barducci 2022)

And Putin would know since he worked for them. Putin is no paragon of actual virtue, but very often our biggest critics even inadvertently light a pathway of constructive criticism. And rather than give in to the temptation to attack him ad hominem, I just evaluate the crux of his argument—the woke West's similarity to Bolshevism of a century ago.

Diversity taking first chair in the orchestra of priorities is a direct assault on individualism and merit. The vision diversity activists seem to espouse is that the more representation from about five specific intersectional group identities (not all groups are equally revered), the better the product will be. It doesn't seem to matter whether there is skill or experience. Is this just Utopian wishful thinking? If armies or sports teams were built on this principle, they would lose every single time. The reason today's mainstream Western culture frequently vilifies successful people, such as with Representative Ocasio-Cortez's Met Gala dress, or Western governments frequent "tax the rich" plans whenever they need more funds (Gordon and Smith 2021), is because their existence disproves the radical left ideas that we are all the same, and that hard work and talent are artificial societal constructions designed to keep the oppressors in power and the oppressed on the bottom.

Race is perhaps the most common dimension brought into cultural conversations about diversity today. Specifically, the racial social justice movement in the US has brought attention to long-standing issues, but what are their solutions? They have propagated the term "white guilt," which describes the feelings of shame and remorse some White people experience when they recognize the legacy of racism and racial injustice ("White Guilt" n.d.). This is gaslighting on a cultural level. It is effective because there are kernels of truth in every narrative, but it is an incomplete story. Some other considerations to factor in include the White Americans who fought to end slavery in the Civil War; that slavery was ubiquitous cross-culturally, but it was actually the Western ethic that brought it down (following the biblical idea that we are all made in the image of God); that there are more slaves now than at any time in human history (Hodal 2019), and if one truly finds the idea of slavery repugnant, why is this not the leading social issue of our time?

Are White Americans collectively supposed to be born feeling guilty for their immutable characteristics? Isn't that the very definition of racism?[22] Google's anti-racism initiative claimed that America is systemically racist. They had an allyship training module encouraging people to rate themselves in racial and gender identities, then rank themselves in a hierarchy of power and privilege. In a video from guest lecturer Ibram Kendi, director of the Center for Antiracist Research, he claimed that "to be raised in the United States is to be raised as racist . . . the heartbeat of racism is denial, and the sound of that denial is 'I'm not racist'" (Shapiro 2021c). The core of this quote echoes throughout many of Kendi's teachings. So if you believe you're racist, then you're racist. And if you don't believe you're racist, you're also racist. This is a Kafkatrap. While it's possible that racists aren't self-aware, there needs to be objective criteria for racism. But for the radical left, the subjective world takes primacy. And what follows from Kendi's anti-racism training is tacit approval of discrimination against White people.

Martin Luther King Jr.'s dream of color blindness is truly sinking in the face of so-called diversity mandates. "I have a dream that my four little children will one day live in a nation where they will not be judged by the color of their skin but by their character." The good reverend also warned against Black supremacy. But in 2024, skin color is perhaps the most important determinant of cultural status. By calling attention to, even fixating, on skin color, this is the opposite of color blindness. Fighting discrimination with more discrimination is only perpetuating the tool of discrimination. It will do nothing to right historical wrongs, and it will only leave us more divided.

However, in Ibram Kendi's book on how to be a good person (the actual title is *How to Be an Antiracist*), he instructs: "The only remedy to past discrimination is present discrimination" (2019). Is this Freudian reaction formation? I believe his implication is that you can give preferential treatment to Black people and discriminate against White people. But just because you are racist against White people does not make you a good person; actually, it makes you racist. As an example, McGill University professor of chemistry Patanjali Kambhampati believes he is being denied research grants on the justification that "the Equity, Diversity and Inclusion considerations in [his] application were deemed insufficient." He was clear in his application that he would hire based on merit and not skin color. He believes what's implied is that he can't mentor straight White men as equally as others (Azar 2022).

A school board in Ontario defines and disparages color blindness in a draft document targeting grades 2 and 3:

> . . . an approach to reduce interracial tension which proposes that "racial categories do not matter and should not be considered when making decisions such as hiring and school admissions. The primary tenet of this approach is that social categories should be dismantled and disregarded, and everyone should be treated as an individual." This ideology posits itself on the premise of equality for all, rather than equity, and thus, at its core is an insidious practice of racism in itself. (Hamilton-Wentworth District School Board 2021)

Very clearly, this document demonstrates that equal outcome matters over equal opportunity; that the group you belong to matters more than who you are as an individual. I believe that the culture war ultimately boils down to these two questions: 1) Should society prioritize equal outcomes over equal opportunities? and 2) Should group identity matter more than one's individual qualities? You cannot side with both, as they are opposites; instead, you must choose between Enlightenment and anti-Enlightenment values.

Another Ontario school board (York Region, a suburb of Toronto) has a hiring policy under the penumbra of diversity that is emblematic of quota-based policies around the Western world, like in Hollywood: "The Board commits to hiring more Black staff while at the same time creating work environments that are identity-affirming, inclusive, and anti-racist. The [school board] will prioritize the hiring of Black teachers and other Black staff" (York Region District School Board 2021). I wonder whether other teachers will initially doubt new Black hires' skills and be predisposed to believe that they got the job because of the color of their skin rather than their capabilities. I also wonder what happens if in some instances this actually is the case and the teacher is unable to do a competent job. Wouldn't that hurt students, some of whom could be Black? Isn't such a policy insulting to Black teachers who feel they can advance on their own merit? How many excellent non-Black teachers were passed over, discriminated against, because of their skin color? Would you accept being operated on by a surgeon who got the position mostly because they met a quota, even though they cannot perform surgery well? While I recognize the merits of having people from a community preferentially hired as a beacon of hope to others of the same community, this hiring policy, like many others on diversity, makes no mention of balancing intersectional identity with skill.

Equity

Now we are left with equity. What is the difference between equity and equality? It is confusing, and there is an overlap in meaning. Equity, by definition, adds the dimensions of justice and fairness ("Equality vs. Equity: What Is the Difference?" n.d.). In the last few years, equity has become a very popular buzzword. In execution, however, I believe it means equal outcome, and this is the idea I want to critique.

You can't have equal outcome and equal opportunity at the same time; they are not the same thing. Equal opportunity maximally gives people the chance to differentiate themselves; after all, aren't we supposed to celebrate diversity? The drive for equity, or sameness, is also antithetical to this supposed diversity.

Hypothetically, those who tout equity as among the highest ideals in society do so out of love of those who are not as successful in a number of dimensions. But what if you tried to apply equity to every facet of society? I'm not sure how people can ask for equal outcome economically and not also apply this to professional sports. Why does LeBron James get more time with the ball than his teammates? Do you want to watch sports where everything is equal? Further, why don't people like you and me get a chance at playing professional sports? How is that fair? Equity is definitely not the modus operandi of professional sports. Play time and salaries are based on performance alone.

Stepping outside of this exclusive, high-achieving realm, studies have shown that as countries have increased equal opportunity for careers, there have paradoxically been more—not less—differences in gender preferences (Falk and Hermle 2018). Specifically, the countries with the highest levels of gender equality have some of the largest STEM (science, technology, engineering, and math) gaps in higher education (Stoet and Geary 2018). This suggests that when presented with equal opportunities, men and women tend to make distinct occupational choices, often leading to more women pursuing fields like nursing and more men gravitating toward fields like engineering, rather than an even gender distribution across all professions.

You also can't have both equity and diversity. Jordan Peterson says,

> All you have to bring to the world is what is unequal about you. You'd think that people who push on the diversity end of things would recognize that above all else. By forcing equality, you actually destroy what everyone has to bring to the table to trade. That's terrible because you punish them then for

> the best thing they have, and you deprive everyone of the opportunity to benefit from what everyone bringing what's unique about them to the table. (J. Peterson and Weinstein 2021).

Essentially, recognizing individual differences naturally leads to diverse paths and outcomes, rendering uniform results unrealistic. If everyone were identical, diversity wouldn't even be a topic of discussion. However, celebrating our unique qualities involves embracing differential achievements and unequal outcomes.

Equity, or aiming for equal outcome, discriminates based on immutable characteristics. For example, the Department of Justice investigated Yale University admissions and found that Asian American and White students are one-tenth to one-fourth as likely to be admitted as Black students with comparable academic resumes (Department of Justice 2020). This is just plain racism under the banner of equity. To paraphrase Orwell, are some truly more equal than others? (1945). Further, most nurses are female. Ninety-nine percent of mechanics are male (J. Peterson 2019b). In the name of equity, should we be forcing those of the minority represented gender into a profession they don't want? What are we sacrificing in the aim of proportional representation based on the population for every profession? Is it even realistic if you add race and other group identity dimensions to this increasingly complicated formula?

Don't forget that some people are particularly skilled, driven, and accomplished, and they can apply themselves to better the lives of the rest of us. We lose this distinction by forcing sameness (equity). We can have an ideal and still celebrate individual differences. We can encourage all to pursue their aspirations while being understanding when they fall short of them.

Further, the way equity is executed culturally is not about redressing all inequalities, it's just about correcting any departure from statistical equality in very select dimensions. The radical left is certainly not trying to even out the overrepresentation of males in prisons, males in the driving or construction industries, or non-Black people in the NBA. I have to wonder whether it's about equality or superiority. At some point, the emphasis on preferential treatment for specific demographics carries within it the idea of inherent superiority for immutable characteristics, that this will produce better results versus merit-based organizations, and that the discrimination of others for their inferior immutable characteristics is justified. This was simply not acceptable up until a few years ago.

The Role of the Radical Left in Diversity-Equity-Inclusivity

I believe the very noble surface intent of diversity, equity, and inclusivity was to foster an environment free of barriers for anyone and everyone to get the same opportunities, though of course skill and hard work (and, to be fair, sometimes cheating) would lead to diverse outcomes. This was based on the stored cultural capital of the Enlightenment, and previously, the Judeo-Christian idea that we are created equal in the image of God. But through the mélange of activism and linguistic ambiguity, a more sinister creature exists within this radical left Trojan horse, one that threatens societal upheaval.[23]

I believe that the uniting theme of the radical left, whether expressed through the welfare state, climate alarmism, social justice advocacy, or its other main avenues, is the tearing down of societal norms, achievements, traditions, and established structures. These actions often stem from the dark underlying motivations of jealousy and resentment. Meanwhile, the motivation for the moderate left comes from a much cleaner, lighter place. They actually feel compassion for the poor and are open to debate. The radical left espouses some sort of revenge justice of righteous payback. Their solutions come from the lowest vibration of places. They are neither practical, nor will they accomplish anything tangible except increase the payoff for being a victim.

It is no surprise that the progenitor of the radical left, Karl Marx, cites Mephistopheles in Faust as his favorite line from literature: "Everything that exists deserves to perish" (Kengor 2020). Embodying the Bazarov (teardown) impulse from Turgenev, the radical left has difficulty seeing that some elements are worth preserving even if there is injustice in the world. Cancel culture, a narcissistic manifestation of the radical left, is the end of the spectrum of censorship; it does not see nuance and cannot (will not?) play devil's advocate. They want to tear down carefully built structures and policies as if to say, "If any part of it is bad, it's all bad!" They advocate for large-scale changes, completely ignoring the law of unintended consequences. There is no forgiveness, and the punishment is wildly disproportionate to the crime (e.g., job loss for a problematic Facebook photo from decades ago).

The radical anarchist tendencies of the extreme left are predicated on the notion that Utopia is a real place. Then, by all means, bring in the wrecking ball; no culture measures up. But if Utopia isn't real, you have to make a more complex decision, weighing out not just the downsides of a system but also the upsides. Using America as a proxy for our judgment of the West, the radical left says that America is a terrible, oppressive country. Compared to what? Is there another major country that is clearly preferable? Is every sinew of America bad and irredeemable, or are some aspects worth keeping and tweaking? Could you be scapegoating or projecting your own shadow onto it, or your own depression and anger, at least to some extent? So unless Utopia truly exists, even the next best world will have elements to improve on. You can never stop upgrading what you have, but be careful that in your resentment you don't destroy the good parts as well.

Conclusion

The diversity-equity-inclusivity slogan achieving cultural dominance perhaps represents the pinnacle achievement for the radical left. That it is undebatable and vaguely defined should make people at least privately question its motives. There is a divergence between its marketing—the intrinsic goodness of the words—and the reality of how it plays out. Meanwhile, previous culturally accepted values such as color blindness and merit have fallen out of favor. If you are going to pay homage to diversity-equity-inclusivity in any capacity, at least do so after defining the words for yourself and considering the criticisms brought up. Say no to being compelled to swear allegiance just because it is a shortcut to virtue.

Note: While inherent, even metaphysical, assertions of superiority based on race and other immutable characteristics still exist, which is the cardinal feature of the radical right, they do not have any effective cultural sway. This book focuses on the radical left because it has the power of mainstream media and Big Tech behind it, and its credos have deeply penetrated our institutions. People lose their jobs for having right-leaning views, not left-leaning ones. But we must still be wary of radical right ideology. Ideally, we can move back to the center with open minds and hearts.

Chapter 8:

VICTIMHOOD AS A REPLACEMENT RELIGION

Ajax was perhaps the strongest of the Greek warriors in the Trojan War. He was a demigod and Achilles' cousin. After Achilles' death, Greek leadership debated on who to award his armor to, a huge honor, and ultimately decided on Odysseus over Ajax. Ajax now faced a dilemma. He was a hero in the soon-to-be victorious army of a great war, yet he felt ashamed and beyond upset. So Ajax killed himself. Even though he was viewed as a champion by his peers, in that moment, what mattered most was that in the mirror he saw a victim. While his ending is an extreme example, Ajax's dilemma is universal in that we are constantly faced with opportunities on how to interpret hardships. Sometimes life isn't fair. And yet whether you are a prince or a pauper, there are better ways of dealing with the rigors of life than ending it.

Victimhood is a common replacement religion in the 2020s. A victim is defined as someone who is subjected to oppression, hardship, or mistreatment ("Victimhood" n.d.). Victimhood acts as a replacement religion when you espouse the idea that not only do you lack agency and responsibility, but you also seek to receive clout for being a victim. In this inverted hierarchy, the more victimized you are, the more social status you have, and the more power there is in your viewpoints. It is both childish and low vibration. It has become culturally trendy and an informal social credit system.

Origin and Payoff of Victimhood Culture

The ultimate origin of the coddling culture of victimhood in the West lies in Jean-Jacque Rousseau's *Émile*, his guide on the education of children. In it, Rousseau argues that children are born naturally good and that their education should be largely self-directed ([1762] 2010). This proto-Montessori philosophy was a break from the older Christian idea that we're born instead with original sin, and we must develop the internal discipline required to resist our sinful desires. The opening sentence sets the tone well: "Everything is good as it leaves the hands of the Author of things; everything degenerates in the hands of man" (Rousseau [1762] 2010). That's a much nicer notion than the Christian view that man was born imperfect but could and should strive toward the ideal (i.e., Christ). The goal instead shifted to restoring men to their original and natural state of goodness and happiness, thus inviting social engineering on a huge scale. Perhaps Rousseau drew on the biblical idea that people are made in the image of God, without balancing this with the idea of original sin. Giving in to your child's whims is a convenient idea to buy into if you are a busy parent.

Fellow French philosopher Michel Foucault took this a step further in the twentieth century with his denial of free will. "None of us chose our brains, bodies, families, or communities in time and space. How could we be said to have free will at all?" (Shellenberger 2021a). From these ideas, the ideology of victimhood has grown.

Today it has never been more advantageous to be a victim. There is often a payoff for lying (or at least embellishing) and a price to pay for being truthful. Being a victim is an easy pathway to positive emotions. There's a pity party in your name everywhere you go. Suddenly you can put on the cloak of invulnerability (inspired by Jonathan Haidt; Haidt and Rogan 2019) and infallibility. You can do no wrong. Instead, others praise you. The bigger the victimhood status attained, the bigger the praise, and the more impervious your cloak. At higher echelons, you might even be called "heroic." You wear your victimhood as an honor badge. To loosely paraphrase Winston Churchill, a blanket of feathers has descended upon the West.[24]

As a victim, you get at least the following:

1. Moral immunity that shields you from criticism, including about the means you might use to satisfy your demands. You can morally justify lying, cheating, and even violence. For a blatant historical example, Stalin scapegoated the kulaks, Soviet farmers who owned over eight acres of land, under the banner of oppression and other leftist platitudes. Millions starved in the resultant famine

("Kulak" n.d.). For a more recent example, recall prominent journalist Nikole Hannah-Jones's endorsement of the destruction of property (Wulfsohn 2020).

2. You become less blameworthy. Instead, for example, it's society's fault.
3. It elevates your psychological standing, the subjective sense of legitimacy or entitlement to speak up. In this manner, you can reject or ignore any objections by nonvictims to the unreasonableness of your demands (Ok et al. 2021).

There's an ABCDE formula to easily transform yourself into a hero who can do no wrong:

A—Find a group that is historically, currently, or even just **A**llegedly oppressed.
B—Use **B**inary thinking to find a corresponding oppressor, a group that one can be envious of for historical or even fabricated reasons.
C—The more marks of **C**ain you anoint the oppressors with, the better. Call them racist, sexist, hateful, or Nazis. Liberally insult anyone who tries to have dialogue with you on the issue to silence them. As Vladimir Lenin said, "We can and must write in a language which sows among the masses hate, revulsion, and scorn toward those who disagree with us" (Eastman 1955).
D—Cite **D**iversity, equity, and inclusivity as your north star.
E—Cite **E**nvironment, social, and governance as a bonus.

A good example of this is the Black Lives Matter organization.

A—The oppressed group is Black people.
B—The oppressor is the system and White people.
C—Those who disagree, or even just want dialogue on the topic, are deemed racist. People lose their jobs for even questioning them (such as the author of a study of the effect of de-policing) (Kriegman 2021).
D—Diversity is one of their thirteen guiding principles (Black Lives Matter 2022).
E—They link environmentalism to racial justice, championing the concept that "climate justice is racial justice" (Black Lives Matter 2021).

Black Lives Matter's fulfillment of these criteria lends them plenty of moral immunity, so here are some criticisms that do not get mainstream attention: Regarding their demand to defund the police, Black people themselves, when polled, have revealed that they don't want this. A 2020 Gallup poll found that 61 percent of Black Americans prefer that the police spend the same amount of time in their area, and 20 percent wanted more (L. Saad 2020). There is also some evidence of increased murders of Black people as a result of de-policing, estimated at 2,500 additional murders per year (Kriegman 2021). Further, if the focus is on advocacy for Black people, it is unclear why the organization promotes transgender and environmental activism, is against the nuclear family, and is even staunchly pro-Palestinian in the Middle East conflict (Black Lives Matter 2022; Gonzalez 2021).

Black Lives Matter has done an outstanding job of calling attention to tragic injustices, but the organization has failed to foster an environment where solutions can be debated, and it has left many to wonder about their intentions. No one is against Black Lives Matter's semantically endowed name, but the organization has some questions to answer.

The payoff of victimhood is so big that many celebrities also go to great lengths to acquire such status. In 2019, Jussie Smollett paid two Black brothers to physically attack him, shout racial and homophobic slurs, and place a noose around his neck. Smollett had the right idea. Trying to amass as much virtue capital as possible, Smollett went for racist and homophobic victimhood status. Together, they would power him like a rocket straight to the top of the victimhood hierarchy. Sadly, the mistake Smollett made was doing the "crime" near a security camera. In December 2021, a jury found him guilty on five of six counts of felony disorderly conduct.

Professor of marketing Gad Saad jokes that only expert judges in oppression Olympics could adjudicate two people vying for victimhood supremacy. In his book *The Parasitic Mind*, he discusses which markers are the greatest for victimhood (2020). I believe that in the era of lived experience and subjective truth, he or she whose truth wins out is whoever claims greatest victimhood; the dominant narrative is awarded to the gold medalist victim.

There is emerging literature behind the concept of competitive victimhood, whereby various social groups try to claim ever greater degrees of victimhood as a resource extraction strategy. It also helps them even more fully justify seeking retribution against alleged oppressors. Further research suggests that individuals or groups can gain an advantage in the "victim space" by emitting signals that convey not only need but also moral worth and deservingness (Ok et al. 2021).

A culture of offense has taken shape, where it pays to be a member of the perpetually offended. We've essentially weaponized being offended. This has created an ever-growing number of offense archaeologists, whose primary mission in life is to say "I'm offended" as often and as loudly as possible. Saad articulates it well: "The Oppression Olympics (also known as Victimology Poker) is the arena wherein this competition of victimhood takes place, using identity politics and intersectionality . . . to establish the 'winners' of this grotesque theatre of the absurd" (G. Saad 2020).

Feeling offended is, to a certain extent, a reflection on how you feel about yourself. If you're easily offended, your poor self-confidence shines through. Grounded, centered people that are more concerned with elevating themselves than tearing others down don't easily get offended. If you're offended often, maybe you should look inward to your insecurities first. There is even a term that has been invented to allow you to still feel offended even when there are absolutely zero external, objective indications: microaggression (Orr, Ahmed, and Peterson 2022).

On a macro-cosmic note, countries can also have razor-thin emotional resilience. China, for example, gets angry and confrontational whenever anyone questions their way. This is called wolf warrior diplomacy, after a Chinese action film franchise (Maddeaux 2021). Anything that can be perceived as a slight will be taken as one. Minor incidents are treated as existential threats and grave offenses. Here are some examples from the 2020 Olympics in Tokyo: China attacked NBC for displaying an "incomplete map" of the country that didn't include Taiwan or the South China Sea; Reuters for publishing an "ugly" photo of Chinese weightlifting gold medalist Zhihui Hou; CNN for mentioning a Chinese gold medal win and COVID-19 in the same headline; and a Japanese broadcaster for implying that Taiwan is a country. For such a powerful country, they are awfully insecure (Maddeaux 2021).

The concept of lived experience is central to victimhood. It is often used to declare that one's truth is equivalent to objective truth, or that objective reality itself doesn't exist. It's true that no one can lay a claim on your subjective experience, but this truth can be used in an infantile manner. Author Coleman Hughes exposes the flaw of the primacy of lived experience:

> The only way to count every life equally is actually to look at data . . . to elevate your own personal history to the point where you don't feel you need to look at any facts or evidence is extremely narcissistic and implic-

> itly counting your life as more valuable than other people's lives. It's the opposite of a defensible moral stance towards all of humanity. (Hughes and Jaimungal 2020)

To illustrate how lived experience is often used poorly, CNN host Don Lemon interviewed the acting director of the National Hurricane Center, Jamie Rhome, in 2022. The interview was to discuss the impact of Hurricane Ian as it was making landfall in Florida. Lemon kept trying to link it to climate change, and Rhome kept rebuffing him, saying, "On the whole, on the cumulative, climate change may be making storms worse. But to link it to any one event, I would caution against that." Lemon refused to accept Rhome's empirically responsible statements. Lemon retorted, "Listen, I grew up [in Florida] and these storms are intensifying—something is causing them to intensify" (Griffin 2022). A study on US hurricane landfall frequency and intensity denies any significant increase since 1900, corroborating Rhome's data-based point of view (Klotzbach et al. 2018). Are we interested in an objective truth? What if other people like Lemon who grew up in Florida had a different lived experience? Should those people all vote on whether hurricanes are increasing, and then should everyone accept the poll results as fact? Likewise, the lived experience of every human is of a flat Earth, and very painfully only centuries ago did we realize that wasn't true.

To illustrate how lived experience can be used effectively, I use it in my daily medical practice in chronic pain. Many chronic pain conditions have no obvious objective measurement modalities. Unless there is a motive for secondary gain, such as for insurance money, I cannot dispute when my patients say they are in a lot of pain. In fact, their feedback is essential to the formulation of my medical plans to address their symptoms.

Thanks to a culture of victimhood and modern technology, anecdotes have never been more powerful. With smartphones now ubiquitous, videos of tragedies circulate to the masses quickly. Our minds instinctively and uncritically extrapolate these videos as evidence of incontrovertible trends. The conclusions we draw quickly become imbued with a sense of black and white, good versus evil. Once we identify with them, it becomes difficult to challenge the prevailing narrative with any amount of scientific skepticism and data. Therefore, our rationale is increasingly defined by black truths. I don't think we've adapted well at all to the meteoric rise of social media. Like icebergs, there is far more to social media narratives if you look under the surface, but these days stories, emotions, feelings, group identity, and lived experience trump data, facts, and the once powerful scientific process.

Financial Dimension of Victim-Based Culture

How does entrenched victimhood manifest financially? Programs such as social services, welfare, and the overall safety net for those at the socioeconomic bottom are absolutely necessary. But how robust should they be? And are there any negative consequences? The downside to overly generous social services is that they murder the urge to strive in those who struggle the most with it. In those who are the least self-motivated, you cannot thereafter fan the embers of striving. This is a problem of socialism in general. When you already have trouble motivating yourself, and you discover that the reality that forty hours of work per week will make you just so slightly better off after taxes compared to social assistance, this extinguishes the beginnings of motivation; it keeps people from finding meaning and purpose in their lives.

Criticism of the central paradox of welfare goes back as far as Benjamin Franklin, who felt that the English system paradoxically produced more poverty compared to the less generous American (then known as the thirteen colonies) system (1780). Fellow American Founding Father Thomas Jefferson recognized that when you cannot keep the rewards of your work, you are going to be less productive; this is human nature ([1858] 1998). Of course we must have taxes, but there is an innate trade-off. The more taxes, the more the erosion of the principle of private property. Socialism is a spectrum, and of course the end of the spectrum, communism, called for the abolition of private property. Maybe society is better off with 5 percent of this idea implemented, but we need to negotiate where that line is drawn.

American economist and writer Thomas Sowell says the bigger cause of Black Americans' problems today is the government welfare programs initiated in the 1960s. "The Black family, which had survived centuries of slavery and discrimination, began rapidly disintegrating in the liberal welfare state that subsidized unwed pregnancy and changed welfare from an emergency rescue to a way of life" (2004). Welfare payments are generally lower if married, thus discouraging two-parent households (Rector 2015). The poverty rate among Black married couples is only 7.5 percent compared with Black people in general at 22 percent and White people in general at 11 percent. With this stat, Sowell emphasizes the poverty-reducing effect of marriage (Sowell 2018). Lack of father involvement is a big predictor of multiple key stats for children, such as lower high school graduation rates, poorer adult mental health, engaging in risky behavior, lower self-esteem, and lower achievements (McLanahan, Tach, and Schneider 2013). But this narrative is suppressed in the mainstream media because it would be impossible to attain equal outcomes for this inequality.

Universal basic income is taking this nanny state approach supernova. I see one argument in favor of state assistance based on automation rendering more people unemployed, hence the need for some way of taking care of basic needs. But I am firmly against this idea for the following reasons:

1. It does nothing for the deeper problem of purpose. "Man shall not live on bread alone" (Matthew 4:4).
2. We already have welfare for those on the bottom. Why does everyone else need handouts?
3. It further disincentivizes the pursuit of employment.
4. Western nations cannot afford it outside of running massive deficits. Are these deficits wise or even sustainable?
5. Many people won't spend money where they ought to (i.e., education and food). If you had some random hardship and lost your finances, you might use the money well to rebuild. But many people have a completely different blueprint. Some are predisposed to self-destruction, particularly those struggling with addiction. Poverty is a complex problem that isn't solved by just throwing money at it (though throwing other people's money at it makes us feel virtuous). Further, as discussed in the levels of energy section in chapter 3, some individuals have energetic ceilings. When their life circumstances improve, their self-sabotage instincts, akin to those of a relapsing gambler, often kick in. They struggle to maintain happiness or stability, which underlines why solutions like welfare and universal basic income don't always succeed in elevating people out of their challenging situations.[25]
6. People on the socioeconomic bottom won't just suddenly write poetry (Shapiro and Rogan 2019), and this is the prime target population of the policy. That these people will swiftly put their lives together if given this equal opportunity is a Utopian vision. Their underground complex will find some other way to rid themselves of the funds unproductively.
7. Universal automation isn't here yet.
8. Are people in countries with more extreme forms of the nanny state, such as the oil-rich United Arab Emirates, any happier?

Handouts can become a whole way of life. I first became aware of this idea when I started to see patients as a resident doctor, training at a general practitioner's office. In our patient population, there was a large group of patients who were fixated on getting welfare and disability forms filled out, without any ambition to one day lift themselves out of this status. Welfare was not a means to an end; for them, it was the end. Like flies caught in a spider's web, welfare status becomes a trap from which you may never escape. Once you are a have-not, it's difficult to muster the willpower to become a have. Your life may never have meaning again. And to numb all that pain, you'll form a bad habit commensurate with the degree of suffering that you're in, your underground complex made manifest.

Western countries have engendered a culture of expectation—even entitlement—and not appreciation. This fostered the greatest addiction of our time: to handouts. For a real-life example, if you counted the seven large federal welfare programs in 2013 available to Californians, a single mother of two was eligible for benefits that were the equivalent of a job paying $16.96/h in California ($35,287/year), only 8 percent below the median salary in the state (West 2015). In this situation, unless that job was beyond fulfilling, how could you justify working?

To be clear, the argument that the welfare state is keeping poor people down is correlation, not causation. But it makes me wonder about the deleterious effect on human striving. The central paradox of welfare remains that resource distribution needs to be carefully managed to avoid becoming pathologically altruistic and thus ultimately harmful to the poor. Next, let's take a look at how people deal with trauma.

Levels of Trauma Processing

Meghan Markle went from mediocre actress to princess to victim. It's quite the journey. Speaking more frankly, she and Prince Harry are exemplary of the culture of victimhood being elevated to higher status. Somehow she convinced a guy who was born into unbelievable wealth and fame that his family had trapped him and that he needed to escape their oppressive firm (a term often used to refer to the British monarchy). They live in a $14 million mansion, had a deal with Netflix originally worth an estimated $100 million, are surrounded by celebrity friends, and still manage to generate sympathy. Their lives are utterly unrelatable.

I am not completely without sympathy, as money does not solve every problem (and maybe not even most problems). And I really admire some of their work. I watched *The Me You Can't See*, a series on Apple TV on mental health, co-produced by Prince Harry and Oprah and released in 2021. The quality of the production was first-rate. They had in-depth looks at celebrities and refugees alike. But there was something that bothered me throughout that I could not put my finger on until I had some time to reflect. Meta-theme #1 seemed to be something like "You should feel absolutely comfortable speaking up about your mental health issues." Fantastic. Meta-theme #2 was "You should also identify fully with your mental health issues and never let them go."

I conceptualize three levels of trauma processing with respect to victimhood, and this can be loosely related to levels of energy:

Level 1: You are completely crippled by trauma. You are unable to even speak about it. In that case, identifying and being praised for being a victim can raise you up. Prince Harry, his wife, and Oprah do a great job of empowering people to move past this level.

Level 2: You are already victim-identified and speaking freely about it. Here you are at a crossroads. It is wonderful to have arrived here if you have been stuck at Level 1. Therapy can be quite effective. However, there is a chance that you stay here, fixate on therapy, and never move on. You have a choice here to stay bitter or to get better.

Level 3: You are transcending your trauma. It is a part of you and always will be, but it is not you. You accept what happened and let go. You are not a fragile victim. You are a victor, or even a champion. As a tip, being grateful for what you do have in life can greatly catalyze your transition to Level 3.

The reality is that no matter what your cross is, there is always someone who has it easier and someone who has it worse. I have met people at death's door who left this world with a smile. They were the ones upholding the rest of their families mourning their last moments. I also had a patient whose family members were recently murdered. You would never know looking at him since he carried himself as if while he acknowledged the tragedy, he was still grateful for life, for his being.

You must strike the right balance between processing history and dwelling on it. Too much dwelling will render you completely incapable of moving forward in your life. If you never process it, however, you are doomed to repeat it, or stay in the victim-identified state. Victimhood should be a temporary stage, but this concept of Level 3 is completely thrown out in modern victim ideology.

Meghan Markle has since introduced Prince Harry to ancestral healing to break the cycle of genetic and generational suffering, the emotional freedom technique from tapping therapy, and so on. I have no problem with any of these, but I do with the sheer quantity of therapies and the fixation on being a victim. I think the goal for this power couple sadly is for them to always remain victims. I don't think they will ever transcend their traumas and reach Level 3.

I use Prince Harry and Meghan Markle to illustrate the point that even those in the most luxurious and prestigious life situations can view themselves as perpetual victims, and it does them no good. More commonly, there are people who were previously in bad relationships who feel used or even abused. And in my medical practice, I encounter many people who were in car accidents that left them with pain. And while they should seek recompense, I absolutely notice a trade-off in quality of life when the pursuit of such drags on. Speaking about the trauma to process it, then transcending it with gratitude, can help celebrities and everyday victims of trauma alike.

The Dark Triad

Author and environmental policy consultant Michael Shellenberger believes that the secular religion of compassion has gone completely crazy. He covered the topic in depth in his 2021 book *San Fransicko*, his research into the tailspin of San Francisco. "Victims are treated as sacred and thus good. The demand that we not enforce laws against people defined as victims is an attack on a foundational principle of our democracy—equal justice under the law" (2021a). Shellenberger has caught on to the benefits of playing the victim, which he calls "victim signaling." It appears to be working better than ever. Society's definitions of trauma and victimization are broadening. Like moths to a flame, people fight for greater victim status, allowing them to portray themselves in simplistic oppressor-oppressed narratives, whereby they, the oppressed, can do no wrong.

Research also suggests that those with dark triad traits more frequently signal virtuous victimhood (Ok et al. 2021). The dark triad traits are Machiavellianism (manipulation), narcissism, and psychopathy (short-term gain without any regard for others).[26] The dark triad is a well-studied cluster of socially aversive traits such as selfishness, glibness, short-term thinking, aggression, and exploitation. Such people are devoid of a moral compass, and it's no surprise that a dark triad personality is also linked to poor life satisfaction (Kaufman et al. 2019). In my professional experience, those addicted to opioids often exhibit dark triad traits.

A group of psychologists examined the link between victim signaling coupled with virtue signaling and the dark triad in a series of studies. They developed and validated a victim signaling scale that includes statements such as, "Spoke about how people who share my identity are criminalized by society." They found that the virtuous victim signaling can facilitate nonreciprocal resource transfer from others to the signaler. In other words, you can get material resources (e.g., money or jobs) and symbolic ones (e.g., respect or tolerance) in a one-way exchange. Moreover, they showed that those with dark triad traits more frequently signal virtuous victimhood, even when controlling for demographic and socioeconomic variables commonly associated with victimization in Western societies. Finally, they showed that the frequency of emitting virtuous victim signals predicts a person's willingness to engage in and endorse ethically questionable behaviors (e.g., lying to earn a bonus, or making exaggerated claims about being harmed in a social context) (Ok et al. 2021).

I believe that one reason the virtue signaling impulse is so strong in many people is that by projecting the image of being a good person, it excuses you from having to actually be one. This was the faith of the Pharisees in the Bible. Doing good deeds is infinitely harder than saying nice things. The power of virtue signaling has been rising along with the elevation of victim status. If you can attain the image of goodness and its accompanying shield of virtue, why bother going to the trouble of actually doing good deeds? And every competent evildoer knows that virtue signaling is a must to distract from deeds they do not want others to see.

Shellenberger decries the "don't blame the victim" staple of victim ideology. This means that some people are essentially victims, and they should only receive without anything ever being asked of them. It's the withdrawal of all demands for taking responsibility (Shellenberger 2021a). I believe that perpetual victims and the people who hypothetically advocate for them don't want to answer this question: Are they responsible for their situation in any way?

Pathological Altruism in Victimhood

Pathological altruism features prominently in Shellenberger's *San Fransicko*. First defined by professor of engineering Barbara Oakley in 2011, it is behavior that attempts to promote the welfare of another or others and results instead in harm that an external observer would conclude was reasonably foreseeable (Oakley et al. 2011). It's essentially excessive compassion. By pathological, I mean that this behavior is maladaptive and rigid to the extent that it interferes with their ability to live their life, leading to functional impairment and with little awareness.

Jordan Peterson refers to such excessive compassion as the "Freudian Oedipal nightmare." This attitude keeps the target of your care an infant (Shellenberger and Peterson 2021). In the attempt to make everything safe, you harm your children, leaving them incapable of fending for themselves in the world.

One major hallmark of the ideology of victimhood is a desire for cosmic justice. This term was coined by Thomas Sowell. It's an idea that everyone should receive the same life chances (2002). "Universe, make right!" It's Utopian in nature. Cain also saw an anomalous, unequal outcome by comparison to Abel. He certainly believed he deserved better. Under the guise of cosmic justice, he corrected things. Sowell explains, "If there is not equality among people born to the same parents and raised under the same roof, why should equality of outcomes be expected—assumed—when conditions are not nearly so comparable?" (2019).

The problem with pathological altruism is that it disrupts the supposed victims' internal drive, and they are likely already struggling with motivation. It also interferes with their already diminished incentive to strive. In Ayn Rand's *Atlas Shrugged* (published in 1957), Hank Rearden is a steel industrialist. The "looters," government bureaucrats who pass inefficient laws, make it harder for him to be productive. However, he accepts their ideas that he's fundamentally obligated to serve others, at least for the bulk of the novel. He loves his work and wants to meet whatever unrealistic quota is set by the wisest and best. A friend asks why Rearden carries so many people, why he's willing to work and let others feed off his energy. He replies that it's because they're weak, and he doesn't mind the burden. The bureaucrats use Rearden's own guilt against him. This exposes a key paradox of socialism. The bureaucrats need the productive to produce so their society can continue, but to do so well, they need to be free enough. If they get out of line, the only recourse the government has is force. When this same friend asks what he would say if he saw Atlas[27] holding the weight of the world but losing strength, when Rearden doesn't answer, the friend posits, "To shrug," a nod to the novel's title.

"Atlas (Roman Statue 2nd Century AD)," photograph by Lalpua, n.d.

Ultimately Rearden lays down his burden and ceases to believe it's his duty to bear so much weight for so many who don't try. He joins the general strike, the Ayn Rand solution to a corrupt system beyond any point of saving.

Boxer from Orwell's *Animal Farm* (published in 1945) is also pathologically altruistic. At the behest of his pig masters—he constantly repeats about the head pig, "Napoleon is always right"—he continually increases his workload. Like Rearden, he believes that any problem can be solved if he works harder. Unlike Rand's character, Boxer ultimately collapses and is taken to be killed. In life, Boxer's motto was, "I will work harder!" It never dawned on him that he was enabling a parasitic situation in which others became effectively disabled. The bureaucrats of the world want the productive to march to the slogan "*arbeit macht frei*," which, in a coincidental confluence of ideologies, the Nazis emblazoned on their concentration camps. I wonder whether seeing the words "work makes you free" enough times makes one believe it.

The gate of Sachsenhausen concentration camp just north of Berlin (jpatokal n.d). This image is licensed under the Creative Commons CC BY-SA 1.0 License: https://creativecommons.org/licenses/by-sa/1.0/deed.en/.

Orwell, who started by fighting in the Spanish Civil War for the socialist faction, gave this scathing warning later in life to sympathizers:

> . . . socialism inevitably leads to despotism, and that in Germany the Nazis were able to succeed because the socialists had already done most of their work for them, especially the intellectual work of weakening the desire for liberty. By bringing the whole of life under the control of the state, socialism necessarily gives power to an inner ring of bureaucrats, who in almost every

> case will be men who want power for its own sake and will stop at nothing in order to retain it . . . The only salvation lies in returning to an unplanned economy, free competition, and emphasis on liberty rather than on security . . . collectivism is not inherently democratic, but, on the contrary, gives a tyrannical minority such powers as the Spanish Inquisitors never dreamed of. (Orwell 1944)

Like Rearden and Boxer, pathological altruism is rampant in the medical profession. We are so collectively tilted toward compassion and high in agreeableness that it blinds us to second-order thinking. By obeying every bad government decision on healthcare, we think we can make up the gaps in patient care by working harder. The last generation has seen an increasingly fractured relationship between the government and physicians in Canada. We have essentially no private healthcare, and in an age of increasingly marvelous yet expensive technology, where people are living longer than ever with more medical conditions, what the government is willing to pay physicians has decreased with respect to inflation. Most Canadian medical practices function on a small business model where the government pays doctors for services rendered, and doctors pay a percentage to the clinic. That percentage goes to overhead for healthcare delivery. This includes staff salaries, office leases, utilities, medical supplies, equipment, and so on. With successive sub-inflationary pay raises, increasingly clinics do not break even. For example, when I started a medical clinic, it was a year before it broke even, and there were times when it might have gone bankrupt.

More and more medical clinics are closing in Ontario; this is Atlas shrugging. But this was all allowed to happen because, as a profession, we agreed to successive bad deals with the government. I protested the ones in 2016 and 2017.[28] But government guilt-tripping always wins with a profession that is innately altruistic, and pathologically so in these examples. Every system needs some checks and balances, and because we cannot provide these, it is ultimately our patients who suffer. Canada now has one of the worst healthcare performances in the developed world (Moir and Barua 2022).

Antagonizing Resilience, Self-Esteem, and Antifragility

Another meta-issue with the worship of the victim is it has compromised the pathway for the development of self-esteem. "You're fine the way you are, no matter what!" If you think the goal is to cultivate self-esteem directly in children, you're crippling them. If kids have high self-esteem but it's unstable, then they're more likely to be violent and have more problems. Instead, you want to build capacities; you want to teach them abilities and skills so they do things that indirectly give them self-esteem (Haidt and Rogan 2019).

There are problems in making every space a safe one. First, it's impossible. Some nature-induced tragedy can still get you (e.g., cancer). Second, you cannot build up resilience to life in this manner. Overcoming some adversity is necessary to face the innate rigors of life. Excessive safe spaces make you even more fragile; you need some volatility, as author Nassim Taleb suggests in *Antifragile*.

> Antifragility is a quality which has propelled human progress from the earliest times. It allows systems to grow and improve in an unpredictable and volatile world. However, modern society is in the process of trying to dismantle the volatile environment that is vital for antifragility. In doing so, we are making ourselves more fragile. (Taleb 2012)

Antifragility is more than just resilience. The resilient person resists shocks and stays the same, while the antifragile person gets better. Like muscle hypertrophy in weightlifting, the antifragile individual adapts, learns, and grows stronger when exposed to challenges and stressors.

I was bullied a lot as a kid. I was a nerdy, quirky student at an all-boys music school. Some of the teasing was likely for the good grades I got, but I also think much was due to my choices of reading *Star Trek* books at recess or being extra socially awkward even when accounting for my age. "D'Souza D'Loosa" was one of my nicknames. I would sometimes cry at night wondering why I did not fit in.

Very soon after starting university, I would look back at my elementary and high school years and not regret the bullying at all. Not only did it help me grow a thicker skin—one more conducive to the rigors of life—but it also really socialized me. I suspect it had a big role in developing the extraverted bent of my personality, and I seemed to be able to fit into groups better. Jordan Peterson believes this is the role of Nelson Muntz, the school bully in *The Simpsons*. His role is to be a corrective function; "If he bullies you, there's a pretty high probability that you're doing something stupid and contemptible" (J. Peterson and Willink 2021). I was surely guilty of this, as my awkwardness, introversion, and preference for reading science fiction books during recess, instead of playing with other kids, made it difficult for me to fit in with my peers.

It's incredibly challenging to determine when and how much to help someone in their victimhood. Are you robbing them of a developmental opportunity? Perhaps the right amount is just as much as absolutely necessary, and they must be trying as well. They have to have some skin in the game. You certainly can't be helping with something they're perfectly capable of handling themselves. This is also analogous to the concept of hurt versus harm in my chronic pain practice. In select patients who exhibit pain-focused behavior, when they fear basic physical activity but I know they won't hurt themselves or make things worse, I challenge them. The point is, there is a trade-off with coddling. Coddling steals your opportunity to build resilience and antifragility, to develop confidence in overcoming adversity.

Do you ever think if you love your kids too much it will actually harm them? Helicopter parents are pathologically altruistic; they have the propensity to over-coddle. Education systems can also have policies that seem wonderful on the surface, but when you look under the hood, they can set kids up for failure. Here are two more examples:

"The [York Region District School] Board recognizes that silence and inaction not only deny the lived realities of Black students, families, and staff, but also create experiences that can be unsafe and retraumatizing" (York Region District School Board 2021). This policy falls under the woke rubric of "silence is violence."

"Please be aware that race is a heavy burden many racialized students carry even at a very early age due to their lived experiences. If a racialized student is unwilling to share, participate, or even be present for these conversations, it may be due to personal triggers. Thus, enforcing them in a conversation about race they don't feel safe to participate in may cause added harm to such students" (Hamilton-Wentworth District School Board 2021). With such policies, how are students supposed to be given opportunities to build resilience and antifragility, let alone self-esteem? Ontario introduced Bill 67 in 2021 to the legislative process to make policies such as these mandatory across all educational institutions.

Caring for someone is like water, and having a firm hand is like the bottle that contains it. Every time you don't give firm but loving encouragement, your boundary—the bottle—breaks, and there's a little leak of that care. Do it enough, and that care, that love, spills; it will not be able to manifest. When you care for or even love someone, sometimes you need a firm hand. In pathological altruism, there is no bottle, and the water is completely spilled. To properly love someone, you need a balance of maternal and paternal energy, of mercy and judgment. Have you ever seen someone with potential waste it? It is truly heartbreaking.

There are actual victims in this world. Tragedies are part of the universal human experience, and some people assuredly have it worse. But it requires judgment to determine who is a victim and to what extent. A lived experience saying so is not sufficient; the false victimhood narrative is too rampant in our society. The criteria can't be so wide that anyone who wants to join the club gets in. This current process is discriminatory against actual victims. For example, in October 2022, the Supreme Court of Canada ruled that mandatory listing of repeat sex offenders in a registry is "an unjustified infringement on their liberty that is not rationally connected to the goal of investigating or preventing sexual crimes." The explanation is that putting even one person who does not re-offend on the list is unconstitutional, even though this loosening of the law increases the risk of sex crimes. Thus, by portraying repeat sex offenders as victims, it makes a mockery of actual victims of sexual assault. This is the hierarchy of victimhood at play (Agar 2022b).

We have elevated the status of the suffering victim to the highest rung, so much so that people are clamoring to be the top victim. Even if it were true that this is objectively the most victim-filled time in history, blaming others and taking no personal responsibility is no way to empowerment. Moreover, depriving people of agency is the best way to keep them down.

You can't escape pain, but suffering is optional. Being a victim is the most painful way to live, full of purposelessness, nihilism, anxiety, depression, and short-term thinking, but it's also the easiest. Taking responsibility is incredibly hard, but it also sets you free.

Chapter 9:

CLIMATE CHANGE ALARMISM AS A REPLACEMENT RELIGION

Captain Planet was a popular children's cartoon in the 1990s. It portrayed five children from various parts of the world who, along with their superhero, Captain Planet, fought against the evil adult polluters in the name of saving the planet (Turner and Pyle 1990). To this day, I still catch myself spontaneously singing its very catchy theme song. I suppose it's unreasonable to expect nuance in a children's show. But was this a form of indoctrination?

Today, climate alarmism is one of the most popular replacement religions, rife with Trojan horse thinking—ideas that appear attractive and appealing on the surface but can be catastrophic with further exploration.

Climate change alarmism clearly fits the mold of a replacement religion—it is an attempt to find meaning and purpose, to fulfill people's top values. It can be a foundational belief. It puts subscribers on the side of the moral good, awarding plenty of automatic virtue points. Its theology also labels a convenient enemy. The solutions to the issues brought up are radical and unrealistic, but that's not the point. Actually solving the problem would deprive ideologues of this value, so there's no practical attempt to do so.

I first came across the idea of climate change alarmism as a replacement religion from Michael Shellenberger. He believes that it filled the void of a new apocalyptic threat at the end of the Cold War:

> After the dissolution of the Soviet Union, people in the West no longer had an external enemy against which to direct their negative energy and define themselves. Being the sole winner in a conflict means concentrating on oneself all the criticism that could earlier be deflected onto others. (Shellenberger 2020)

Like me, Shellenberger also believes that a deeper cause for this replacement religion is the death of God and subsequent nihilism (Shellenberger and Peterson 2021). He calls it the dominant secular religion of the educated upper middle-class elites (Shellenberger 2020). Author Marian Tupy says this new religion has saints like Greta Thunberg; a Garden of Eden, which was the pre-industrial world; and even indulgences, like the Catholic Church did centuries ago. So long as you say the right things and donate to environmental causes, you can still fly on a private jet, and all your sins are washed away (2022).

Climate alarmists are not actually trying to solve the problem. They do a poor job of articulating it, hence their frequent censorship by labeling anyone who wants a more detailed discussion as a climate denier. Many activists prefer to reduce the entirety of the problem to each individual's carbon footprints, while claiming to be our moral betters. Shellenberger believes they are opposed to the obvious solutions because their motivation is to destroy the whole system. I also believe that there is a deep psychological fear of losing the alarmism as a replacement religion. If the problem was addressed appropriately, subscribers would have to seek an entirely new replacement religion. As we'll see in chapter 13, people would rather eliminate the solution to their grievance than give up their faulty belief system.

There's a strong unconscious romantic appeal to nature. People imagine that what's natural is better than the built environment—so sunshine, wind, and water are often the first things that come to mind. But this is a fallacy, and I believe it represents unsophisticated thinking. Arsenic and cyanide are also natural. While the sun may be from nature, how about the toxic chemicals from solar panels? Wind may also be natural, but turbines may affect bird and insect migration paths that have evolved over centuries (Shellenberger 2020).

Conversely, climate alarmism is also taking a toll on its adherents' mental health, to the extent that "eco-anxiety" is a new term now recognized by the American Psychological Association, defined as anxiety or worry about climate change and its effects. A 2021 *Lancet* study surveyed ten thousand young people from ten countries, the largest study to date on the topic of climate anxiety. It showed that the psychological (emotional, cognitive, social, and functional) burdens of climate change are profoundly affecting huge numbers of young people around the world. Nearly 60 percent were very/extremely worried. "Climate change makes me feel sad > afraid > anxious > angry > powerless > guilty" were all commonly cited, each of these identified by at least 51 percent of respondents (Hickman et al. 2021). The authors might as well have copied the bottom of Dodson's levels of energy graph. So I ask, is demoralizing our youth serving to move us closer to a solution? Or is it making a huge and passionate voter demographic vulnerable to being preyed upon by virtue signaling politicians?

Climate Alarmism

Climate alarmism is the belief that the changing climate will bring about the end of humanity within the next few decades (Spratt and Dunlop 2019). Climate alarmists believe that anecdotal evidence like the prevalence of hurricanes and fires provides irrefutable proof and that their anger and panic are justified. They say the only way to prevent our civilization's destruction is a radical and equitable resetting of our way of life. They say yes to solar and wind power, and no to oil, gas, coal, and nuclear power. If anyone dares disagree, they are climate deniers and should be censored. Given the severity of the problem, they say every last tax dollar should be thrown at this problem without any nuance. They believe the wealthy (a term ill-defined along with everything else in this ideology) bear disproportionate guilt. There are of course variations on this theme, but this is the most extreme version of climate alarmism. It clearly meets the criteria of an ideology, as it purports to explain everything and denies debates.

Global warming has become the convenient narrative for any natural disaster or extreme weather event. With the advent of modern clickbait news, it may feel like the climate is changing at a faster rate, but this is hardly the most objective perspective. Further, the UK's Institute for Public Policy Research (a progressive think tank) coined the term "climate porn" in 2006 to describe the alarmist rhetoric that permeates today's public discussion about climate change. By this, they mean reporting on worst-case predictions as if they are most likely to occur when they are not at all the most likely to occur (Ereaut and Segnit 2006).

In *Warm Words: How Are We Telling the Climate Change Story and Can We Tell It Better?*, commissioned by the aforementioned think tank, the authors concluded:

> Climate change is most commonly constructed through the alarmist repertoire—as awesome, terrible, immense and beyond human control . . . It is

> typified by an inflated or extreme lexicon, incorporating an urgent tone and cinematic codes. It employs a quasi-religious register of death and doom, and it uses language of acceleration and irreversibility. The difficulty with it is that the scale of the problem as it is shown excludes the possibility of real action . . . by the reader or viewer. It contains an implicit counsel of despair—"the problem is just too big for us to take on." (Ereaut and Segnit 2006)

But like any serious topic, there is nuance to the impact of climate change. As we've discussed before, making a single issue apocalyptic is a dangerous strategy. So what are some of the thornier subtopics to consider that could turn this ideology into a debatable, actionable issue?

Electric Vehicle Policy Is a Trojan Horse

Electric vehicles look amazing for not emitting gases. But depending on the jurisdiction, where does the electricity they charge with come from? My home province of Ontario is powered by low-carbon fuels (thanks in large part to its nuclear capability), yet China has so many coal-powered plants that electric cars worsen local air. It's estimated that in Shanghai, pollution from an additional million electric vehicles would kill three times as many people annually as an additional million gas cars (Lomborg 2020).

What about the battery? Building electric car batteries and later disposing of them are both carbon intensive. They're larger and heavier than regular car batteries. Further, only 5 percent or less are recycled (Woollacott 2021).

Even if every nation achieves all their ambitious electric vehicle targets, emissions will be reduced by about 0.1 percent by 2030. If this reduction is maintained throughout the century, temperatures will be reduced by 0.002°C by 2100 (Lomborg 2021b). Over a gas car's ten-year lifetime, the International Energy Agency believes that it creates thirty-four tons of carbon (if you include production and disposal), and they have roughly estimated that an electric car creates twenty-six tons. Given that the average subsidy spent on electric cars globally is $10,000 per car, we have to ask ourselves whether these eight tons saved are cost-effective (Lomborg 2020). For reference, the Canadian carbon tax in 2024 is $80 per ton. Regardless, Canada has planned to ban the sale of new fuel-burning cars starting in 2035, and many other Western nations have similar commitments.

A 2017 study by the Montreal Economic Institute called electric vehicle subsidies a waste. They are expensive and have little effect on emissions (Goldstein 2020b; Belzile and

Milke 2017). It's clear that politics, not practicality, is the driver behind the push for mass adoption of electric vehicles.

While Congressman Dan Crenshaw is in favor of energy subsidies, he believes they should be technology-neutral for carbon reduction and should include oil, gas, and nuclear (Crenshaw and Peterson 2022). In this manner, subsidies would apply to any sector of energy for emissions reduction, as that is the overarching goal anyway. This makes the most sense. He explains that assessing trade-offs is a primary tenet of conservatism:

> It's a process-oriented governing philosophy that seeks to solve problems within a set of limiting principles. Limiting principles means we ask questions, like what are the second and third order consequences, what's the cost-benefit. That's really what the climate change debate should be about. Instead, it's about if you're a denier or a killer, or you want to save the planet like a good person. (Crenshaw and Peterson 2022)

The reality is that, with their immense political appeal, wind and solar receive almost all energy subsidies (Environmental Progress 2021).

Anti-Nuclear Climate Policy

"Personally I am against nuclear power . . . extremely dangerous, expensive, and time-consuming," says Greta Thunberg (Shellenberger 2019).[29] Not every climate alarmist is anti-nuclear, but many are. This is understandable given how large Chernobyl, Fukushima, and to some extent Three Mile Island live in the public consciousness. How dangerous were these accidents?

Only thirty-one people died as a direct result of Chernobyl's accident. The WHO and the UN have estimated that in total the long-term death toll will be about four thousand (UN Press 2005). Fukushima's death toll was one person (who died of radiation-induced lung cancer). There has been an increase in thyroid cancer rates in children, but the WHO believes this is due to increased screening. Five hundred and seventy-three people died from the stress of the evacuation of people around the reactor (i.e., moving long-term-care patients) (Ritchie 2017). Finally, the full reactor meltdown of Three Mile Island produced no harmful levels of radiation. Those standing near the plant got less radiation than they would get from an X-ray (United States Nuclear Regulatory Commission 2022). By comparison, hydro dam construction has killed hundreds of thousands of people in the last fifty years (Watts 2010; "1975 Banqiao Dam Failure" n.d.).

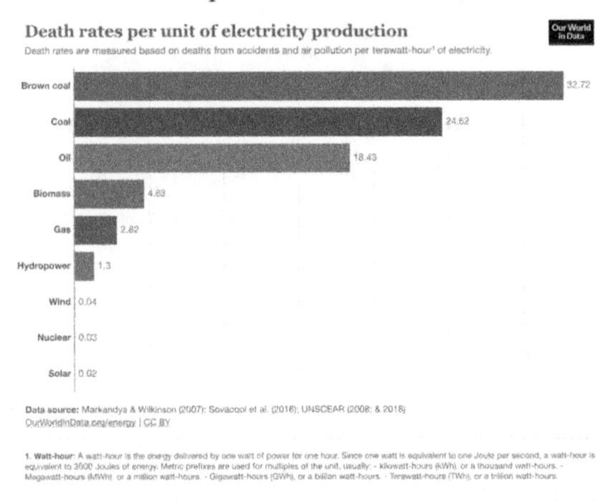

Ritchie and Rosado (2020) created this graph based on information compiled from the following sources: Sovacool et al. (2016), Markandya and Wilkinson (2007), and UNSCEAR (2008). Image courtesy of Ritchie and Rosado (2020), Creative Commons License CC BY 4.0: https://creativecommons.org/licenses/by/4.0/.

But what do we do with nuclear waste? According to the Nuclear Energy Institute, all of the used fuel ever produced by the commercial industry since the late 1950s would cover a football field to a depth of under ten yards (Nuclear Energy Institute 2019). By comparison, solar panels contain toxic heavy metals. They produce three hundred times more waste than nuclear reactors when providing the same energy (Shellenberger 2021b). Experts at the Institute for Energy Research are concerned that solar panels will be shipped to poor countries to be disassembled, and the toxins will leach out into the environment and possibly pose a public health hazard if they get into the groundwater supply (Institute for Energy Research 2018). The National Renewable Energy Laboratory estimated that it costs \$20–\$30 to recycle a panel, versus \$1–\$2 to send it to a landfill (Agar 2022a).

Further, we know that fossil fuel particulate matter kills. How many lives have been saved by nuclear power displacing fossil fuels? It is estimated at 1.84 million lives between 1971 and 2009 (Kharecha and Hansen 2013). Moreover, deadly air pollution shortens the lives of seven million people/year (Kuehn 2014). A 2019 analysis concluded that Germany's nuclear phaseout has led to 1,100 avoidable deaths (along with \$12 billion in social costs) per year due to increased air pollution (Jarvis, Deschenes, and Jha 2022; 2019).

The cultural supremacy of solar or wind power represents Trojan horse thinking. Journalist Robert Bryce puts it best: "If you are anti-carbon dioxide and anti-nuclear, you are pro-blackout" (2011).

Virtue Signaling with Emissions Targets

Governments around the world have set goals to reduce or eliminate carbon emissions. For example, in 1988, Canada's emissions were 588 megatons, and they rose to 729 megatons in 2018 (Goldstein 2020a). This occurred despite multiple pledges of emission reduction targets, each of which the government has missed. The problem is that many of these targets are unrealistic, and they're designed to look good in the public eye rather than actually accomplish anything. The Canadian pledges for net-zero by 2050 and full "decarbonization" by 2100 are farcical (Goldstein 2020a).

The UN says that, as a first step in avoiding catastrophic global warming of more than 1.5°C by the end of this century, global emissions have to drop every year from 2020 to 2030 by 7.6 percent. The pandemic only lowered global emissions by 5.4 percent, the largest decrease in emissions since World War II (Goldstein 2021b). So even having a pandemic-equivalent lowering of emissions annually will fall short of this fantasy.

The UN Intergovernmental Panel on Climate Change's (IPCC) seminal document on the 1.5°C limit was its "summary for policymakers report" in 2018. It contains many intuitive statements, such as "Climate-related risks for natural and human systems are higher for global warming of 1.5°C than at present, but lower than 2°C (*high confidence*)." It also realistically discusses how challenging it will be to stay under 1.5°C: "Pathways limiting global warming to 1.5°C with no or limited overshoot would require rapid and far-reaching transitions in energy, land, urban and infrastructure (including transport and buildings), and industrial systems (*high confidence*)." As for the pop-culture-ingrained nightmare of Greenland's ice sheet melting after hitting a point of no return, while this could result in a multi-meter sea level rise, this would occur over hundreds to thousands of years. For good measure, the document does include one politically contaminated doublespeak term, "Climate-Resilient Development Pathways," which are "trajectories that strengthen sustainable development at multiple scales and efforts to eradicate poverty through equitable societal and systems transitions and transformations while reducing the threat of climate change through ambitious mitigation, adaptation and climate resilience" (IPCC 2018).

To abide by the Paris Agreement guidelines (7.6 percent annual reduction) would cost equal or greater than $20,000 income loss per family by 2035 and a total aggregate

GDP loss of $2.5 trillion, as estimated by the Heritage Foundation. Even if the US eliminated all emissions, there would be less than a 0.2°C reduction in global temperature (Dayaratna, Loris, and Kreutzer 2016; Lomborg 2016). Put another way, the IPCC found that if every country kept its nationally stated mitigation ambition until 2030, Earth would still warm at least 3°C by 2100 (IPCC 2018).

Climate Policy's Effects on the Poor

US climate envoy and climate alarmist icon John Kerry says that no one is being asked for a sacrifice (Lomborg 2021a). Yet Western climate policy locally and globally makes electricity bills more expensive. Energy poverty is defined as when utility bills take up too high a proportion of income, so people have to either cut energy or cut spending on other essentials (e.g., food). A 2016 Fraser Institute study, which set energy poverty at over one-tenth of income, found that 19.4 percent of Canadian households already experience energy poverty (Green et al. 2016). Yet Canadian Prime Minster Justin Trudeau keeps increasing the carbon tax. According to the Canadian government's own report, the second carbon tax "would disproportionately impact lower and middle-income households . . . as well as households currently experiencing energy poverty or those likely to experience energy poverty in the future" (Department of the Environment 2020). An environment ministry report last year warned that the tax will increase energy poverty in Canada, disproportionately impacting low-income households, seniors, single mothers, rural Canadians, oil, gas, and freight transport workers, single-family homeowners, and tenants (Goldstein 2021a).

Speaking globally, a 2018 IPCC report claimed that "the regions with the greatest potential to leapfrog to low-carbon development trajectories are the poorest developing regions" (Agrawala et al. 2014). This includes dams, natural gas plants, and nuclear plants, as well as decentralized energy sources such as solar panels and batteries. However, Shellenberger contests that the report didn't cite other economists who have debunked leapfrogging (2020). It does seem that the world's poor aren't taken into account when considering energy policy. Western climate policy is a good example of the existence of the underground society, analogous to the underground man. It is self-destruction due to our boredom with prosperity.

Believing that we can suddenly stop using fossil fuels and rely solely on renewables is a luxury belief, a concept developed by psychologist Rob Henderson. A luxury belief is an idea or opinion that confers status on the upper class while often inflicting costs on the lower social classes (Henderson and Peterson 2021). It is virtue signaling of the most elite. Jordan Peterson surmises the point: "What's wealth? Energy. Make energy cheap, there's no poor people. Why? Because work requires energy, and work produces everything" (Shellenberger and Peterson 2021). Fossil fuels have raised our living standards. Meanwhile, left-leaning political parties, particularly the more extreme ones, support the renewables-only narrative, as there's an intrinsic anti-capitalist component. This is why, despite the discordance between the idea that the left is supposed to be advocating for the poor, and the disproportionately harmful effects of Western climate policy on the poor, the anti-capitalism sentiment wins out.

Sensible Solutions

Solutions to climate change do not exist in slogans, catchphrases, or clickbaitable terms. The central paradox of climate policy is the trade-off between green energy and finance. The debate we should be having should center on how much of our finances we should sacrifice for stabilizing temperatures. People also absolutely need to clarify their intentions.

Nobel Prize–winning economist William Nordhaus calculated the optimal point for targeting temperature warming while balancing economic harms. He claims that the costs of mitigating global warming to under 2°C over the course of the next century far exceed future damages. Instead, he suggests that allowing for 3.5°C increase by 2100 is optimal (Nordhaus 2018).

Bjørn Lomborg, president of a think tank called the Copenhagen Consensus Center, has written extensively on the intricacies of climate policy. He presents a five-point approach to climate change: 1) carbon tax; 2) innovation; 3) adaptation; 4) geo-engineering; and 5) prosperity (Lomborg 2020).

1. Lomborg actually proposes a small carbon tax. This will motivate people to eliminate the low-hanging fruit usage (e.g., not heating the patio while not in use). He certainly doesn't believe in an ever-increasing government cash grab under the banner of carbon tax.
2. Innovation is the most important of Lomborg's proposed solutions. He believes that governments should invest billions into many small ideas. Only a few of them will pay off, but that's all you need. Some examples of climate innovation that have helped: fracking has allowed for more easily accessible natural gas (which burns at half the carbon intensity of coal); the catalytic converter mini-

mized auto pollution in LA in the 1970s; and there's a process in development for carbon capturing algae on the ocean surface that turns into oil (Lomborg and Peterson 2021).

3. Adaptation is Lomborg's third general approach to dealing with climate change. Humans are excellent at this. Holland has been sinking under the sea level for centuries, yet their system of dikes is first-rate.
4. Geo-engineering is the deliberate and large-scale intervention in the Earth's climate system. It's the ability to rapidly alter the climate in an emergency, and it's just a backup plan.
5. The final Lomborg solution to climate change is prosperity. There's a clear connection between making a country richer and helping them fight climate change, even though the price can be larger emissions. Compare and contrast the flood adaptation history of Holland and Bangladesh. If Bangladesh becomes wealthier, they'll be better able to handle sea level rise.

Nuance and math are needed in every complex problem, and they would be helpful to deconstruct our Trojan horse beliefs. You can't be a radical climate change activist and anti-poverty at the same time. Ultimately climate alarmists will have to choose between clinging to their depressive replacement religion or trying to solve the problem.

Now that we have covered several replacement religions of the left, in the next chapter, we will explore one from the political right.

Chapter 10:

VACCINE HESITANCY AS A REPLACEMENT RELIGION

Vaccine hesitancy can also be a replacement religion.[30] Not all those who are vaccine hesitant are ideologues, and there can certainly be pro-vaccine people who are ideologues. However, I am going to dive deeply into the vaccine-hesitant position, given that it was the minority one during the COVID-19 pandemic. One of the generic payoffs of ideologies is in giving the subscriber a sense of tribe. Minority ideologies are more effective at this than majoritarian ones; the club is more exclusive.

In my many conversations with patients on the topic in 2021, I tried to look for consistent leitmotifs. The vast majority of patients whom I've seen on a regular basis and who 100 percent trust me on every other single issue, I was unable to probe or ask questions about their vaccine hesitancy. I respectfully challenged the ones who were open to the conversation, and no matter what their answer was, I was proud that this minority within a minority gave it real thought. This chapter is not for those who played devil's advocate on the topic; they are not ideologues.

Vaccine hesitancy ideology gives its adherents deep meaning and purpose, such as a feeling of saving the world from a conspiracy. It also encompasses the appeal to nature fallacy. It is different from climate alarmism. It believes that science (or "the science") and government have tricked us, and this is a conspiracy. It is a reaction to Big Pharma and the shadow side of capitalism, and it fulfills deep spiritual and psychological needs.

Quite simply, an ideology is a low-resolution universal explanation. The same people have exactly the same talking points. There is 100 percent certainty. Subscribers start with their conclusion, then seek confirmation bias; some of my patients locked onto any news of downsides to the exclusion of any news on upsides. Given that the dogma is unassailable, the ideologue becomes agitated easily when simple questions come their way. Since it's an ideology, it only has unsophisticated arguments (e.g., "The vaccine is dangerous").

Once the ideology has been elevated to replacement religion status, subscribers personally identify with it and will readily raise their voice if questioned. The shouting is not only to silence others but also the doubting voice within themselves, the part that wonders whether indeed this truth is all there is to know, that this truth is absolute. Now the priority becomes being right, not seeking truth, which is always going to be nuanced. Sometimes there is even a hint of moral hegemony in their position, which justifies protesting outside hospitals and harassing healthcare workers. There is a clear oppressor-oppressed narrative, with Big Pharma and government being the convenient enemies.

The vaccine and its associated policies threatened to split society in 2021. I suspect future singular government interventions will have a familiar ripple effect. Here are the main arguments I heard from those who were vaccine hesitant.

Disclaimer: Given the rapidly evolving literature on COVID-19, the stats below were the truest to my knowledge at the time of writing, and they will have evolved by the time of publication, let alone reading.

Main Arguments for Vaccine Hesitancy

1) "It hasn't been out long enough."

How long is long enough? Two years, three months, and four days? The technology is not new. mRNA and adenovirus vector technology have been in development since the 1980s for cancer and HIV (Dolgin 2021). Forty-two days after COVID-19's genome was sequenced in spring 2020, Moderna had their mRNA vaccine ready (Verbeke et al. 2021). They did not skip any steps, going through all phases from pre-clinical work to animal trials to human trials (Reuters Fact Check 2021). This illustrates the speed at which vaccines can be developed when the entire world is working toward a common goal and funding is not an issue.

This argument is a subset of the idea that doubters can identify a study and cherry-pick its conclusions, and then their point of view is thereafter infallible. Science that supports their viewpoint is acceptable, and science that doesn't is flawed. Instead, we must all be humble and not assume that there are 100 percent no doubts in our minds, hence the need to be open to free speech. I found it odd that many laypeople started quoting studies without any experience or training in critically appraising the literature. Physicians and scientists learn how to do this in school. That being said, I'm not advocating for blind trust, but there has been no public conversation about differential expertise in interpreting studies.

2) "Don't tell me what to do."

There seems to be a common theme of resentment toward the government for forcing the issue, which is entirely understandable. But this is not actually relevant when trying to discern whether the vaccines are good for you or not. "If all your friends jumped off a bridge, would you do it?" Most children who think about this for more than a few seconds immediately realize doing what they're asked by a parent in this instance is actually good advice, even if it is imposed on them to some degree.

I found that while many vaccine-hesitant patients marketed to me that the science is flawed, I got the sense that they really meant they wanted to stick up for their principles. I'm all for standing up for your principles, but at least be conscious that this is why you resent the vaccine, instead of trying to deceive yourself that it's indisputably flawed science.

3) "I'm young and healthy."

Admittedly this is a harder argument to evaluate than for older patients; the confidence intervals are wider. First, what is the social responsibility we owe each other versus complete freedom of choice? Even the most ardent vaccine-hesitant people obey red lights when driving as part of the social contract. But is this giving up too much individual freedom for the group? Vaccinated people possibly transmit less (Fisman, Amoako, and Tuite 2022) (admittedly, this point has been hard to quantify and has been generally controversial), and the higher the proportion of the population that is vaccinated theoretically leaves a smaller reservoir for this virus to mutate (Goldman 2021). The delta variant spread more easily and had a higher burden of disease than the original virus. The omicron variant also spread more easily, though it was less severe.

The Canadian Institute for Health Information data shows that COVID-19 hospital admissions cost on average three times more than a heart attack, almost on par with kidney transplant patients (Canadian Institute for Health Information 2021). If there is a safe way to reduce this financial burden, do we owe it to our society to do this?

4) "I don't owe anything to anyone. My body, my choice."

Okay, let's just take this maximized libertarian standpoint and imported abortion slogan at face value. What about long COVID? The more time has elapsed since the pandemic, the more data accumulates on this admittedly still unclear post-viral syndrome. Young, low-risk patients still get these consequences, feeling fatigued and breathless, and dealing with headaches and abnormal blood markers of organ dysfunction for months afterward. According to one study conducted in the pre-vaccine era (2020), 13.3 percent of COVID-19 cases got long COVID (Sudre et al. 2021). Two doses of the vaccine decrease the risk of long COVID by 50 percent (Antonelli et al. 2022; Tsampasian et al. 2023). Moreover, there is evidence that even mild COVID survivors are at increased risk of an array of neuro-psychiatric disorders (e.g., depression, opioid use disorder, cognitive decline, insomnia; Xie, Xu, and Al-Aly 2022), a constellation of cardiovascular pathologies (e.g., stroke, heart failure, abnormal rhythms, etc.; Xie et al. 2022), chronic nerve pain (Odozor et al. 2022), diabetes (Xie and Al-Aly 2022), irritable bowel syndrome (Marasco et al. 2023), hair loss, ejaculatory difficulty, and reduced libido (Subramanian et al. 2022).

Former Australian Deputy Prime Minister John Anderson believes that in a democracy, we enter into a contract in which we say that we'll surrender rights temporarily, but only as long as absolutely necessary to secure the rights and freedoms of others, and only in the most temporary manner possible. His historical example was that during the Battle of Britain, Londoners had to have black curtains drawn so the Luftwaffe bombers couldn't have targets. No light could escape from houses. The police had the right to barge into your house to cover the windows up. There was no right to conscientious objection (Anderson and Peterson 2021). The proportionality of the vaccine mandates was of course debatable, but this is an analogous albeit more extreme situation, illustrating when individuals have a duty to the group.

5) "I don't want a blood clot."

Great, take the vaccine. The risk of a blood clot is much higher with COVID-19 than from any of the vaccines. One study estimated deep vein thrombosis at 20 percent of those admitted to hospital with COVID-19 (Malas et al. 2020).

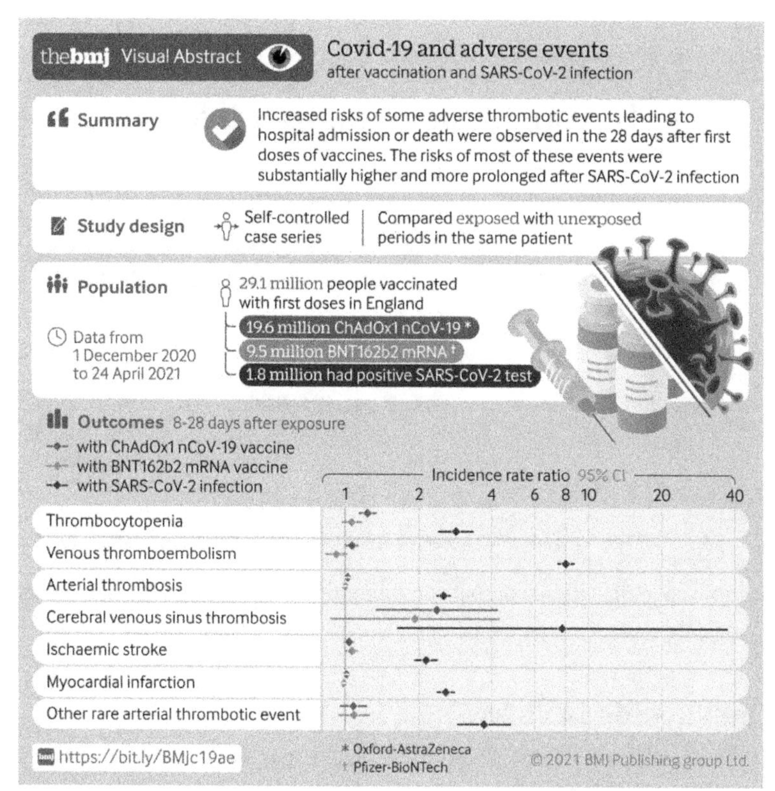

Illustrates the risk of adverse outcomes for those with vaccines versus the infection itself (Hippisley-Cox et al. 2021). This image is licensed under the Creative Commons CC BY 4.0 License: https://creativecommons.org/licenses/by/4.0/.

6) "I don't want myocarditis."

Again, take the vaccine. The risk of myocarditis is sixteen times higher in those with COVID-19 (Boehmer et al. 2021).

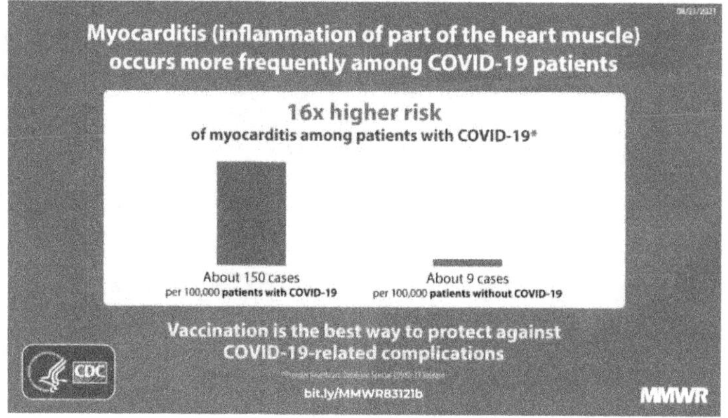

Boehmer et al. 2021

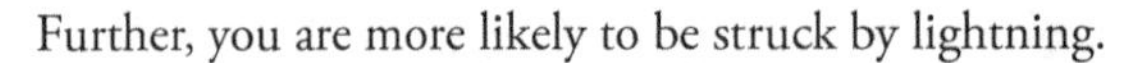
Further, you are more likely to be struck by lightning.

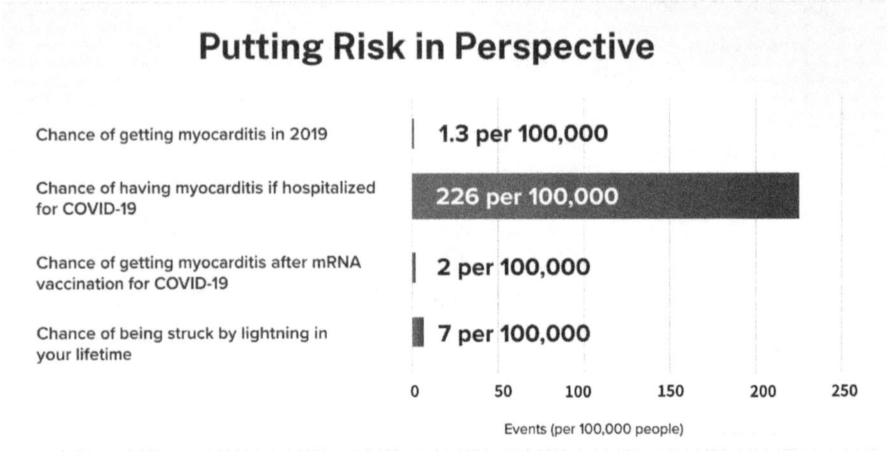

Q&A: COVID-19, Vaccines, and Myocarditis Research" National Institutes of Health 2022

I acknowledge that these comparisons should adjust for the fact that not everyone gets COVID-19.

7) "The vaccine is risky."

There is absolutely no zero-risk proposition, but that is an existential reality. Walking across the street has some risk. For this argument to carry through, you must completely ignore the risks of COVID-19, as my vaccine-hesitant patients always do without exception (at least before a hearty debate). Understandably, the power of anecdote has never been stronger, and when you are vaccinating billions, of course there will be some sphincter-tightening stories (e.g., 1.11 in 100,000 risk of serious allergic reaction; Xie, Xu, and Al-Aly 2022). If vaccine-related side effects grip you, look for COVID-19 anecdotes for balance. You absolutely need to if you are at all interested in a complete story. On the balance of risks in particular for older adults, there is no contest.

8) "I don't trust the government."

Everyone can sympathize with this. The mixed messaging has not helped, and this topic has proved particularly thorny in separating the science from the politics. But it is fallacious to think the government is always wrong and also that you should never trust the government. If you buy food at the grocery store, drink city water, or send your child to school, there is some implicit degree of trust. Moreover, in generations past, governments compelled far riskier propositions (e.g., conscription).

9) "Why should I take a vaccine to preserve hospital beds for those with unhealthy lifestyles?"

This is a great argument. I encountered significant resentment among many people toward those who smoke, drank, and ate unhealthy diets, as these individuals disproportionately occupy ward and intensive care beds for their lifestyle-related diseases. Of course, governments should foster more preventative medicine approaches, and there should be more personal responsibility in healthcare use. These are not quick changes, and the vaccine presented a single intervention that was easily deployed to keep our critical care hospital beds below capacity, the true limiting factor in the pandemic.

Engage in Debate

The vaccines are a scientific miracle produced in less than a year, a feat to be envied by generations past. Pfizer and AstraZeneca vaccines were 88 percent and 67 percent effective, respectively, against symptomatic disease caused by the delta variant, and they were even higher for the original virus (Lopez Bernal et al. 2021).

During the height of the pandemic, you couldn't be pro-business and anti-vaccine; this was an oxymoron. The vaccines were the best route through which we could resume a regular economy and stop governments from imposing lockdown measures.

There is a real payoff for subscribing to ideology. You instantly have a tribe. You gain oppressed status in some dimension, which has never been more beneficial than in our times. But you have to trade in truth, objectivity, the scientific method, and in this case, your health.

PART 3:

Finding a Way Forward

Chapter 11:
PROGNOSIS FOR SOCIETY

In the previous section, we covered several examples of ways people go about trying to find meaning. But replacement religions will never completely satisfy the human need for meaning. The opioid epidemic is the manifestation of a widening gap between how much meaning we require and how much we get, our delta (Δ) meaning. We manifest our underground complex to fill this void—the most extreme way of doing so being opioid addiction. Other bad habits can be enough for many, though an increasing number of people reach for opioids to cope with their existential pain.

So what is the prognosis for society? Are we moving toward rediscovering God and therefore improving our satisfaction with life? Or do we continue to stab his corpse while searching for a meaningful replacement? In which direction is the needle moving? How can we help society to move in a positive direction?

I firmly believe that we are going in the wrong direction. With the seminal pathology of the problem being advancements in science, this process has accelerated the way our day-to-day life changes. Evolutionary biologists Bret Weinstein and Heather Heying coined the term *hyper-novelty*, defined as the out-of-control process by which the acceleration of change outstrips the capacity to adapt. Weinstein and Heying explain that the amazing rate of change we've created is deranging us and making it harder to be human (Weinstein, Heying, and Peterson 2022; Heying and Weinstein 2021). Essentially, the world changes by the time kids become adults, and then it changes again every few years.

Not only is this making life materially easier for us, but it's also leading us closer to the technological singularity. This is a hypothetical point in time at which technological growth becomes uncontrollable and irreversible, resulting in unforeseeable changes to human civilization. Specifically, author Ray Kurzweil predicted that due to exponential growth in artificial intelligence, in a few decades, artificial intelligence will exceed that of human brains (Kurzweil 2005).

Whatever dystopian future this might conjure up is besides the devastating impact further automation will have. The more things are automated, the more empty we are spiritually. And how will it affect employment? People derive a large part of their life meaning from their jobs (many in a healthy way, but some in a pathological way as a replacement religion if it compromises family, friends, community, and other dimensions of a more well-rounded life). Impending car automation is the biggest threat, as driving is the biggest employment category for men. Jordan Peterson's take on mass unemployment: "A lot of them take opioids. People drop out of the employment race, they get very depressed, they develop chronic pain problems, especially if they're men, because chronic pain and depression are very much the same thing, and then they take opioids. This is what happens to people for whom there's nothing to do" (2017b).

I've seen this firsthand as a chronic pain and addiction specialist. Oshawa, the suburb of Toronto where I had my chronic pain practice for several years, was greatly affected by General Motors layoffs and the company's eventual departure. Some of my patients used to be more pain-free and more generally functional in life, they told me, when they had jobs. But their lives seemed to spiral downward after becoming unemployed. Then it became a cycle of pain, addiction, and existential suffering. This is an unfortunate recurrent theme in my practice.

I believe that Aldous Huxley predicted this exact problem. In *Brave New World*, there is a real battle between having freedom and meaning, versus numbing yourself with pleasure to be "happy." For the people of Huxley's dystopian world, pleasure = happiness = life purpose. But something is terribly wrong. Whenever they are unhappy, they take the drug soma—happiness in a pill (1932). Soma is the ultimate magic pill manifestation, literally a magic pill. "If you're not happy, you're nothing at all" is the tagline in the 2020 TV series adaptation of the novel (Weiner 2020). The characters try to cover up every existential suffering with more and more soma. Just pop another pill! Their lives are about having no responsibility and only experiencing impulsive pleasure. But there is no meaning, and the reader or viewer can tell they are beyond miserable. The character of John the Savage poses a very different question to members of Huxley's soma society. "Choose—do you want to be happy or free?" In echoing Dostoevsky's underground man, he struck a chord with his audience, who then threw out their soma and rebelled (Weiner 2020).

Huxley's character John voices his manifesto: "I don't want comfort. I want God, I want poetry, I want real danger, I want freedom, I want goodness, I want sin . . . I'm claiming the right to be unhappy" (1932). This is the rallying cry we need today.

We all need responsibility to have purpose and meaning in our lives, yet the technological situation of the world moves us in the opposite direction. And soma exists in today's world. It has many forms—including the replacement religions we've discussed—but its most extreme form is fentanyl. I fear that as the opioid crisis progresses, one day we will all be on various sorts of drugs to deal with our existential pain. Sadly, the train has left the station and is picking up steam. Is there any hope of putting our world in reverse?

I believe there is, though it won't be easy. The rest of the book covers the keys to restoring meaning to life—and bringing the end of the opioid crisis.

Chapter 12:

PROMOTING FREE SPEECH

Free speech is the kryptonite of ideology. Ideologues are allergic to the truth. Let's define truth as the best point estimate of objective reality. Only God can know this fully, but our best efforts to get as close as possible include numbers, the scientific method (essentially repeated rigorous tests trying to disprove your hypothesis), and an articulate, compelling argument.

We need free speech because we cannot see past our biases. (A bias is something that systematically moves you away from truth.) Every word or thought is clouded by our own biases. They will always confound searches for truth. Outside opinion is needed to see our blind spots, though critical thinking is required to discern what is actually true and free from other peoples' own untrue biases. Approaching a challenging conversation with an open (yet discerning) mind and heart is the best way to free yourself from this matrix. But this has to be your choice.

Free speech is the mechanism that allowed for the truly oppressed to rise. Abolitionist Frederick Douglass said, "Slavery cannot tolerate free speech. Five years of its exercise would banish the auction block, and break every chain in the South" (1860). Society improves via free speech.

Have you ever worked for a company where even constructive criticism wasn't tolerated? Or been in a relationship where you couldn't speak your mind? When I speak of the importance of free speech, I mean that not only at the societal level, but also within businesses, families, friendships, romantic relationships between two individuals, and every other level of analysis. The quality of any relationship is directly proportional to how much free speech is permitted.

It takes guts to open yourself up to criticism. Especially when it is an ideological position that is even to a degree a replacement religion, a belief that you identify with, your natural instinct will be to stamp out any argument you can't easily win. People are eager to preserve their points of view at all costs, to leave their sense of security in place. We have been on the brink of annihilation with weapons of mass destruction in order to preserve our collective belief systems at the societal level.

Professor of marketing Gad Saad believes that free speech is one of the main reasons for the rise of the West. "The guaranteed right to debate any idea (freedom of speech and thought) coupled with a commitment to reason and science to test competing ideas (the scientific method) are what have made Western Civilization great" (2020). Certainly some things may be off-limits. You shouldn't be able to libel or incite violence or crime. But I believe there is a necessity to keep the safeguards as thin as possible.

Saad advocates for free speech absolutism:

> If you truly understand the meaning of free speech, then you agree with the following: "There is simply no better alternative than to allow those with unpopular views to express them and to allow those wishing to hear them to do so." The "I believe in free speech but" crowd violates the foundational ethos of what it means to have free speech. Usually, what comes after the "but" is an appeal to refrain from hurting people's sensibilities and feelings. The general idea is that we must weigh our freedom of speech against the right of others to not be offended . . . Occasionally being offended is the price that one pays for living in a truly free society. Your feelings might get hurt. (G. Saad 2020)

I believe the corollary to this is true. Trying to phrase things in a manner that offends the fewest people will stifle thought.

Building on this point in a later dialogue, Saad continues:

> In a free society, there's always room for racists, imbeciles, idiots, false spreaders to exist. I'm Jewish. There's no more greater offensive lie to say than to deny the Holocaust. The most documented historical event that has

> led to a systematic eradication of a people in the most industry-level way, yet I support the right of Holocaust deniers to exist. I may not invite them on my show because I think it's fruitless and pointless for us to debate, but they have a right to exist. So what does it mean that someone is going to adjudicate misinformation, disinformation? No, let the auto-corrective process of debate and the scientific method decide that. (G. Saad and Rogan 2022)

Take the idea of banning hate speech. What do you think constitutes hate speech that should be banned? Now let's get answers from everyone else in the world and then combine them all into a list of things that are hateful. Can people even speak to each other anymore? There is no single way to define hate speech. Therefore, there's no way to ban it without destroying free speech. If we mandate a world free of hate, then we won't have a free world at all. I prefer the White supremacist speak publicly and embarrass himself or herself, rather than let pernicious thoughts and actions go underground due to censorship.

Political Correctness

North Korean escapee Yeonmi Park's mother used to tell her when she left for school, "Take care of your mouth. Remember, even when you think you're alone, the birds and mice can hear you whisper" (Park and Vollers 2016). This may be an extreme example to illustrate the principle in question. But is freedom of speech more important than freedom from offense? Maybe not, but you're going to have to choose a stance on this, and how does prioritizing freedom from offense prevent those who are insecure, angry, or depressed from quenching any meaningful dialogue?

Author Ben Shapiro deduced the three-step process the radical left has used to effectively close the Overton window (the range of discussion that is permissible). I believe this has occurred consciously and unconsciously, and certainly collectively. Step 1 was the cordiality principle. "Anything considered offensive ought to be barred." This aids the radical left in their main tools of silencing and double standards. They also get to define what is considered offensive. Step 2 was fostering an environment where speaking up against mainstream (their) point of view amounted to a form of violence. At this point, it was okay to be silent. All you had to do to not draw their ire was to be silent. But then came Step 3, where silence began to be equated with violence. "If you're not obviously with us, you're against us" (Shapiro 2021a). Being a heretic became the default, so we increasingly have to, for example, sign emails with our preferred pronouns, a litmus test for being a good person. Allowing this three-step process to congeal has given unlimited power to those who are quickest to rise to offense.

Building on Shapiro's inferred formula, I believe the radical left collectively exhibits dark triad traits. They are narcissistic (they're always right and there's no debate). They are Machiavellian (manipulative), using stories and emotions to monopolize the narrative; also using gaslighting and Freudian projection to weaponize guilt in conscientious people (who tend to be conservative temperamentally and thus are prone to taking responsibility). They are at least on the spectrum of psychopathy with their glibness (superficial charm), drive for short-term gain, and firm belief in *exitus acta probat*, that the ends justify the means. As Solzhenitsyn warns, "The vileness of the means begets the vileness of the result" ([1974] 2006). Finally, the radical left frequently signals virtuous victimhood, which has a clear link to dark triad personality traits.

Recent psychological research corroborates this assertion, revealing narcissism and psychopathy as predictors of left-wing authoritarianism. A 2023 study suggests that a segment of activists uses their cause as a pretense to exercise violence to satisfy their own ego-focused needs and that they don't actually care about social justice and equality (Krispenz and Bertrams 2023). In effect, they are pretend-altruistic. The authors elaborate that "certain forms of activism might provide them with opportunities for positive self-presentation and displays of moral superiority to gain social status, to dominate others, and to engage in social conflicts and aggression to satisfy their need for thrill seeking" (Wilford 2023).

The problem with a culture tilted toward never offending through compulsive self-censoring is that you'll always be chasing a rainbow. There are no limits to someone declaring that they're offended. With the shifting sands of political correctness, the threshold of causing offense will keep changing so that you're always guilty. There's also the question of how you can get through life without having a meaningful (difficult) conversation with your spouse, kids, parents, or peers. In the Venn diagram of offense and truth, some things that are offensive are often also true. "I don't like when you eat cookies in the bed. It's messy, and I have to clean it up frequently." Is it preferable to just ignore this and be resentful? For very insecure people, there is no Venn diagram. Instead, offense and truth overlap entirely. The corollary of this is that if you're offended or triggered, start with examining your insecurities instead of lashing out like a child.

The term *microaggression* has emerged to allow people to claim to be offended when there is nothing objective or tangible occurring. Any act that makes the recipient uncomfortable, no matter how uncomfortable, can be considered offensive, regardless of the intent of the other person. Imagine giving someone advice because you care and still being called offensive! How is this not about amplifying the so-called victim's cry in order to gain leverage? Jordan Peterson believes that the legal system is moving to eliminate intent in the system. Therefore, presumption of innocence will increasingly no longer apply (J. Peterson and Blatchford 2018). Instead, if someone claims harm, you are guilty. The most fragile among us become judge, jury, and executioner in the ministry of truth.

Yeonmi Park cries when she speaks about her experience as an undergrad at Columbia University:

> That four years I learned to censor myself all over again. And it became ridiculous, like I literally risked my life to say what I think is right, and now I . . . have to learn to create a safe space and be sensitive enough . . . did I become free? Where am I? Is there any truly free space in this world right now? . . . What am I doing, this is not why I escaped. (Park and Peterson 2021)

Notably, Park wouldn't be surprised if the plan for America is to "rebuild into a communist paradise" (Sahakian 2021). Her worry is justified, as a 2020 YouGov survey showed that 22 percent of millennials (ages 24–39) and 28 percent of generation Z (ages 16–23) have favorable views of communism, compared to 6 percent of baby boomers (Victims of Communism Memorial Foundation 2020).

The Redeeming Jester

Comedy can be a vehicle for personal development, and it can move you toward free speech. All jokes are de facto microaggressions; otherwise they're not funny. Jordan Peterson commented on the current state of comedy:

> Comedy can't exist without the potential to cause offense, and neither can truth. Comedy is almost always truth. A comedian says something funny, and it's true in a way that people didn't expect, and they know it. They're also teasing the boundaries of tolerance. (J. Peterson and Doyle 2021)

Comedians often dare to say what others know deep down to be true but cannot voice, especially these days. Historically, that was the traditional role of the jester (Peters, Peterson, and Peterson 2022). People don't freak out and claim offense on things that are absolutely absurd. If you tell someone the sky is purple, they probably won't overreact. But if you tell someone they need to work better with others, if they get offended or upset, it's highly likely they know consciously (or more likely unconsciously) that there's truth to this statement.

Author Salman Rushdie speaks of the importance of not making topics off-limits:

> The idea that any kind of free society can be constructed in which people will never be offended or insulted, or in which they had the right to call on the law to defend them against being offended or insulted, is absurd . . . The moment you say that any idea system is sacred, whether it's a belief system or a secular ideology, the moment you declare a set of ideas to be immune from criticism, satire, derision, or contempt, freedom of thought becomes impossible. (Rushdie 2005)

I believe that Rushdie advocates for us to stay grounded when someone claims offside and to not overreact.

Internationally renowned Canadian comedian Russell Peters voices what a lot of comedians likely feel:

> My intent is never to offend, it's only to make others laugh. If someone gets offended by something I said, then they have their own personal issues to work with. I just happened to trigger them and realize there's a problem for them, and maybe they need to see a psychologist. (Peters, Peterson, and Peterson 2022)

And perhaps the next time you're offended, before lashing out at your so-called oppressor, maybe you should look inside to see whether there's some truth to it. Can their "oppression" be a pathway to improving yourself?

Society should be frowning upon the censorship of comedians. They should be protected from political correctness at all costs. Comedians joking freely is a sign of a healthy society. Jokes offer a pathway to individual development. If you are triggered, there is something deep within that you know is true that you aren't willing to confront but you should. When the kids in school used to joke that I was too nerdy, over time I found a way to bring out the more socially appealing side of my personality. When there's a stereotype about Canadians being too nice, that can be taken as constructive criticism that often we're collectively pushovers (again, except in hockey). Sometimes the jokes can be crass, but if it's funny, you can probably find the diamond in the rough of criticism. That doesn't mean jokes won't ever hurt, but this is a winning mentality, all the while expanding societal capacity for free speech.

This isn't to say people should go out of their way to offend. As Ben Shapiro says,

> To be politically incorrect means to say that which requires saying, not to be a generic run-of-the-mill jacka**. There is a difference between making an argument against same-sex marriage and calling someone an ugly name. In fact, conflating the two grants the authoritarian Left enormous power: it allows them to argue that nonliberal points of view ought to be quashed in order to prevent terrible behavior. Fighting political correctness requires a willingness to speak truth and the brains to speak the truth in cogent, clear, and objectively decent language. (Shapiro 2021a)

Sadly, Russell Peters hints at the dismal future for his profession. He believes there's no room for political correctness in comedy, the last frontier of free speech (Peters, Peterson, and Peterson 2022).

As a general guideline, I believe there are two criteria to measure whether you should feel guilty if someone claims offense. First, the statement has to be true. In the scenario where you think your friend is about to make a grave economic mistake, "As best as I can tell, this is going to be a major financial error." Second, it has to come from a good place, one of good intent. Of course, there is nuance to this, but if you're not projecting or displacing your own insecurities or frustrations, you're doing them a favor. "I want to tell you what you want to hear, but I really care that you don't put yourself in a worse financial situation." This might be agape love. Indeed, as Proverbs 27:6 reminds us, "Wounds from a friend can be trusted, but an enemy multiplies kisses."

John Stuart Mill

John Stuart Mill predicted all the meta-arguments we are having over free speech's place in our world. He also provided the best succinct rationale for its defense in *On Liberty* (published in 1859). In it, he divides opinions into orthodox (mainstream) and heretic (dissenting).

Mill does this with three straightforward arguments. 1) The other person's idea might be right. 2) Even if you are mostly right, you can hold your position more rationally and securely as a result of the challenge. "He who knows only his own side of the case, knows little of that." 3) Both views might contain a portion of truth, which then need to be combined. "Conflicting doctrines share the truth between them" (Mill [1859] 2002).

He summarizes his points with this quote:

> The peculiar evil of silencing the expression of an opinion is, that it is robbing the human race; posterity as well as the existing generation; those who dissent from the opinion, still more than those who hold it. If the opinion is right, they are deprived of the opportunity of exchanging error for truth: if wrong, they lose, what is almost as great a benefit, the clearer perception and livelier impression of truth, produced by its collision with error. (Mill [1859] 2002)

On wrong opinions and practices, he says, "[They] gradually yield to fact and argument, but facts and arguments, to produce any effect on the mind, must be brought before it" (Mill [1859] 2002).

So, as free speech absolutists, should people be allowed to shout and call names at those who disagree with them? Mill also answered this question. He believed that stigmatizing the unpopular opinion as bad and immoral (which happens these days all the time) is a weapon only the orthodox opinion holders can wield. Moreover, abusive language "really does deter people from professing contrary opinions, and from listening to those who profess them. For the interest, therefore, of truth and justice, it is far more important to restrain this employment of vituperative language" (Mill [1859] 2002).

Essentially, Mill is explaining the difference between being civil without being censored. There comes a point in the way you can speak that effectively dissuades the other side from voicing their opinion; the downstream effect is silencing:

> Those who desire to suppress [an opinion], of course, deny its truth; but they are not infallible . . . To refuse a hearing to an opinion, because they are sure that it is false, is to assume that their certainty is the same thing as absolute certainty. All silencing of discussion is an assumption of infallibility. (Mill [1859] 2002)

The realm of being civil without censoring is absolutely a gray area. Who defines what is civil? Won't people self-censor to some degree in an effort to be civil? How do you calibrate to those who are particularly insecure and easily triggered?

The perfect guideline may not exist, and there will unfortunately be some degree of subjectivity in judging on a case-by-case basis whether or not someone is censoring with their words and tone. Intent, however, is likely key. If silencing the opponent or distracting the debate is the goal, then the speaker is offside. If it is an honest mistake, or the opponent is deliberately trying to silence by claiming offense all too easily, then the civil standard has been maintained.

Be careful about apologizing too easily when you're not sure what you did wrong. If, after some reflection, you stand by your words, you can instead do an apologia, a formal defense of your opinion, position, or action ("Apologia" n.d.). This is what Socrates did in his trial, after which he was ultimately sentenced to death. With an apologia, you're elaborating on your position and standing up for your principles, instead of groveling to groupthink.

Try as I might, I may not have met this civil-without-being-censored benchmark in every line of this tome. I think this speaks to the difficulty Mill found in articulating this territory. Readers are welcome to call me out, and though this doesn't guarantee I will accept their assertions, I will self-examine with an open mind and heart.

Mill goes so far as to claim that banning heretics most harms the censors:

> But it is not the minds of heretics that are deteriorated most, by the ban placed on all inquiry which does not end in the orthodox conclusions. The greatest harm done is to those who are not heretics, and whose whole mental development is cramped, and their reason cowed, by the fear of heresy. Who can compute what the world loses in the multitude of promising intellects combined with timid characters, who dare not follow out any bold, vigorous, independent train of thought, lest it should land them in something which would admit of being considered irreligious or immoral? (Mill [1859] 2002)

I have made it a practice to praise people who express disagreement with me civilly and encourage them to elaborate; I am absolutely open to seeking truth together. But be warned if you think this is a tactic. If you are not genuine in your intention, people can easily see through this.

And if you find yourself silencing someone else, consider whether it's the spirit that possesses you (and not you) trying to maintain its grip. Challenge yourself to civilly explain to whomever you are conversing with why you disagree with them, and try to steelman their argument. If you cannot explain your argument calmly to them, perhaps you are at least in part wrong.

In the reverse situation, if you find your opponent trying to shout you down or call you names, take it as a compliment. People only do this when they know deep down (unconsciously more likely than consciously) that your argument has some real merit.

Jordan Peterson often refers to Matthew 22:21, where Jesus says, "So give back to Caesar what is Caesar's, and to God what is God's." Peterson quotes this verse in the context of illustrating the importance of the separation of church and state and not contaminating politics with the religious (J. Peterson, Kaczor, and Petrusek 2021). I believe that in the specific context of dialogue, the worst thing that you can do in a conversation is elevate your opponent to the status of evil. This unfortunately happens all the time in political debates these days. Those in low vibration naturally have a strong scapegoating impulse. Liberals label conservatives as evil, or at least morally reprehensible, and vice versa. It is an easy temptation to make your opponent out to be evil; then you are the hero saving the day from the great Satan. It can also effectively silence them. However, how on Earth (or anywhere else for that matter) are you supposed to come to an understanding with the other side? If you make out the other side to be evil, you can't have a real conversation with them. And maybe you don't want to. Because when you're a nihilistic youth, the opportunity to wear a mask and bring a baseball bat to a protest riot in the name of a good cause tugs at your messianic impulse far more effectively than debating the pros and cons. As Vladimir Lenin said, "It is, of course, much easier to shout, abuse, and howl than to attempt to relate, to explain" (1917). However, if political parties are going to try to govern together, if we as a society are going to try to live with our family and friends, we all need to stop this contamination. Be wary of demonizing your interlocutor.

Instead of relegating your opponent to the status of evil, attack the idea rather than the person. Calling your opponent an arrogant jerk is not helpful. Strip your language of emotion and religious terms, especially marks of Cain. Try to remain as objective as possible. This will give your argument more power, at least with people who are debating in good faith, with some degree of open minds and hearts. If they are just trying to win by shouting you down, then you will be like two ships passing in the night, and dialogue was never possible to begin with. Finding common ground inevitably requires two invested parties. However, if you remain sober with your words, this may win over the observing, undecided third-party audience. I have very much tried to remain true to this spirit in the writing of this book.

Diversity on the political spectrum is even baked into our DNA. Research indicates that political orientation is partly nature (genetic) and partly nurture (environment) (Alford, Funk, and Hibbing 2005). MRIs can even suggest where you are on the political spectrum. Greater liberalism was associated with increased gray matter volume in the anterior cingulate cortex, whereas greater conservatism was associated with increased volume in the right amygdala (Kanai et al. 2011). Personality plays a role as well, with those high in openness more likely to be liberal, and those high in conscientiousness more likely to be conservative, though there are more factors at play of course (Hirsh et al. 2010).

TABLE 1. Reported Brain and Behavior Affiliations for General Conservative Versus Liberal Orientation With Implications for Political Ideology[a]

Brain and Behavior Affiliations	High Conservatism	High Liberalism
Personality	Stability; opposition to change	Novelty
	Conformity	Unconventional; self-expression
	Tradition	New experiences and sensations
	Order, structure, and closure	Flexibility and variability
	Favor less complexity; harder categorization	Tolerance for uncertainty and ambiguity
	Purity	Minimization of harm
	Authority	Equality
	Conscientiousness	Empathy
	Distinctions with out-groups	Universal community
	Expressions of power	Expressions of warmth
Cognitive	Negativity bias	No clear bias
	Greater sensitivity to threat or loss	Greater sensitivity to cues for altering habitual response patterns
	Sensitivity to disgust	
Physiological	Greater activation of right amygdala	Greater conflict-related anterior cingulate cortex activity
Neuroimaging	Increased gray matter volume in right amygdala and other right anterior structures	Increased gray matter volume in anterior cingulate cortex

[a] References and studies for cognitive, physiological, and neuroimaging discussed in the article text.

Conservatives need liberal opinions, and liberals need conservative opinions. The eternal tug of war will keep our society optimally functioning. You need one foot in tradition and the other in innovation. I believe there is not enough philosophical bedrock or self-evident truths between today's right and left, such as shared definitions and belief in objective reality, which is why dialogue between the two sides is increasingly dysregulated. For this we all pay the price.

There is research that indicates that the disconnect is not fifty-fifty, that conservatives have a natural advantage over liberals in mutual comprehension. Conservatives can accurately predict how liberals will respond, but the same isn't true the other way around. Psychologist Jonathan Haidt reviewed the anthropological literature cross-culturally and derived five moral foundations upon which human societies are built. They are harm, fairness, authority, ingroup, and purity. Liberals have moral intuitions mainly based upon the first two factors, while conservatives tend to value all five (Haidt and Graham 2007).

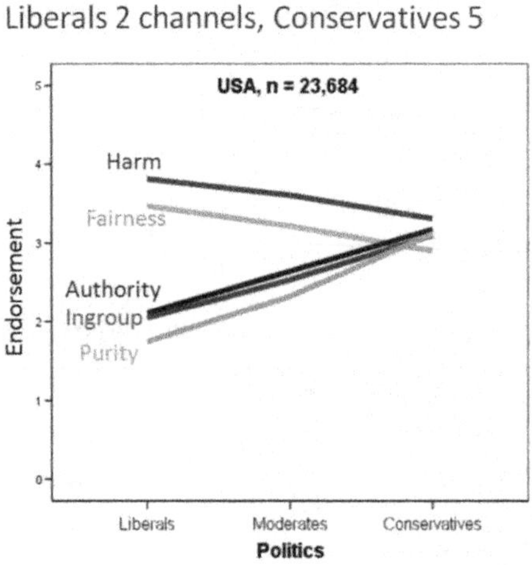

Liberals 2 channels, Conservatives 5

Jonathan Haidt's research revealed that liberals have a five-channel moral foundation, while conservatives have a two-channel moral foundation (Haidt 2012).

Social justice can manifest when the moral domain is limited to harm and fairness. However, the other three foundations are historically essential. For example, loyalty to the group, respect for one's elders, rules about sex, and so on are pervasive in the Koran, Old Testament, and non-Western religious and philosophical scriptures (Haidt and Joseph 2004).

It's easy to designate someone as evil and to disregard authority, ingroup, and purity. For a recent societal example, it's easy and convenient to label the over seventy million people who voted for Trump in both the 2016 and 2020 elections as hillbillies and bigots than to try to understand why they did so. But it's also easy to shift the mindset to have productive dialogue. First, recognize that all sides are morally motivated. Second, try to frame appeals in language that may trigger new intuitions on the other side. For example, in the context of arguing for gay marriage to very conservative minds, emphasize the additional social order and stability this brings (Haidt and Joseph 2004).

Four Steps to the Difficult Conversation

What should you do if you want to have dialogue with someone gripped in ideological possession, or someone who simply won't discuss their point of view in good faith? If the person is moralizing, elevating you to the status of evil, or reducing the issue to binary thinking, the short answer is you can't. But there is a process you can and should do to ensure that you have actually tried, and maybe you'll be surprised.

Step 1: Actively listen.

Actually listen to the other person. Seek first to understand. You must start with this step to avoid being the one steeped in ideology and squashing debate. If they are sincere about dialogue, psychologist Carl Rogers gives us the advice of restating what they're saying (J. Peterson 2021). This is active listening. Play devil's advocate to your own perspective. A mature two-way conversation will be obvious if they are doing the same to you and you are both empathetic to each other's opinions. In many cases, however, this won't happen. Instead, a one-sided conversation emerges, effectively a monologue. In this case, move on to Step 2.

Step 2: Pay attention.

Let them do most of the talking while you pay close attention. You'll want to be assessing how entrenched their position is. Are they possessed by their idea completely, or is it 50 percent? You are also watching for their motivations. Are they just trying to win no matter what's true? To silence you? Maybe the scapegoating impulse is at play, making you or those with your point of view the enemy. Are they really so imbued with their idea, or are they stressed out for some other reason in life and thus displacing their frustrations on you? Is there projection going on to cope with their own misdeeds or to gaslight you?

This is the step where you must start paying attention to the context the dominant conversation partner puts forth underpinning the entire conversation. Words are just the surface layer. One context I often encounter is that, thanks to the internet, a patient who has looked at a few websites understands a disease just as well as a physician does. We call this "Dr. Google." Understanding what context the other person is trying to put forth is critical for subsequent steps. Ideally, you are both aiming for a context of free speech, humility, and nuance, and this is the context you generally want to emote. But there can only ever be one context underlying an interaction, so when two different ones collide, the stronger context absorbs the weaker one.

Step 3: Feel out if there is enough good faith conversation to salvage, or if this will be a dead end.

FBI hostage negotiator Chris Voss uses a tactic to set the tone of conversations: employ a late-night FM DJ voice. Make your speech straightforward with a soothing, downward tilt, and imbued with warmth. It is similar to the tone used when talking to a two-year-old. Two-year-olds and ideologues often share the same solipsistic demeanor, and the late-night FM DJ voice is a great speech pattern to calm them down (Voss and Raz 2016). Reassure your conversation partner that they drive the bus (that they're in charge) if this fits contextually, and say basic true things that they will agree with (e.g., "I know this is a very important issue"). This buys you discourse capital, so then perhaps you can say something proportional that they won't like (e.g., "I have to be honest, this treatment won't 100 percent eliminate your pain"). This will give you a good idea about how open they are to different perspectives. Further, challenge them gently with problems that their ideology does not solve or contradictions inherent in their belief (e.g., "Why can't climate conferences be held virtually to save on emissions?"). At this stage, you're still not really trying to win the argument. Instead, every question you ask has a purpose, and that purpose is solely to tease out the fruitfulness of this conversational endeavor. Here's a tip: if you need to spend a lot of time in your late-night FM DJ voice, you already have your answer—this is a conversation to nowhere.

Usually a bit of back and forth with a late-night FM DJ voice is enough to tease out whether this will yield dialogue or a dead end, but if you're still not sure, here are a couple of other strategies to prod your interlocutor into declaring themself. One is showing an ideologue that they already agree with you. This requires some swift on-the-fly deep thinking. For example, to someone whose golden calf is keeping personal carbon emissions down, while they're promoting electric vehicle subsidies, you can point out that in a jurisdiction where most of the energy is not clean, the electric vehicles are still generating emissions from the electricity they charge with. So instead, by their own principles, that money is better spent elsewhere. Another strategy is to get the other person to agree early on to discuss both pros and cons and thus engage in a more nuanced argument. The pride of ideologues is such that they think their belief explains everything, so of course they won't be the one to admit they can't get into the weeds. And then, as the debate unfolds, if they try to stymie debating both positives and negatives, you can call them out on this.

In the specific scenario where they are sticking to their beliefs but cannot silence you or leave, such as in a formal debate, pay attention to where they are reacting the most.

What is getting them riled up? They know deep down their argument has weaknesses in these very positions. It's like the insecurities within that comedians uncover. Keep asking simple questions that don't quite fit their beliefs, as you shake their tree of ideological certitude. The closer you are to the trunk, the core belief, the more they react. Follow this trail.

Throughout any difficult conversation, tread carefully in the gray zone of being civil without being censored. Your honest point of view should be phrased courteously and should not be slurred with a mark of Cain or ad hominem attack. If called offensive, quickly examine your words and tone, but also the intent of the accuser. Is it to silence you? Decide on an apology or an apologia. Do not get into an "I'm sorry" ladder, where it appears you are apologizing repeatedly. If you are, then you have been subsumed into their context that you have overstepped and that your argument holds no merit.

The best-case scenario in any of these steps is you can snap them out of the software that's running them and talk to the real person. These are truly wonderful moments. But if this belief is a replacement religion, you'll know pretty quickly following these steps, so move onto Step 4.

Step 4: Get out.

Once you have determined that dialogue is not possible, don't engage in the argument at face value. This is where context comes into play. Don't argue back from their paradigm, otherwise you buy into their context and lose. In the previous scenario on carbon emissions, for example, quit trying to argue against the minimization of personal carbon emissions as the sole metric of success. Further, don't keep trying to have the conversation you wish to have—in this case, a detailed debate on the nuances of climate change, causes, effects, and implications. You are talking to a wall. Instead, give a simple reply (e.g., that there is far more to climate change than just personal carbon emissions), laugh it off, or, if feasible, get a third-party mediator. Don't appear unnerved. And finally, don't negotiate with terrorists. You were never going to have a real conversation with this person to begin with. You tried forthrightly, so you can just walk away.

In the right context, call their bluff. In perhaps the singular joke that made Russell Peters famous, he tells the story of his childhood where once, when his dad was going to discipline him, Russell threatened to phone Children's Aid. "Let me get you the phone," came the reply. Young Russell was perplexed, wondering why his dad wasn't scared. His father explained, "I might get into a little bit of trouble, but I know that it's going to take them twenty-two minutes to get here. In that time, somebody gonna get a hurt real bad"

(Peters 2016). The principle of "calling their bluff," as humorously illustrated by Russell Peters, also applies in more serious contexts where decisive action is required in the face of intractable opposition. Let me share a personal experience that highlights this approach.

In February 2020, I began renovating my condo, but the pandemic lockdowns forced a halt to the work. When renovations resumed, the person living below me constantly complained about the noise. Despite my efforts to accommodate her, including offering noise-canceling headphones (which she returned unused), her complaints persisted. It became clear she was not interested in a solution but perhaps sought financial compensation. She had already established a pattern of complaining to the building management about external construction noise, and now seemed intent on stopping my renovation process. It is common for people in low vibration to displace their negative emotions externally. This situation dragged on, as management took her side in not allowing me to resume in the hopes of appeasing her, thereby exacerbating my inconvenience as I was living with relatives during the renovation.

Realizing that a reasonable negotiation was impossible, I involved a lawyer who sent a legal letter to the building manager, clearly stating my rights and the building's obligations. This intervention shifted the dynamics, compelling the building to treat my case with fairness and allowing me to resume renovations in limited hours. This experience underscored the importance of recognizing when a genuine dialogue is unattainable and taking decisive action to protect one's interests. It was a practical application of American president Theodore Roosevelt's principle "speak softly and carry a big stick" ("Big Stick Ideology" n.d.). In this case, the "speak softly" was my attempt at helping her with the noise (e.g., headphones), and the "big stick" was the involvement of legal action, a necessary assertion of strength underpinned by a calm and reasoned approach. This situation was an opportunity to apply the concept of shadow integration, using assertiveness and legal means to address the issue, akin to the controlled use of low-vibration emotions in a high-vibration manner.

But I Will Lose My Job If I Speak

It appears to many that the radical left has silenced their detractors. Solzhenitsyn would say,

> We have so hopelessly ceded our humanity that for the modest handouts of today, we are ready to surrender up all principles, our soul, all the labors of our ancestors, all the prospects of our descendants—anything to avoid

> disrupting our meager existence . . . We do not even fear a common nuclear death . . . but fear only to take a civic stance. ([1974] 2004)

Those who speak their minds are absolutely more at risk of becoming social, economic, and cultural pariahs. But knowing that self-censorship warps thought and action, is there any way to walk a middle path? Fortunately, Solzhenitsyn again lights the way. He acknowledged to his followers in the Soviet Union that they can't exactly speak their minds. However, they can refuse to say what they don't think, refuse to speak lies, and refuse to assent to lies spoken around them. He believed that personal nonparticipation in lies is the most accessible (and practical) key to liberation. His rules for responsible conduct might help you navigate this tightrope:

1. Will not write, sign, nor publish in any way, a single line distorting, so far as he can see, the truth.
2. Will not utter such a line in private or in public conversation, nor read it from a crib sheet, nor speak it in the role of educator, canvasser, teacher, actor.
3. Will not in painting, sculpture, photograph, technology, or music depict, support, or broadcast a single false thought, a single distortion of the truth as he discerns it.
4. Will not cite in writing or in speech a single "guiding" quote for gratification, insurance, for his success at work, unless he fully shares the cited thought and believes that it fits the context precisely.
5. Will not be forced to a demonstration or a rally if it runs counter to his desire and his will; will not take up and raise a banner or slogan in which he does not fully believe.
6. Will not raise a hand in vote for a proposal which he does not sincerely support; will not vote openly or in secret ballot for a candidate whom he deems dubious or unworthy.
7. Will not be impelled to a meeting where a forced and distorted discussion is expected to take place.
8. Will at once walk out from a session, meeting, lecture, play, or film as soon as he hears the speaker utter a lie, ideological drivel, or shameless propaganda.
9. Will not subscribe to, nor buy in retail, a newspaper or journal that distorts or hides the underlying facts. (Solzhenitsyn [1974] 2004)

So how many of these do you currently follow? If the answer is not all nine, perhaps you can set a goal to improve that number. And if the answer is zero, Solzhenitsyn asks that you are honest with yourself. "Let him say to himself plainly: I am cattle, I am a coward, I seek only warmth and to eat my fill" ([1974] 2004).

In his book *Live Not by Lies*, journalist Rod Dreher tells the story of Father Tomislav Kolakovic, a Catholic priest who worked in Slovakia during World War II. In 1943, he told his congregation he had good news and bad news. The good news was that the Germans were going to lose the war. The bad news was that the Soviets were going to win and that they would definitely come after the church. He had studied Soviet doctrine, and he foresaw the persecution to follow. His fellow priests criticized him for fearmongering, just like the flack social commentators take for warning of the consequences of today's cultural flocking to what are fundamentally Marxist ideas. But he took it a step further than just sounding the alarm bells. He made concrete plans to have an underground church, places where people could gather in secret and freely speak about what was going on in the real world. He was the reason the underground church was so strong in Slovakia during the Soviet occupation. Dreher believes we're in the same place now as Slovakia was in 1943, and I agree (2022). The specifics may be different, but it appears we're about to transition to an illiberal society where freedom of thought, speech, and action are choked and compliance to derivatives of Marxist ideology reigns supreme. What underground can we create to cope?

Writing this book is my way of sounding an alarm, but anyone can take a step in the right direction. You can do this by telling your inner circle the importance of living in truth. This could be your spouse, close friends, or even just writing in your journal. Most people can relate to the decrease in societal free speech—this is the reason you are sounding the alarm. Express your commitment to at least not telling lies. If you have a supportive group, ask them to check in with you periodically. You can also evaluate yourself by adherence to Solzhenitsyn's rules. Critically, convince others by your deeds rather than just your words; living in truth must be embodied, not virtue signaled. You can make a difference. If just one person decides to live in truth, then maybe another will, and so on. I believe the cumulative effect of this cascade of truth will produce the most thriving society yet, one well buttressed against tyranny. What a world this would be.

Solzhenitsyn explained that if you had told Russian intellectuals in the 1890s that within thirty years, medieval torture would be introduced, they would have dismissed you. Dreher believes that same parallel plays out today. If you had told Western liberals in the 1980s about the woke ideas from the present day, such as being okay with racism against

White people, a resurgence in popularity for socialism, and the rampant reintroduction of censorship throughout society, they would have laughed at you (Dreher and Peterson 2022).

Be careful even of white lies. If you are in a context in which you must lie, in all likelihood you have put yourself in this position by omitting the truth in a series of events leading up to this. Jordan Peterson gives such an example:

> If you were hiding Jews in your attic in Nazi Germany, if you weren't going to lie, those people would die. However, ten years ago you should've said something about the Nazis when they were first starting to gain power. But you didn't, and now you're in this hellish situation where you have to lie for the good. That means you've already put yourself in a place that isn't tenable. (Peterson and Franzese 2022)

Had I known of Solzhenitsyn's rules and the power of truth, I would have had an easier time dealing with my formal patient complaint from 2013. I would have ensured that I at least did not write and voice with an exaggerated tone how terrible a doctor I was. Instead, I would have stripped my statements of emotion and stayed as objective as possible. That would have earned me the same result of exoneration, without as much emotional turmoil throughout the course.

To thaw frozen conversation, we can reverse the three-step process that Ben Shapiro has exposed of the political correctness aficionados:

Step 1: Recognize that silence is not violence.
Instead, follow Solzhenitsyn's principles. At the very least, refuse to say things that you do not believe to be true. Do not virtue signal out of expediency.

Step 2: Recognize that speaking what you believe is true is not violence either, especially if it comes from good intentions.
Your minority perspective is only going to help everyone get toward the truth. Defend your right to free expression.

Step 3: Recognize that everyone loses when there is censorship under the banner of cordiality.

Recall Mill's three principles, particularly that both views might contain a portion of the truth. Don't slur someone with a mark of Cain, and call out those who do. When someone claims offense, consider intent from both sides. Did they blow the whistle from a place of silencing dialogue, or could you have chosen your words or tone more politely? And, under self-examination, do you think your intent was muddled, or was it honest? In some circumstances, you'll want to apologize. In other circumstances, you'll want to make an apologia to explain yourself further, stand up firmly for your words, and call them out for ill intent. Do not ever let it get to the level of a Maoist struggle session, the "I'm sorry" ladder, whereby no matter how much you apologize, they are never satisfied. And if you're apologizing, always know what for.

Conclusion

Free speech was the mechanism by which minorities got rights in the first place. We should be suspicious of the motives of those who suddenly want to impair free speech under the guise of hypothetically representing these same minorities. We always must be wary of those who censor—censorship is never needed if there is nothing to hide, and it certainly isn't promoted by those winning the argument. Free speech may indeed be dangerous, but it's absolutely necessary.

Pope John Paul II was once asked if all the scriptures were lost and he could only save one sentence, what would that be? He answered, "Truth will set you free" (Naglieri 2018). With this, he quotes Jesus exactly from John 8:32, which may or may not have been intentional. It's quite the opposite of the *arbeit macht frei* slogans on Nazi concentration camps. Tyrannies fall when each individual tries earnestly to the tell the truth, and they can do that by speaking freely. Choose your words carefully to adhere to the strict truth as much as possible. In many contexts today, practically speaking, the very least you can do is not say things you know are not true. Moreover, give space to others by listening well. Do not contaminate conversation with marks of Cain, which is tantamount to monologue. Do not be quick to condemn those who offend you. If someone disagrees with you respectfully, commend them. Via civil dialogue, you will further advance to the truth and elevate your souls.

Speech, thought, writing, and action are fundamentally interconnected. Impede one, and all others suffer. We are all limited beings, subject to many biases that interfere with our search for truth and objective reality. (Confirmation bias might be the chief among these.) Having free and open discourse among diverse opinions is the only way to reliably get there. People who disagree, or even criticize you, are actually doing you a kindness. Don't be afraid of having a strong opinion, but be malleable. Only those insecure in their positions resist a hearty debate. Finally, don't chase the rainbow of never offending the perpetually offended. This pot of gold—the hypothetical destination of pleasing them—will always be just a little out of reach.

Disclaimer: Even though this book has highlighted the flaws of the radical left, much of it applies to the radical right as well. They are also enthralled in ideology, thought suppression, and the idea that the ends justify the means. The book's focus on the radical left is, however, because they hold the levers of power in the West; they are culturally dominant. The mainstream (and legacy) media is predominantly left-leaning, as is Big Tech. Further, the radical left has control of language, hence is the bigger threat. Ideally, we can all be centrists, believing in free speech to sort out our differences, though peace and prosperity is a far less compelling story to sell than righteous discrimination from the political extremes.

Chapter 13:
FINDING MEANING THROUGH TRADITIONAL RELIGION

The solution to the unholy trinity of nihilism, atheism, and depression is meaning. Speaking of meaning, there is nothing better to provide it than a sophisticated, traditional religion.[31] To loosely paraphrase Winston Churchill again, traditional religion is the worst form of belief system except for all the others.

The rationality borne out of the Enlightenment has given our world so many wonders created by our own human hands. But it doesn't mean the religious impulse—and the human need for it—has suddenly disappeared. But when we try to satisfy this thirst with replacement religions, it doesn't work—and eventually leads to destruction. Instead of using increasingly harmful substitutes to address our meaning deficit, we can increase the meaning in our lives. What people need is a deep, real religion that embraces mystery, connects us to each other, and gives us a sense of meaning based on truth.

The Brothers Karamazov

Meet Ivan, from Dostoevsky's *The Brothers Karamazov* (published in 1880). Ivan is another one of Dostoevsky's rationalist-nihilist types. He puts forth an amazing argument against the existence of God, or at least a loving, good God:

> Listen: if everyone must suffer, in order to buy eternal harmony with their suffering, pray tell me what have children got to do with it? It is quite

> incomprehensible why they should have to suffer, and why they should buy harmony with their suffering. (Dostoevsky [1880] 2003)

Ivan reasons that if God exists, he doesn't really love humanity. We should reject him because he torments us, rather than worship him. The argument effectively boils down to that God cannot be good if he indeed exists because children suffer in the world.

> Perhaps the entire cosmos is not worth a single child's suffering. How can the universe be constructed such that pain is permitted? How can a good God allow for the existence of a suffering world? (Dostoevsky [1880] 2003)

There's one truth that Ivan shows us: you can't rationalize belief in God. The mystery and mystique of traditional religion requires faith, and somehow this has satisfied the spirit for millennia. Religious ritual challenges Ivan's logic. Ivan is so possessed by his intellect, he recites his nihilism, but it isn't that clear that he believes this deep down. When his atheist philosophy influences another character, Smerdyakov, to kill a man named Fyodor, Ivan is faced with the possibility that he is in some way responsible for murder, for suffering. Unable to cope with the contradiction, he hallucinates and becomes mad. His absolute rationality led him down this pathway, and he is completely lost.

In contrast, Ivan's main philosophical rival, his brother Alyosha, is not silver-tongued or quick-witted, but he is religious, a staunch believer in God. Even when he is unsure of himself, he simply reverts to doing good as per his faith. He is greatly influenced by the monk Zosima, and he just tries to be a good person in life. He simply can't debate Ivan.

The monk teaches Alyosha:

> Above all, do not lie to yourself. A man who lies to himself and listens to his own lie comes to a point where he does not discern any truth either in himself or anywhere around him, and thus falls into disrespect toward himself and others. Not respecting anyone, he ceases to love, and having no love, he gives himself up to the passions and coarse pleasures, in order to occupy and amuse himself, and in his vices reaches complete bestiality, and it all comes from lying continually to others and to himself. (Dostoevsky [1880] 2003)

Lying to yourself is a slippery slope. Psychologist and concentration camp survivor Viktor Frankl believed that deceitful inauthentic individual existence was the precursor to social totalitarianism.

Jordan Peterson surmises the philosophical conflict between Ivan and Alyosha:

> Alyosha can't address any one of Ivan's criticisms. But Alyosha continues to act out his commitment to the good, and in that manner, he's triumphant. It doesn't matter that he loses the arguments, because they aren't exactly the point. They're the side issue. The existential and main issue is not what you believe as if it's a set of facts, but how you conduct yourself in the world. (J. Peterson 2017e)

The conflict between faith and rationality is the central theme of *The Brothers Karamazov*. In his books, Dostoevsky frequently puts the counterargument in the form of his most objectively admirable character, in this case Ivan, and then has it play out as he writes. In this case, his actual argument is in the form of Alyosha. It's like David and Goliath. At the beginning of the book, who would bet on scrawny little David? But as the story plays out, Alyosha's faith wins out over Ivan's rationality.

The story shows that while objectivism, empiricism, and free speech are the best tools to seek truth, they are not everything, and we simply cannot reason out every facet of existence; we must have faith. Dostoevsky's great tale toys with the devil's advocate position: that there is no unknowable landscape of knowledge; that everything can be intellectually discovered. However, Ivan's mental collapse at the end of the book represents the victory of faith over rationality in a way only a story could tell. Explicit doctrine would not do this justice.

Faith is harder to choose. There are no rational reasons to believe, but that's just it by definition. If you have faith, you do so in spite of its lack of justification. You have to defy the many reasons to doubt. As in *The Brothers Karamazov*, a life of faith and of meaning, is happier than a life of doubt and of hyper-rationalism.

The Brothers Karamazov is so deep, there is even a story within a story. Ivan tells Alyosha the story of the *Grand Inquisitor*. During the Spanish Inquisition, Jesus returned to Earth but was arrested. The inquisitor believed he was acting in humanity's best interest and sentenced Jesus to death.[32] They speak together in his cell. He explains that Jesus's rejection of Satan's three temptations in the Gospel gave humanity free will, which is beyond burdensome. For example, had Jesus accepted the final temptation and ruled over all the Earth, everyone would be saved (perhaps meaning there would be no conflict or suffering). In parallel to his narrator Ivan, the inquisitor makes an amazing argument. In parallel to Alyosha, Jesus has no counterargument. He simply kisses the inquisitor, the man who has sentenced him to death, on his lips; this is perhaps the most powerful kiss in literature. The inquisitor is stunned, then simply opens the cell and releases Jesus, telling him never to return. This one kiss demonstrates the power of love and faith in a way that is similar to the mysteries of traditional religion. The kiss is more profound than words can explain, inexplicably overcoming the inquisitor's grand argument. Whereas Ivan sees free will as the metaphysical albatross on humanity, the story extols the necessity of free will. Being good and having faith needs to be a choice. This is impossible without free will.

In echoing Ivan's claim that "without God, everything is permitted," Solzhenitsyn surmises his central thesis of why so many people suffered and died in the Soviet Union: "Men have forgotten God" (1983). If Ivan ever had the humility to ask Solzhenitsyn for advice, the reply would have likely been: "The price of selling your God-given soul to the entrapments of human dogma was slavery and death" (Solzhenitsyn 1974).

Viktor Frankl believed that the last human freedom is the ability to choose one's attitude in a given set of circumstances ([1959] 2014). With this, he paraphrases Nietzsche's famous saying, "He who has a why to live can bear almost any how" (Nietzsche [1889] 2008).

Pope John Paul II also explains the necessity of pairing faith and reason:

> Faith and reason are like two wings on which the human spirit rises to the contemplation of truth; and God has placed in the human heart a desire to know the truth—in a word, to know himself—so that, by knowing and loving God, men and women may also come to the fullness of truth about themselves . . . With the light of reason human beings can know which path to take, but they can follow that path to its end, quickly and unhindered, only if with a rightly tuned spirit they search for it within the horizon of faith. (John Paul II 1998)

Dogma versus Spirituality

"I'm not religious, but I'm spiritual." This is a common statement. Is being spiritual enough? What in fact does it mean to be spiritual?

There seems to be a spectrum between dogmatic religion on one end and abstract spirituality on the other. As fewer people believe in traditional dogmatic religions, more people claim to be spiritual (Routledge and Peterson 2021). The problem with dogmatic religion is that it's really easy to criticize because it's explicit. By comparison, being spiritual is more abstract, and every individual can customize it fully. However, the problem with being just spiritual is that there is no coherent structure. Since it's so individually tailored, it cannot unite people. In dialogue, we can push each other on the edges of what we disagree on, but if we have to debate the meaning of every word, we can't have a coherent conversation. That the sun rises in the east, that you have to work to earn a living—these are examples of dogmatic bedrock. I believe this is why the right and the left can't speak to each other anymore: they lack any uniting principles.

I had a relative who was a staunch lifelong atheist. He didn't believe in God or organized religion. One day late in life he explained to me his belief in the force. I was stunned. I thought he actually didn't believe in anything but the physical world. Yet denial of traditional religion led him to something spiritual.

Being spiritual is easier and is definitely less judgmental, but it lacks critical elements people need to create meaning in their lives. Psychologist Clay Routledge explains, "A lot of new age alternative beliefs are motivated by the need for meaning, but they don't seem to do a good job of providing it, as they're inversely correlated with the presence of meaning" (Routledge and Peterson 2021). If the whole point is filling oneself up with meaning, then being simply spiritual is useless. It is an attempt at a replacement religion, and the hungry ghost will never be satiated. Into this meaning deficit, our Δ meaning, our underground complex goes to work, and for the most nihilistic, that means the solution is opioids.

Instead, religion can work as a prix fixe menu, giving you the parameters for life so you don't have to be paralyzed by every little choice. By this reasoning, having normative parameters for living your life, such as the Ten Commandments, or the importance of marriage before children, actually frees people to focus on what they truly want. Maybe all that is traditional isn't outdated, but rather deep ancient wisdom that is still relevant today.

Clarify Your Goals and Beliefs

One of the major tenets of the Entropy Model of Uncertainty (EMU), a theoretical framework by psychologists designed to better understand uncertainty-related anxiety, is that the adoption of clear goals and belief structures helps constrain the experience of uncertainty by reducing the spread of competing affordances. It's like driving on the highway of life with the lane markers clearly painted.

Another tenet of the EMU is that anxiety is associated with more adrenaline release. In this manner, adrenaline is released in response to uncertainty, unexpectedly not getting the outcome you want, and cues of impending punishment (Hirsh, Mar, and Peterson 2012). When you have a clear goal and things are going according to plan, adrenaline is released according to its phasic mode. It has a low baseline firing rate, and it is specifically released in short bursts when you experience goal-relevant information. This enhances task performance.

So when your foundational belief structure (which has inherent goals) is in place, you are far more effective—your adrenaline level stays low. But when your beliefs are attacked and crumbling, your adrenaline rises, and accomplishing minor tasks becomes arduous.

The authors of the EMU have their own take on religion versus ideology:

> It has long been argued that one of the functions of religion is to reduce uncertainty about the meaning of the world. However, the EMU predicts that any strong interpretive structure (e.g., political ideology) would constrain the behavioral and perceptual affordances associated with an experience and, therefore, serve a similar uncertainty-reducing fraction. The uncertainty-reducing function of such belief systems becomes even more pronounced when an individual lives within a community of like-minded others, who are consequently more predictable and less likely to provoke uncertainty. It is worth pointing out that while strong beliefs and well-structured social environments will help to reduce uncertainty, they may also result in dogmatic forms of rigidity if taken too far . . . Indeed, excessive rigidity and a reluctance to explore and confront uncertainty have been associated with a variety of pathological outcomes and the failure to adapt to changing circumstances. (Hirsh, Mar, and Peterson 2012)

Thus, using ideologies as foundational belief structures is like basing your financial stability on fool's gold. They may work in the short term, but as time progresses, you will inevitably pay a price.

For example, believing that you are so good at managing your finances that you tune out constructive criticism will preserve the ego for now. However, if you are actually bad with money, this faulty belief system will crumble when you are bankrupt. If, instead, you have a functioning belief system in place, such as a traditional religion, you will gladly evaluate advice for its merits and play devil's advocate against your own pride. In the next section of this chapter, we cover the features of a functional belief system.

There's another reason for the importance of a dogmatic, traditional, sophisticated religion. What's the alternative? Rationality without limitation leads down a pathway of nihilism, atheism, and the destructive effects of poor mental health. They are all inextricably linked. Religion isn't the opioid of the masses, but rather the refuge from the ultimately self-destructive avenue that replacement religions eventually lead to. Such nihilistic, rational thoughts entered the minds of the characters Bazarov, Raskolnikov, Stavrogin, and Ivan, all of whose stories ended in catastrophe.

Having deep meaning is a meta-solution[33] to the unholy trinity of nihilism, atheism, and depression. Research reveals that meaning reduces the risk of depression, addiction, and suicide, while encouraging social flourishing.

> Meaning in life reflects the feeling that one's existence has significance, purpose, and coherence. A growing body of research identifies meaning in life as a fundamental human need that strongly influences both psychological and physical well-being. Individuals who perceive their lives as full of meaning live longer, healthier, and happier lives than those less inclined to view their lives as meaningful. (Routledge and FioRito 2021)

Again, while my most frequent example of a system of deep meaning is Christianity, any traditional faith likely works; due to my Christian background, I am just not very familiar with other religions.

How to Identify a Functional Belief System

How does one identify a religion that can provide meaning, produce baseline life satisfaction and happiness, and quench the search for more meaning? How does one identify a belief structure that isn't a cheap imitation?

I don't believe this to be a comprehensive answer to such a complex question, but there are two hints from a conversation between Jordan Peterson and theologian Nigel Biggar. 1) It locates evil within rather than without, and 2) the Socratic insistence upon ignorance (Biggar, Orr, and Peterson 2021). To these two criteria, I will add 3) it's challenging, and certainly not the path of least resistance, 4) the ends do not justify the means, 5) it does not rely on lies, 6) it offers a genuine pathway to atonement, and 7) free will exists and you are responsible.

Most replacement religions identify a convenient enemy and create a narrative structure within which its adherents are on the side of the good. For social justice warriors, the convenient enemy is essentially anyone who has more success than they do. Or sometimes it's just blaming White people for all the problems of the world, which is the very definition of (classical) racism. This isn't to say you can never identify someone else as evil, but be very careful, and make sure you have thoroughly played devil's advocate. (How often do people unfavorably liken their opponent to Hitler these days?) Because are you sure the evil person isn't you? Before you declare *exitus acta probat*, that the ends justify the means,

> Why do you look at the speck of sawdust in your brother's eye and pay no attention to the plank in your own eye? How can you say to your brother, "Let me take the speck out of your eye," when all the time there is a plank in your own eye? You hypocrite, first take the plank out of your own eye, and then you will see clearly to remove the speck from your brother's eye. (Matthew 7:3–5)

Part of why the scapegoating impulse is so strong is that it distracts you from fixing yourself. When the narrative you subscribe to points to an external enemy, you can neglect any enterprise for self-improvement. It's hard to know sometimes when your attention needs to be inward before trying to solve an external problem, and certainly those who take this passage from the Gospel of Matthew seriously might be prone to being taken advantage of via gaslighting. People of low vibration are often experts at weaponizing guilt. But as long as you are aware of both internal and external enemies, have faith that you will strike the right balance in your focus and that your rare external vilification is justified.

The Socratic insistence upon ignorance is essentially having the humility to recognize the limits of your knowledge. Replacement religions (particularly ideologies) push the opposite belief, that all there is to know can be explained by their simplistic set of rules (e.g., *The Communist Manifesto*, which is less than fifty pages). Socrates always insisted on being cognizant of how much he didn't know. No matter how much science can explain the world, there will always be an inexplicable domain. "I am the wisest man alive, for I know one thing, and that is that I nothing." Socrates isn't declaring that he knows absolutely nothing and is a complete idiot. Rather, this is epistemic humility, a declaration on the limits of rationality. Faith in God in the Judeo-Christian tradition means in part having the humility to admit our human limitations in being, knowledge, and life. Practically speaking, have a great relationship with objective reality. Do this by playing devil's advocate, steelmanning the opposing argument, and of course, free discourse. Have an open mind and heart when seeking feedback from others and the world. Don't have an ego about it.

Perhaps another property of a functioning religious structure is that it isn't easy. Being vaguely spiritual is too easy, as is being a victim, but being part of a deep religion or faith is not. There are duties, roles, and rules, and a modicum of faith is required. And maybe this is by intelligent design. "Enter through the narrow gate. For wide is the gate and broad is the road that leads to destruction, and many enter through it. But small is the gate and narrow the road that leads to life, and only a few find it" (Matthew 7:13–14).

The ends can never justify the means. It's too easy to follow the slippery slope and become the evil you seek to root out. From Dostoevsky's Raskolnikov to Anakin Skywalker from *Star Wars*, the road to hell is paved with good intentions.

Moreover, a deep belief structure cannot rely on a foundation of lies (e.g., a master race or the deification of your country's leader). Like the head of a hydra, lies multiply. You cannot lie for the greater good and not risk falling into the abyss. Any belief system that relies on a lie is accompanied by existential malaise. Only God knows fully what is false. But we can try to get as close to the truth—the best point estimate of objective reality—as possible by using the scientific method and having an articulate, compelling argument that withstands the scrutiny of playing devil's advocate and free speech. A wholesome belief system encourages debate. Ask a friend to critique your belief, or, even better, ask someone you generally don't agree with. Have an open mind and heart. And in the spirit of John Stuart Mill, may your belief be refined and strengthened, and, thus, be as far away from a lie as humanly possible.

Further, a true religion offers a real and practical step for the forgiveness of your sins. This idea is from British comedian Konstantin Kisin and does not apply to values such as pride or money being replacement religions, but it definitely does for ideologies. In the world of diversity-equity-inclusivity, if you're White, there's nothing you can do about it. The same applies to Jews for Nazism and wealthy people for communism. In climate alarmism, there isn't a practical carbon reduction solution to satisfy, both for individuals and societies. By contrast, Catholics have confession at which you are granted absolution. There is inherent in this process a moment of self-reflection and an explicit penance to make, such as saying a few prayers. You can leave the confessional with the desire to be a better person and the road map to do so.

Finally, I believe that a truly functioning religion places abundant agency on you. You have free will. You are responsible for your actions. Even though everyone is born into different circumstances, you cannot just blame society, God, or the universe for your life. By the same token, you should take credit for the burdens you successfully lift, moral and otherwise. We'll look more at the idea of personal responsibility in the next chapter.

A deep and functioning belief system fills you with meaning, and thus there is no instinct to seek out replacement religions. It is oriented to objective reality and acts as a bulwark against nihilism, atheism, and depression. It provides a guidebook on how to live your life, relieving you of the burden of figuring out every micro-decision. For example, you automatically know it's wrong to steal or murder, that you should probably commit to a life partner for optimal happiness, and that you should honor your parents. Any belief system that does not fulfill these seven criteria mentioned in this chapter is likely a replacement religion. Only belief systems steeped in tradition have a hope to qualify as sources of true meaning.

Chapter 14: ENCOURAGING PERSONAL RESPONSIBILITY

In the Trojan War, Achilles, the greatest of Greek warriors, was at one point living a blissfully happy life with his wife and child. The Greeks were trying hard to convince him to fight, knowing how much of their fate lay in his hands. The gods presented him with a dichotomous option. If he didn't fight, the Greeks would lose, but he would live essentially happily ever after, and when he died, no one would remember him. But if he fought, he would die, the Greeks would win, and he would be remembered forever with everlasting glory. Hands up if you would choose option A . . . My, there are a lot of you. You are in good company. This is what Achilles chose . . . at least at first.

Personal responsibility is a big part of the cure for nihilism, pathological entitlement, and for this crisis of meaning we are all in. For this goal, judgment needs to be resuscitated to a more nuanced connotation. The biggest addiction in the West isn't opioids—it's handouts. We need an ongoing adult discussion of how much welfare the state should supply, without banning concepts such as personal responsibility. Social services should be enough to help those willing to rise, but not so much that it incentivizes them to stay down. Of course this is far easier said than implemented. Discourse shouldn't vilify the side opposed to excessive welfare, so policy can be constructively debated. It does no one any good to elevate these discussions into good/evil binary narratives. We need a balanced carrot-and-stick approach, protecting and encouraging simultaneously, with both maternal and paternal energies; with mercy and with justice.

Back to the story of Achilles: after some time feeling unfulfilled and the death of his best friend at the hands of the Trojans, he realized he wanted meaning and purpose in his life. In picking up his sword, he took on the heaviest responsibility he could and fulfilled his potential. While he died in battle, he made it count, and he set in motion events that ultimately led to the victory of the Greeks. We remember him today for Achilles' heel, the only vulnerable part of his body. We are often faced with Achilles' dilemma, the same meta-choice between meaning and the easy life, though fortunately it is almost never so dramatically life and death. The question remains: How much responsibility do you want to bear?

I have seen people try to abandon more and more (personal) responsibility, and as a consequence, they have become increasingly miserable. Then, suddenly, when responsibility is thrust on them, they thrive and are happy. This is a strange phenomenon.

Have a Family, the Most Time-Tested Way of Adopting Responsibility

Committing to a partner for life and having a family is the prototypical way of having responsibility, adventure, and meaning in human history. This avenue is available to everyone, though of course I am not saying that achieving it is easy. Further, there are specific challenges unique to modern times, such as increased years of education and cost of living, which delay marriage and family planning. But you don't need to save the world to have the requisite responsibility to fill your life with meaning. Had Achilles stayed home with his wife and raised his kids, he could have had his cake and eaten it too, so to speak.

Finding a life partner itself is a challenge. Develop yourself into a person who someone you'd want to marry would be attracted to. Superficiality, such as looks or money, cannot be the central focus. But living a life of purpose and meaning in the other aspects of life, in a way where you develop yourself to your full potential, will at least put you in a good position. Keep in mind, as the Bhagavad Gita says, "You are only entitled to the action, never to its fruits." In other words, focusing on what you can control, not the results, is a practical way forward. Further, once you marry, keeping your relationship in good health while raising children also requires effort. But nothing worthwhile comes easy.

The government can play a positive role to this effect, particularly focusing on the beneficial childhood outcomes of the nuclear family. First, stop discouraging two-parent households with welfare policies. As an example, a single mother with two children who earns $15,000/year will receive about $5,200/year from a particular American food stamp program. If she marries someone with the same earnings level, that subsidy goes to $0. Instead, that program should maintain the same subsidy (Rector 2015).

Second, the government can go a step further and incentivize nuclear families with children. In light of declining birth rates, a common feature of developed nations today, Hungary gives us a template. Hungary has invested heavily in the family in the last decade, increasing spending to 3.6 percent of GDP compared to the 2.43 percent average of developed nations. There is special funding targeting families through loans and subsidies, which increase in value by the number of children born. There are subsidies for mortgage payments, homes, and cars. There are childcare fees to grandparents. Student loans are canceled with the third child. There is a newlywed tax break. Personal income tax decreases, and the rate of decrease varies like many of these policies with how many children born; for those with four or more children, they pay zero income tax for life (Government of Hungary n.d.).

Hungary created this policy so that having children is not the financial pyrrhic victory that it is in many other Western nations. By comparison, it is estimated that total expenditures to raise an American child born in 2015 to a middle-class family with two children to age seventeen would be $310,605. Hungary's policy also encourages people to marry and stay together, and it encourages women to not only get educated but stay in the work force. Since 2010, the number of marriages has almost doubled, the number of divorces has decreased by 57 percent, the number of abortions has fallen by 41 percent (120,000 more children were born), and the fertility rate has increased by 24 percent. Moreover, female employment went up from 54.6 percent to 67 percent (Cabinet Office of the Prime Minister 2021; Van Maren 2021; LifeSiteNews 2021).[34]

If your basic necessities are met, and you have a life partner and a fruitful family life, I would be reluctant to call you poor no matter what your bank account says. And maybe then if you had space to pursue a career, hobbies, and self-care, I would call you fabulously rich. Endeavoring to marry and have children is a formula backed by millennia of evidence for requisite responsibility to fill your life with meaning. While there are other dimensions to wealth, this can be the foundational piece.

Factor Incentive into Social Policy

What does extra taxation for the purpose of increasing social services do to the productive? Critics of socialism historically warned about the incentive issue. If people are just getting paid from each according to his ability and to each according to his needs, why would a super-productive person exert himself or herself so much? The socialists countered that in a socialist society, there would be a new Soviet/socialist man. I believe this would be somewhat modeled on Chernyshevsky's Rakhmetov. They believed that greed and self-centeredness wouldn't exist in true socialism, and that it existed in capitalism because that's how people in those decadent systems survived (Murphy and Peterson 2021). It was the perfect argument that could never be disproven because they could never quite get to Utopia.

This scenario played itself out early in Ayn Rand's *Atlas Shrugged*. The book started with a factory where income became based on need, not performance. Somehow the productivity plummeted, and the factory eventually closed. Ability had become a liability; those who were more productive were just given more work but not more income. It's not hard to see how this would play itself out likewise in the real world. Suddenly everyone would have high needs and little ability.

With this, Rand gave a cartoonlike narrative of what happens when unions get too powerful, but she did this to explain the point. Social policy should factor in the more realistic human nature, that incentive is a driving force of productivity. In a real-life scenario, during my emergency room work, on sunny days we would routinely be short-staffed of nurses as a consequence of unusual amounts of sick calls (and yes, I admit there are real limits to anecdotes). With a very powerful union, they effectively had unlimited sick days. Unfortunately, on those days, the burden of carrying forward the emergency department was shouldered by fewer staff.

We need sick days, parental leave, and benefits. It is optimal to put those who aren't as productive in a position to give their best efforts. But it cannot be to such a degree that it harms the product by disincentivizing—let alone demoralizing—everyone. Trade-offs should be recognized, and where to draw the line on each social policy needs to be debated under the rubric of free speech.

Other Areas of Life in Which You Could Take More Responsibility

Work is a prime area in which to take increased responsibility. Are there merit-based opportunities for advancement, where someone displaying hustle and talent can get recognized? If so, this would be a worthwhile endeavor. Put in more hours, stay late, and think of ways to be more productive with the hours you already spend. Of course, some jobs have minimal reward for extra efforts, or even punish them. I have had such jobs, where innovation and hard work were frowned upon. If this is the case, in the short term, do not throw pearls before swine; find other dimensions of life in which to take increased responsibility. And in the medium term, start working on finding another job. Low-vibration environments and high-vibration workers do not mix. I ultimately left each job that did not foster an environment of excellence.

On a macroscopic level, do you consider your work a job or career? Surely there is a spectrum, but ideally you want to put yourself in the position where your work is something that is meaningful, a skill you can hone for the rest of your working life, and something you identify with, as opposed to a temporary situation to pay the bills.

How much responsibility do you take socially? Do you have a good group of friends? What can you add to the lives of others? Are you someone they can depend on? When someone is sick or just having a bad day, are you someone they call? Develop yourself into a rock around which the storms of others calm. These should be people who also have your back when you are in a bind. You want to come from an authentic place of giving, rather than just giving to receive; that is manipulation. But mutual appreciation is crucial for long-term relationships.

Do you contribute to your community? This could just be through attendance and engagement with groups. Churches offer opportunities to meet people, and they have innate support networks. Do you help out with any causes you are passionate about? I do not mean activist groups that engage in one-sided arguments and silence debate. Instead, this could be a centrist political party, charity, or other common interest groups. You can participate in athletic hobbies (e.g., sports teams or the local gym), book clubs, cultural interests (e.g., arts shows), and so on.

If you are not in a position to take on more responsibility in any of these dimensions, then what remains is increasing the responsibility of caring for and developing yourself. The self-care and personal development industries are huge, but they are absolutely useless without individual motivation. Let's start with health. Do you use alcohol, cigarettes, or drugs? If so, does it come from a place of celebration or pain? Do you generally eat healthily and exercise regularly? What are your hobbies? Do you carve out some time routinely to attend to these? Is there a new skill you would like to learn? What are your stress levels like? You can gauge this regularly with validated questionnaires such as the Perceived Stress Scale (Cohen 1988). Chronic stress is linked to many adverse health outcomes (Kopplin and Rosenthal 2023). Finally, do you sleep well? Chronic sleep deprivation is associated with a host of other pathologies, including compromised cardiovascular and mental health, interpersonal relationships, and decision-making. If that's not enough to motivate you, sex drive also decreases by 30–40 percent with poor sleep (Parsley 2016). So if you can't give yourself at least a passing score in the domain of self-care and growth, chances are any attempts to advance in the other ones will be suboptimal.

It requires some self-reflection to decide in which domain you want to pursue increased responsibility and to what degree. Your spouse or friend can also help you discern which area you should tackle to get out of your comfort zone. Be sure to drop the ego and ask for feedback from people you believe are insightful and have your best interests at heart. The proximal task should not be too easy, but it should also not be crushingly challenging. Instead, it should adhere to the Goldilocks principle of being "just right," an optimal load. You will also get well-earned, wholesome dopamine hits as you progress.

Beware of trying to tackle too many areas at once. Your attention is an invaluable resource. Dabblers spread themselves too thin and accomplish little. Being laser focused on one or two areas at a time will give you a much higher chance of succeeding, and then you can move on to other areas.

As an example, you can choose the domain of self-care and the specific goal of being less stressed overall. You can small chunk it into the steps of being disciplined about bedtime, taking regular exercise three times a week, praying or meditating briefly when you wake up and before bed, and, if you are to some extent a workaholic, setting limits on how much time you can spend each day working. You can even sign up for a weekly yoga class, which, as a bonus, might enter into the domain of community engagement.

The Death of Judgment

In the last twenty years, to echo Nietzsche, I believe that we as a society have killed judgment, and we will never find enough tissue to wipe away the tears. "Don't be judgmental" is a common mantra. Being judgmental about immutable characteristics should be condemned. But how far are we taking nonjudgment? Does this also mean not having standards or ambitions? Is everyone and everything just fine as they are? There is a hopelessness to this hymn.

You can't be alive and not make judgments. You're making choices in every moment based on your values and preferences. Journalist Bari Weiss believes that "good vibes only" doesn't work: "Judgment is discernment, saying that some things are worthy and some things aren't . . . Some ideas are worthy of being heard by the world. Non-judgment is the pathway to insanity" (Weiss and Peterson 2021). Further, to never have an opinion on a controversial topic is intellectual cowardice. Even if it is understandable in our censored times, it is to be a peacemaker of the Chamberlain kind.[35]

I define radical nonjudgment as the elimination of judgment completely. As a consequence, you also eliminate values, standards, rank-ordered preferences, striving, encouragement, mentorship, merit, excellence, ideals, achievement, the positive aspect of discrimination, improvement, focused attention, and so on. This is in contrast with not judging immutable characteristics, which is a realistic and laudable endeavor. Radical nonjudgment is a prime feature of the radical left (even though the end-spectrum of their movement supposedly believes in nothing, like Bazarov).

Jordan Peterson says, "Part of the critique of the radical left is that ideals themselves are discriminatory. There's truth in that; the question is whether they're arbitrarily discriminatory. If you say yes, then what do you strive for? The answer is for everyone to be equal" (Carolla, Prager, and Peterson 2021). In a separate discussion, Peterson further illustrates his argument with an example:

> The data is absolutely clear that children with intact two-parent families do far better . . . It seems impossible in our society to have a discussion about the fact that some forms of families are better for children than others . . . because we think of any imposition of a value analysis of that sort as discriminatory. And you know in some sense it is discriminatory because when you say that one thing is better, you're also saying at the same time that the opposite of that is worse. (Henderson and Peterson 2021)

However, the data makes a stronger argument that this is true in this instance.

When discrimination is derided, I believe what's really meant is unjust discrimination, such as for immutable characteristics. This is the negative side of the coin of discrimination. But its positive dimension is to sort out good from not good, or even best from just okay.

Everyone discriminates and judges. Somehow you judged that spending time reading this book was better for now than the infinite array of other choices available to you. As another example, you don't sleep with everyone who wants to sleep with you; that's a form of judgment and discrimination. And of the various group identities that have not slept with you, you surely don't believe that the government should rectify this cosmic injustice.

Nonjudgment is on the precipice of being taken to academic extreme. In some California school districts, high school students may no longer be given failing grades. The news report explains, "Educators are hoping to transition to a more equitable grading system, especially for those hit hardest by remote learning in the state—Black, Latino and low-income students." What's the rationale? During the pandemic, the academic gap between Black and Latino students on one side, and White and Asian students on the other, widened (Postmedia News 2021). Thus, there was an opportunity to seek virtue points under the banner of equity. The assistant principal of Fremont High in Oakland, Nidya Baez, said, "Our hope is that students begin to see school as a place of learning, where they can take risks and learn from mistakes, instead of a place of compliance." They continue to explain that if a student fails a test or doesn't do their homework, they get the chance to retake the test or be given more time respectively, so as to not impair their chances at educational advancement (Postmedia News 2021).

Is the goal that everyone feels good by the time they graduate, or to equip people with the skills to get a job and thrive in life? How does this socialist thrust for radical equality affect the intelligent students who want to be differentially rewarded for pushing themselves? The premise underpinning the socialist, postmodern idea is that intelligence is purely a social construct. The Utopians are sentimentally pushing the idea that with the right supports, everyone could be the next Einstein. While this notion is uplifting, it's quite simply untrue.

When it comes to drug addiction, Michael Shellenberger phrases it well: "The American people are capable of distinguishing between stigmatizing fentanyl use without stigmatizing the sick person who was using fentanyl. The person requires our compassion, but the behavior requires our condemnation" (2021a). The distinction between people and behavior is important as the opioid epidemic moves into higher gear.

Shellenberger even discerns the negative from the positive guise of shame. He explains that it can be manipulated like compassion, but it's essential to enforce social norms, such as picking up after your dog. Like the pain of a sprained ankle might prevent you from further damaging it by running, shame prevents us from wrecking our social interactions (2021a).

Allyship is a term recently introduced into our "wocabulary."[36] Like all other terms we are now taught from on high, it sounds extremely good. Who can be against being an ally? Stating that you're an ally is a shortcut to moral virtue; you don't actually have to help those whom you're hypothetically allied with. However, the concept blends into my idea of radical nonjudgment. "Whatever you do, whatever you are, it's all good." It's so nonjudgemental, it is pathologically altruistic. Being a good ally is telling someone addicted to drugs that they are perfectly fine as they are, that anyone who tells them otherwise is a bigot.

But judgment can be resurrected. Judgment can be your tool to advance yourself. First, distinguish the positive aspect of judgment from the negative aspect. There is no room for judging for immutable characteristics, such as race. Second, what are your goals, and why? Ponder your preferences, standards, values, and talents. How do you spend your time? What are the qualities you like to see in people, such as your spouse, friends, and colleagues? Taking stock of yourself with moments of introspection is resurrecting judgment in its positive dimension, and it makes attaining your goals that much easier now that they are in focus. For example, I make a habit of discerning my preferences and goals every six months in a written document, which allows me to judge my progress on a regular basis.

You can further cultivate your positive judgment through learning and experience. This is ultimately a process about getting to know yourself. Read books that challenge you intellectually. Also, reading the local news is a good habit, especially opinion columns. Do you agree or disagree, and why?[37] Try to stick to a media source that demonstrates balance, which is easier said than done these days. Additionally, the internet has made learning infinitely more possible, though you will run into the paradox of choice. Pick your favorite podcasts from which you learn and stick to them for a period of time. When they no longer resonate with you, cycle through another batch. Further, debate difficult topics with friends with whom you have a wide Overton window. All of these suggestions are like weightlifting for the mind.

Another main way of cultivating your preferences is through traveling with the intent of learning about different cultures. This is different from lying on a beach in the Caribbean or ordering a cheeseburger in India. Life experience paired with introspection is a great formula to squeeze out every ounce of growth. And all throughout this process of maturation, your ideals get chiseled from a mold of clay to something refined, special, and uniquely you.

The Mercy-Judgment Spectrum

Too much judgment is punishing, but too much mercy leaves you in diapers. Jordan Peterson illuminates us with Carl Jung's idea that God rules with two hands, the right hand being justice, the left being mercy.

> The idea was the cosmos couldn't exist without the proper combination of justice and mercy. You should get what's coming to you, but people are fallible and they make mistakes . . . it would be a hell of a world, because you'd be held accountable to an extent that would be unbearable. So this has to be tempered with mercy . . . [but] if it's just mercy, then all is forgiven, you have no responsibility, and you're an eternal infant. (Barron and Peterson 2019)

I believe we need balance on what I call the mercy-judgment spectrum.

The mercy-judgment spectrum: mercy without judgment, you're a pushover; judgment without mercy, you're heartless. You need the right balance to optimally operate in the world with others. The Old Testament was filled with a perhaps overly paternalistic God bent on justice or judgment. Jesus comes along in the New Testament and appears almost pathologically merciful by comparison. And just because the New Testament overcorrects a bit on this spectrum, it ends with the Book of Revelation, a judgmental tome. Peterson conveys that Jung believed that the Book of Revelation was psychologically necessary because any ideal implicitly judges (Barron and Peterson 2019).

On an individual level, the right balance means to love others but have boundaries. Love from the end-spectrum of mercy is unconditional, caring solely for who the person is now without encouraging them to fulfill any potential. It's effectively praising the person with drug addiction who is destitute. "Never change, you're fine as you are!" people tell them as they lie on the street corner, breath rate slowing to fatal levels. By comparison, love from the end-spectrum of judgment is loving purely who that person could be in the best of possibilities. It's telling the student struggling with math who lacks any drive or work ethic, "You are a loser. You have brought shame to your family. What a waste of space!" Ouch.

Instead, how about a firm but loving hand? "You need to shape up. You have so much potential, and you could really achieve and be a light in the world. But the way you're going about school, you could end up on the streets." You need to balance maternal and paternal aspects. You can embrace someone while still believing that they are capable of more.

On the specific notions of decriminalization and safe supply of drugs, I am deeply conflicted. Speaking of decriminalization, which in many proposals is not charging people with possession of limited quantities of illicit substances, I understand that this will save police manpower, which is absolutely finite. But to have no consequences for possession of increasingly harmful drugs, is this not partly sanitizing their use?

Regarding the safe supply of opioids specifically, research clearly shows there are many who are treatment refractory to methadone and buprenorphine, the mainstays of opioid abuse disorders. These patients are instead injected with IV opioids by their addictions doctors. This is a relatively new form of treatment as the opioid epidemic escalates. I believe this form of pharmacotherapy will become more common as the epidemic worsens for the reasons I have outlined. Another manner of safe supply is the government providing untainted opioids for free dispensation. Is it too judgmental to wonder what kind of a life this is? Maybe we are helping some who would otherwise be dead, but maybe there is a portion of this sub-demographic that, knowing this treatment isn't available, would improve to the point where methadone or buprenorphine would suffice. The safety of neighborhoods surrounding these dispensation sites should also be considered. As the needle representing treatment intensity keeps moving in the wrong direction, figuratively and literally, this is an extremely challenging conundrum.

One of Shellenberger's interviewees likens drug addiction in San Francisco to Pleasure Island from *Pinocchio*:

> On one side of the street is food and clean needles, and on the other side all the drug dealers. You think you're having fun, but little by little it's taking away your humanity, and turning you into something you were never meant to be, like how the kids start turning into donkeys in Pinocchio, then end up trapped and in cages. (Shellenberger 2021a)

And now we're back to pathological altruism; we return to the Freudian concept of the Oedipal mother of excessive compassion.

When interacting with others, recognize that some people are more sensitive (prone to negative emotion, which is a personality temperament). They require more mercy than others, but it can't be to zero standards. For example, with my drug addictions patients, I need to have a feel for how to respond when they test positive in their urine samples. How much do I encourage that I know they can do better, and how much do I lay off? Truthfully, it is almost always the latter, but once in a while I can be a bit tougher with the right patients with whom I have great rapport. And with my colleagues, I am usually more on the judgment side, knowing what their performance can and should be. Develop your instinct in interacting with others on how much judgment and how much mercy to convey at each point in time. This social calibration is a honed skill.

You can also apply the mercy-judgment spectrum dynamically to yourself. For example, I push myself very hard at work, but also outside of work, generally trying to squeeze out every last ounce of productivity. I respond well to my own pressure. However, once in a while I need to truly just let go and take it easy; I need to disengage with whatever activity I am doing and spend a moment in silence or relaxing into a show on a streaming service. Know yourself, and how much judgment and mercy to dole out at any given moment. Don't be your own punisher, but hold yourself to a standard.

CONCLUSION

"Hard times create strong men. Strong men create good times. Good times create weak men. And, weak men create hard times" (Hopf 2016). This famous quote begs the question: Where are we in this cycle? In the era of hyper-novelty, now that we've buried God miles deep, the marvels of technological progress will make our lives increasingly easy and devoid of innate struggle; the challenge itself will be finding meaning amid the comparative luxury. It will be ever more difficult to lead purposeful lives grounded in a functioning belief structure, and it will be far more likely to become moored in the unholy trinity of nihilism, atheism, and depression. It is convenient to ignore the warnings of Dostoevsky, Nietzsche, Orwell, and Peterson and instead adopt as role models the characters of Raskolnikov, Bazarov, Stavrogin, and Ivan.

Ultimately, every individual has to decide consciously or unconsciously whether traditional Western values, those of the Enlightenment, are worth defending. These values include equal opportunity, natural justice, colorblindness, merit, free will, primacy of the individual, objective reality, empiricism, effort, appreciation, humility, and nuance. And if they aren't protected, they will subsequently be replaced by equal outcome (equity), presumption of guilt, microaggressions, political correctness, the perpetually offended, Maoist struggle sessions, racial essentialism, intersectionality, determinism, tribalism, group guilt, group entitlement, victimhood, lived experience, postmodernism, relativism, radical nonjudgment, nihilism, rationality, expectation, and pathological altruism.

I believe that free speech absolutism is the foundational value of Western civilization. It allows us to argue along the edges of every debate. Taking it for granted allows "compassionate" authoritarianism to slither in, and, if left unchecked, the inevitable outcome is a return to tyranny.

Part 1 of this book was a journey through how we got to this present-day problem of meaningless living. Poverty rates have declined, we have amazing creature comforts, and yet many people are in existential pain. We set on this course with the death of God, the idea that Nietzsche first proclaimed in 1882. With advancing science, we no longer have a uniting, ineffable, transcendent principle, one that also serves as our moral and philosophical bedrock. We're left with this nihilistic void and its flip side, rationality, the idea that you can reason out all there is to know, that you can be the ultimate source of knowledge.

Dostoevsky revealed a natural link between nihilism, atheism, and depression. Taken to its extreme, nihilism yields a very dark Mephistophelean philosophy, the sentiment that it would be better if being, creation, and life didn't exist at all. Certainly the ease of modern life has diminished our sense of meaning. We all manifest this, our underground complex, from benign habits such as mindlessly binging TV shows, to the end-spectrum—IV opioids. Meaningless living on a societal level is the ultimate cause of the opioid crisis. People self-harm to show the triumph of free will over reason, because we're designed for purpose, and out of a deep desire to be unconscious as a response to our lack of meaning.

In part 2, we explored the search for meaning. A replacement religion is a cheap imitation of a wholesome belief system that you elevate to your top value and identify with. It will not satiate your quest for meaning, and it will lead to your destruction in some sense. Replacement religions can be values—popular ones being pride and money. Young people in their messianic stage of development are particularly susceptible to being seduced by ideologies. Ideologues have exactly the same viewpoints, profess them with 100 percent certainty, default to confirmation bias, and have strong scapegoating impulses. Understanding that speech, thought, writing, and action are connected, ideologues are very particular with language and make ample use of doublespeak.

We then explored several popular ideologies. Social justice warriors believe in the axiom *exitus acta probat*, that the ends justify the means. Diversity-equity-inclusivity is a trendy radical left misnomer that, like all ideologies, places supporters on the side of the good and dissenters on that of the bad. The replacement religion of victimhood is likewise pervasive and is also linked with dark triad personality traits. We also covered climate alarmism, which has many superficial features of a genuine religion with an apocalypse, saints, and indulgences, yet it effectively accomplishes nothing. Finally, we broke down the details of a right-leaning ideology, vaccine hesitancy. The COVID-19 vaccine was a scientific miracle, and many of the concerns could have been better dealt with through conversation, not compulsion.

In part 3, we explored the prime ways of restoring meaning to our individual and collective existence: free speech, traditional religion, and personal responsibility. Mill had three main points in his defense of free speech: the other person might be right; that even if you're mostly right, you can hold your position better as a result of the challenge; and that both views might contain a portion of the truth, which you can then combine. Being civil without being censored is tricky, but intent is key. Start by assuming that the other side is coming from a moral and genuine place. This won't always be the case, and there are four steps to a difficult conversation: actively listen; pay attention; feel out; and, if necessary, get out.

Further, we discovered that just being spiritual doesn't satiate the desire for meaning, and that faith is necessarily paired with reason. Meaning reduces anxiety, allowing us to plan and accomplish our goals more effectively. We covered seven criteria for a functioning belief system. Moreover, you can increase life responsibilities by having a family, hustling at work, helping your social network, engaging with your community, and fundamentally caring for and improving yourself. Finally, we need to find the right balance between judgment and mercy, of being able to show compassion yet hold people to standards we believe they're capable of. Being pathologically altruistic does no one any good.

I now invite people to recognize the problem in today's world and to make a choice to right the ship. Choose dialogue over monologue; free speech over political correctness; gratitude over suffering; hard work over handouts; and virtue doing instead of virtue signaling. Seek first to understand, then to be understood. Be a victor instead of a victim. Choose faith and reason together. Instead of pathological altruism, how about loving encouragement? Beware of Greeks bearing gifts; instead of accepting semantically appealing ideas at face value, think critically about the pros and the cons. Be civil without being censored. Remember that the ends do not justify the means. And take the plank out of your own eye before scapegoating someone else.

What are some practical first steps? Have an accountability partner, such as a spouse or a friend, and choose one of the following actions:

1. Reflect with them on which ideologies you subscribe to, and instead choose steelmanning, devil's advocacy, trade-offs, and nuance.
2. Discuss between yourselves if you honestly have a replacement religion and seek instead a functioning belief system such as a traditional religion.

3. If living in truth is too hard, pick one of Solzhenitsyn's nine rules for responsible conduct, such as to stop saying things you don't believe to be true.
4. Take on more responsibility in a single domain. A simple one is committing to good sleep habits.
5. Develop yourself personally, such as by cultivating a sense of positive judgment and values of your own. For example, read a book that challenges you.

If any of these potential steps resonate in your heart, commit to that one and see it through. Instead of feeling the entire weight of healing society, recall that giant leaps are always preceded by small steps. If even one person takes such a move forward, perhaps another will, and so on. Be an example for the next person. You can make a difference.

Plato and Socrates once discussed the allegory of a cave with respect to the search for truth. In this scenario, a group of prisoners live chained to the wall of a cave their entire lives. They watch shadows projected on the wall from objects passing in front of a fire behind them. While these are only shadows, they believe this is their reality. One day a prisoner is freed (the prisoner represents a philosopher). He explores and finds his way out of the cave. The never-before-seen sunlight hurts his eyes, just as the truth is often painful, but he knows this is closer to objective reality.

Image courtesy of 4edges, Creative Commons License CC BY-SA 4.0: https://creativecommons.org/licenses/by-sa/4.0/.

Excitedly, he tells the prisoners of his discovery, thinking they will all jump for joy. To his surprise, most of them want to stay exactly where they are, in their fantasy world, staring at the wall, no matter how painful it is. Not only that, like the grand inquisitor to Jesus, they will fight and even kill him if he tries to drag them out (Plato, n.d.).

This is my motivation for writing this book. I see the disintegration of the greatness of the West, the taking for granted of our freedoms, the utter lack of appreciation for the good things we have, and an attraction for reality distortion. It's not perfect, and no, Utopia doesn't exist, but if we stop absconding responsibility and denigrating traditional structures of meaning, we might not feel so empty inside; we might even be happy. And if we above all foster dialogue with open hearts and minds among ourselves, we can all together move out of the cave and into the sunlight of reality. If my three meta-solutions were a triangle, the base would be free speech, providing the foundation, while traditional religion and responsibility would form the sides. Free speech will give us the best chance of figuring out not just all the difficult questions this book has brought up, but it is a mechanism for always being as close to the truth as humanly possible. What a world that would be.

ABOUT THE AUTHOR

Dr. Mark D'Souza is a Canadian physician based in Toronto with extensive experience in addiction and chronic pain management. His medical practice, coupled with a lifelong passion for the humanities, provides a unique perspective on societal issues. He has published serial opinion editorials in Canada and has had extensive local media exposure, including TV and radio appearances and advocacy roles in healthcare organizations. Dr. D'Souza is on faculty at Queen's University's Department of Family Medicine.

markdsouzamd.com

GLOSSARY

NB: This glossary is for convenient reference. There is a mix of how I have coined these terms in this book and how they are defined more ubiquitously (e.g., Merriam-Webster's dictionary).

Ad hominem attack: an attack on an opponent's character rather than by an answer to the contentions made ("Ad Hominem" n.d.).

Antifragility: a quality that has propelled human progress from the earliest times. It allows systems to grow and improve in an unpredictable and volatile world. However, modern society is in the process of trying to dismantle the volatile environment that is vital for antifragility. In doing so, we are making ourselves more fragile. Antifragility is more than just resilience. The resilient resists shocks and stays the same, while the antifragile gets better (Taleb 2012).

Apologia: a formal defense of your opinion, position, or action ("Apologia" n.d.). This is what Socrates did in his trial for which he was ultimately sentenced to death. You're elaborating on your position and standing up for your principles, instead of groveling to groupthink.

Bazarov impulse: the impulse to tear down carefully built structures and policies of society. Named after Yevgeny Bazarov, the nihilist in *Fathers and Sons*. There is no building, only tearing things down.

BIPOC: Black, Indigenous, and People of Color.

Black truth: a literal truth that conveys something false due to context or lack thereof.

Climate (change) alarmism: the belief that the changing climate will bring about the end of humanity within the next few decades. Proponents believe anecdotal evidence like hurricanes and fires provide irrefutable proof and that anger and panic are justified. They say the only way to prevent our civilization's destruction is a radical and equitable resetting of our way of life. They say yes to solar and wind power and no to oil, gas, coal, and nuclear power. If anyone dares disagree, they are climate deniers and should be censored. Given the severity of the problem, they say every last tax dollar should be thrown at this problem without any nuance. They believe the wealthy (a term ill-defined along with everything else in this ideology) bear disproportionate guilt.

Climate porn: describes the alarmist rhetoric that permeates today's public discussion about climate change. By this, they mean reporting on worst-case predictions as if they are most likely to occur when they are not at all the most likely to occur. Coined by the UK's Institute for Public Policy Research (a progressive think tank) in 2006 (Ereaut and Segnit 2006).

Colorblindness: the act or practice of treating all people the same regardless of race ("Colorblindness" n.d.).

Dark triad: a well-studied cluster of socially aversive traits such as selfishness, glibness, short-term thinking, aggression, and exploitation. Such people are devoid of a moral compass, and it's no surprise that dark triad personality traits are also linked to poor life satisfaction (Kaufman et al. 2019). These well-studied traits are Machiavellianism (manipulation), narcissism, and psychopathy (short-term gain without any regard for others). Sadism has since been discovered as a distinct psychological dimension, making it a dark tetrad (Međedović and Petrović 2015). There is also research on the corollary, a light triad—humanism, faith in humanity, and Kantianism, the latter being the principle of treating people as ends unto themselves (Kaufman et al. 2019).

Delay discounting: describes the extent to which the value of a reward decreases as the delay to obtaining that reward increases. Lower delay discounting rates, which indicate a preference for delayed gratification, are predictive of better outcomes in social, academic, and health domains. Conversely, higher delay discounting rates, which indicate a preference for smaller, immediate rewards, have been associated with a variety of addictive and impulsive behaviors (Hirsh, Morisano, and Peterson 2008).

Delta (Δ) meaning: the gap between how much meaning we require and how much we get.

Diffusion of responsibility: with the greater number of people present, the less likely any individual will help someone in need, as it's easier to rationalize that someone else will. Coined in the late 1960s by psychologists John Darley and Bibb Latané, who documented such an effect. Also known as the bystander effect (Latané and Darley 1968).

Doublespeak: language that obscures, disguises, distorts, or reverses the meaning of words ("Doublespeak" n.d.). It may take the form of euphemism, in which case it's mainly meant to make the truth sound more palatable. There's intentional ambiguity in language. For example, in an attempt to minimize the controversy of euthanasia, the Canadian government called it "medical assistance in dying" just so the acronym could be MAiD.

Doublethink: the ability to hold two contradictory ideas in your mind at the same time. Orwell coined this term as part of Newspeak in *1984* ("Doublethink" n.d.).

Eco-anxiety: distress relating to the climate and ecological crises (Hickman et al. 2021).

EMU: Entropy Model of Uncertainty; a theoretical framework by psychologists designed to better understand uncertainty-related anxiety (Hirsh, Mar, and Peterson 2012).

Eros-Thanatos spectrum: similar to the levels of energy, the Freudian concepts of Eros and Thanatos can help explain the same phenomenon of vibration along a spectrum, from higher to lower, from peace to hatred. According to Freud, people have a life instinct (Eros) and a death drive (Thanatos) (Freud 1922). In my adaptation of these Freudian concepts, Thanatos describes the compulsion to engage in risky, self-destructive acts. Eros describes life-affirming conduct, a by-product of a high will to live. Those in high vibration are high on the Eros-Thanatos spectrum, while those in low vibration are lower on this spectrum. Someone who is actively suicidal is fully in Thanatos, while someone whose life is brimming with meaning is fully in Eros. Most people are somewhere in between, and they move along this spectrum throughout their lives. Bazarov, for example, was high in Thanatos while he dangerously performed an autopsy without precautions. He caught typhoid fever from this careless act and died.

Exitus acta probat: the ends justify the means (in Latin).

Freudian projection: a defense mechanism in which the ego defends itself against disowned and highly negative parts of the self by denying their existence in themselves and attributing them to others. For example, a bully may project their own feelings of vulnerability onto another ("Psychological Projection" n.d.).

Freudian reaction formation: a defense mechanism in which emotions and impulses that are anxiety-producing or perceived to be unacceptable are mastered by exaggeration of the directly opposing tendency. For example, in Stockholm syndrome, a hostage "falls in love" with the feared and hated person who has complete power over them ("Reaction Formation" n.d.).

Gaslighting: psychological manipulation of a person usually over an extended period of time that causes the victim to question the validity of their own thoughts, perceptions of reality, or memories. Typically leads to confusion, loss of confidence and self-esteem, uncertainty of one's emotional or mental stability, and a dependency on the perpetrator ("Gaslighting," *Merriam-Webster* n.d.). Derived from the 1944 American film *Gaslight* ("Gaslighting," Wikipedia n.d.).

Hyper-novelty: the out-of-control process by which the acceleration of change outstrips the capacity to adapt. Coined by biologists Bret Weinstein and Heather Heying (Heying and Weinstein 2021).

Ideology: a manner or the content of thinking characteristic of an individual, group, or culture; a systematic body of concepts ("Ideology" n.d.). It is a low-resolution universal explanation. That is to say, it is a belief that many things, if not everything, can be totally explained by a set of ideas; thus, in practicality, nuance and granularity are lost.

IPCC: Intergovernmental Panel of Climate Change; a United Nations body charged with advancing scientific knowledge about anthropogenic climate change (IPCC 2018).

Kafkatrap: denial serves as evidence of guilt. Coined in this manner by Eric Raymond in 2010 (Raymond n.d.). Derived from Franz Kafka's *The Trial*, where a man is accused of crimes that are never specified ([1925] 2015).

Levels of energy: a system or scale that maps out how much meaning any individual has in their life. I came across the concept of levels of energy through author Frederick Dodson and medical doctor David Hawkins. Both published books on the topic, Dodson in *Levels of Energy* (Dodson 2010), and Hawkins in *Power vs. Force* (D. R. Hawkins 2014). The concept is nebulous and pseudoscientific. But I have yet to encounter a framework that better correlates with the degree of self-destructive behavior each of us manifests.

Levels of trauma processing: a pathway I conceptualized of processing trauma. 1) You are consumed by your trauma and unable to speak about it. You need to be enabled to speak about it to move to the next level. 2) You are victim-identified and speak freely about it. Therapy will help you process, though eternal fixation on therapy will affix you to this level. 3) You transcend your trauma and let go. What happened is part of you, but not you. You are no longer victim-identified, but a victor or champion.

Lived experience: the subjective experience of a person. Only that person can lay claim to their individual subjective experience.

Luxury belief: an idea or opinion that confers status on the upper class, while often inflicting costs on the lower social classes (Henderson and Peterson 2021). It is a concept developed by psychologist Rob Henderson. For example, advocating for the defunding of the police, particularly while living in a gated community.

Magic pill syndrome: a cultural phenomenon whereby there's a singular cure for all that ails you. For example, fitness supplements are commonly portrayed as magic pills. An example from literature is soma from Aldous Huxley's *Brave New World.*

Maoist struggle session: violent public spectacles in Maoist China where people accused of being "class enemies" were publicly humiliated, accused, beaten, and tortured by people with whom they were close ("Struggle Session" n.d.).

Marks of Cain: labels used on people with the effect of societal shunning (e.g., racist or sexist). In Genesis 4:9–15, God puts a mark on Cain in part so people know he's a pariah. Today they are immensely imbued with reputational damage.

Mercy-judgment spectrum: mercy without judgment, you're a pushover; judgment without mercy, you're heartless. You need the right balance to optimally operate in the world with others. This is analogous to the "carrot and stick" metaphor.

Messianic impulse: the impulse to play a heroic role in saving the world, at least to some degree, and to place yourself on the side of good standing against evil on the moral landscape. I adapted this from Jean Piaget's theory of cognitive development of children, whereby adolescents and young adults "are prone to adopt idealistic and utopian social and political ideas, which they reassert with an almost zealous vigor. Yet, at the same time, and probably due to a lack of experience and an egocentric tendency, they tend to underestimate the difficulties and the ramifications of attempts to implement their ideals in complex, real-world settings" (Rogmann 2021).

Meta-solution: singular approaches that solve a set of problems.

Microaggression: a comment or action that subtly and often unconsciously or unintentionally expresses a prejudiced attitude toward a member of a marginalized group ("Microaggression" n.d.). Any act that makes the recipient uncomfortable, no matter how uncomfortable, can be considered offensive, regardless of the intent of the other person.

Moral foundations: derived by psychologist Jonathan Haidt after reviewing the anthropological literature cross-culturally. They are harm, fairness, authority, ingroup, and purity. Liberals have moral intuitions mainly based upon the first two, while conservatives value all five (Haidt and Graham 2007).

Newspeak: a fictional language in George Orwell's *1984* designed to meet ideological requirements. It is a controlled language of simplified grammar and restricted vocabulary designed to limit the individual's ability to think and articulate "subversive" concepts such as personal identity, self-expression, and free will ("Newspeak" n.d.). There would be no words to commit a "thoughtcrime." (Orwell 1949)

Nietzschean superman: in the absence of God, Nietzsche foretold the coming of the superman, or, literally translated from German (*Übermensch*) "over-man," in 1883 (or super- or over-person today). In a world without a default metaphysical principle, the superman is the person who creates his own values and meaning rather than become nihilistic. He is free from any outside influence or prejudice. Regular people need to put their faith in something, be it God, science, or another replacement religion. The superman, however, puts all his faith in himself, relying on nothing else. This next-level man is an over-man because he has overcome himself; his own whims, influences, biological nature (Nietzsche [1885] 1999). The superman is someone who has their own moral code and acts according to their will completely impervious to any life experience or outside influence, and without consideration for or negotiation with others.

Nihilism: the belief in nothing, that life is meaningless. The root is the Latin word *nihil*, which means nothing. The word was used sparsely for centuries, then popularized in Turgenev's *Fathers and Sons* ("Nihilism" n.d.). There is no objective truth, morality, values, or purpose.

Overton window: the range of policies or discourse politically acceptable to the mainstream population at a given time. This term was named after American policy analyst Joseph Overton ("Overton Window" n.d.).

Pathological altruism: behavior that attempts to promote the welfare of another or others that results instead in harm that an external observer would conclude was reasonably foreseeable (Oakley et al. 2011). It was defined by professor of engineering Barbara Oakley in 2011.

Performative contradiction: when the propositional content of a statement contradicts the presuppositions of asserting it ("Performative Contradiction" n.d.). When actions and words conflict.

Pharisee faith: people who use religion functionally as an ideology. They have strong virtue signaling impulses, as there is a great mismatch between word and deed. They might, for example, pray loudly, or further their own self-interest under the guise of religion. They believe in their own righteousness, but they are inherently hypocritical. They do not embody the deeper, authentic meaning of their professed religion.

Presence of meaning: the sense made of, and significance felt regarding, the nature of one's being and existence (Miconi et al. 2022).

Racial essentialism: your racial characteristics define you. This is the classical definition of racism, where you are treated as superior or inferior based on your race (Shapiro 2021b). Those high in racial essentialism believe that race is a fixed biological property or essence that determines a person's characteristics and abilities (Zeng et al. 2022).

Radical nonjudgment: the elimination of judgment completely. As a consequence, you also eliminate values, standards, rank-ordered preferences, striving, encouragement, mentorship, merit, excellence, ideals, achievement, the positive aspect of discrimination, improvement, focused attention, and so on. This is in contrast with not judging immutable characteristics. Radical nonjudgment is a prime feature of the radical left.

Rationality: the idea that you can reason out all there is to know, that you can be the ultimate source of knowledge.

Religious impulse: the human instinct for deep and satiating meaning. It is the quest for believing in something, for having values, and for having deeper ideals or meaning. It cannot be extinguished whether you like it or not. Pretend not to have one, and it will imbue something in your world inappropriately with religious meaning (e.g., a replacement religion), and you will treat that as sacred.

Replacement religion: an incomplete belief system or prime value elevated above others, designed to give meaning to the world in lieu of a deep, sophisticated religion. But it accomplishes little to quench your thirst for meaning. Instead, it will lead you to ruin in some form or other, at least in the long term, in terms of life satisfaction. Moral hegemony also accompanies a replacement religion, allowing the worshipper to fall into oppressor-oppressed binary thinking. Replacement religions can be values, popular ones being pride and money. Ideologies are also common replacement religions. A good litmus test of whether something is your replacement religion is how strongly you react when it is criticized. Moreover, you can have several possible replacement religions in your value structure, but to truly attempt to replace God with one, it has to be alone at the top of your value structure; you personally and deeply identify with it.

Scapegoating impulse: the human propensity to blame someone or another group habitually with little regard for accuracy. This impulse is convenient and feels good. It is a subset of pride. The narrative of an external enemy not only automatically makes you on the side of the good, but it can unite people psychologically and socially. (There is an idea in the anthropological literature that theorizes that early human societies evolved such an impulse. It minimized intra-group conflict and united them (Riordan 2021; 2017).) Further, the scapegoating impulse ties into the idea of collective guilt, such as the Jews for the Nazis, or those with some degree of wealth for the Communists. This impulse also produces a devil effect whereby the scapegoat can do no right, but it dangerously and inaccurately produces a corresponding halo effect whereby the scapegoat's opponent can do no wrong (Cook, Marsh, and Hicks 2003). Finally, this concept is similar to Freudian projection and gaslighting.

Search for meaning: strength, intensity, and activity of people's desire and efforts to establish and/or augment their understanding of the meaning, significance, and purpose of their lives (Miconi et al. 2022).

Shadow: the dark, more primitive animal instincts (Rogan and Peterson 2017). In analytical psychology, the shadow is an unconscious aspect of the personality that does not correspond with the ego ideal, leading the ego to resist and project the shadow. It is the self's emotional blind spot ("Shadow (Psychology)" n.d.). An integrated shadow is when you are consciously in control of these instincts, as opposed to an unintegrated shadow (J. Peterson 2017a).

Soma: a drug ingested constantly in Aldous Huxley's *Brave New World* that quickly produced a soothing, happiness effect. It had "all the advantages of Christianity and alcohol; none of their defects" (Huxley 1932).

Steelmanning the argument: the opposite of a straw man argument. It is the practice of addressing the strongest form of the other person's argument, even if it is not the one they presented ("Straw Man" n.d.). I strongly encourage the use of this technique to improve your critical thinking. If you are able to articulate the other side of the argument, you can strengthen your position, or at least see its flaws. Then you can revise your position with a more sophisticated argument.

Thoughtcrime: from George Orwell's *1984*. Describes a person's politically unorthodox thoughts, such as beliefs and doubts that contradict the dominant ideology of the country. In contemporary English usage, thoughtcrime describes beliefs that are contrary to accepted norms of society and used to describe the rejection of an ideology ("Thoughtcrime" n.d.).

Trojan horse properties/thinking/ideas: attractive on the surface, but once you fully buy in, they lead to disaster because they are inaccurate and incomplete maps of the landscape, and they leave little room for course correction. Based on the famous Greek ploy in the Trojan War of leaving a wooden horse as a gift for the Trojans, who then took it into their city. The horse contained Greek soldiers who at night left the horse to open the gates for the Greek army, who then destroyed the city.

Underground complex: the things you do (or don't do) that are not logically in your best interest, in order to, unconsciously and psychologically, demonstrate the triumph of your free will over reason. It helps us cope with the feeling of purposelessness and hopelessness. For some it is smoking cigarettes; others watch too many mediocre Netflix series while barely paying attention; and yet others are using dangerous recreational drugs. Your underground complex is inversely proportional to how high you are on the levels of energy scale or the Eros-Thanatos spectrum.

Virtuous victim signaling: virtue signaling while portraying yourself as a victim. This is associated with dark triad traits. It can facilitate nonreciprocal resource transfer from others to the signaler. The frequency of emitting virtuous victim signals predicts a person's willingness to engage in and endorse ethically questionable behaviors (Ok et al. 2021).

Wolf warrior diplomacy: describes a new strain of aggressive, confrontational diplomacy adopted by a country's diplomats and supporters. This ethos encourages angry attacks on any country, brand, or individual who dares question the country's methods. It may also include economic sanctions as a coercive tool. It is named after a Chinese action film franchise (Maddeaux 2021). This coercive style of diplomacy has been adopted by Chinese diplomats during the Xi Jinping administration ("Wolf Warrior Diplomacy" n.d.).

BIBLIOGRAPHY

4edges. *An Illustration of The Allegory of the Cave, from Plato's Republic*. Illustration. Wikipedia. October 24, 2018. https://commons.wikimedia.org/wiki/File:An_Illustration_of_The_Allegory_of_the_Cave,_from_Plato's_Republic.jpg.

"1975 Banqiao Dam Failure." Wikipedia. n.d. Accessed August 17, 2023. https://en.wikipedia.org/wiki/1975_Banqiao_Dam_failure.

"Abraham Accords." Wikipedia. n.d. Accessed August 14, 2023. https://en.wikipedia.org/wiki/Abraham_Accords.

Abrams, Jeffrey Jacob, dir. *Star Wars: Episode IX, The Rise of Skywalker*. 2019; United States: Walt Disney Studios Motion Pictures.

"Ad hominem." *Merriam-Webster*. n.d. Accessed August 17, 2023. https://www.merriam-webster.com/dictionary/ad%20hominem.

Agar, Jerry. 2022a. "It's Time to Be Sensible When We Talk about Moving Away from Oil." *Toronto Sun*, July 18, 2022. https://torontosun.com/opinion/columnists/agar-its-time-to-be-sensible-when-we-talk-about-moving-away-from-oil.

———. 2022b. "Trudeau Keeps Making Life Easier for Criminals." *Toronto Sun*, October 31, 2022. https://torontosun.com/opinion/columnists/agar-trudeau-keeps-making-life-easier-for-criminals.

Agrawala, Shardul, Stephen Klasen, R. Acosta Moreno, Leonardo Barreto-Gomez, Thomas Cottier, Alba Eritrea Gámez-Vázquez, Dabo Guan, et al. "Regional Development and Cooperation." IPCC, 2014.

Alford, John R., Carolyn L. Funk, and John R. Hibbing. "Are Political Orientations Genetically Transmitted?" *American Political Science Review* 99, no. 2 (2005): 153–67.

Allan, G. Michael, Jamil Ramji, Danielle Perry, Joey Ton, Nathan P. Beahm, Nicole Crisp, Beverly Dockrill, Ruth E. Dubin, Ted Findlay, and Jessica Kirkwood. "Simplified Guideline for Prescribing Medical Cannabinoids in Primary Care." *Canadian Family Physician* 64, no. 2(2018): 111–20.

Anderson, John, and Jordan Peterson. "Lockdowns and Location Apps | John Anderson | EP 196." Jordan B. Peterson. October 11, 2021. YouTube video. https://www.youtube.com/watch?v=NoRFaiqiQGo.

Angus Reid Institute. "Canada and the Culture Wars: In the First of a Multi-Part Series, Canadians Weigh in on the Nation's Divided Discourse." *Angus Reid Institute*. September 11, 2023. https://angusreid.org/wp-content/uploads/2023/09/2023.09.11_Culture_Part_One_Speech.pdf.

Antonelli, Michela, Rose S. Penfold, Jordi Merino, Carole H. Sudre, Erika Molteni, Sarah Berry, Liane S. Canas et al. "Risk Factors and Disease Profile of Post-Vaccination SARS-CoV-2 Infection in UK Users of the COVID Symptom Study App: A Prospective, Community-Based, Nested, Case-Control Study." *The Lancet Infectious Diseases* 22, no. 1 (2022): 43–55.

"Apologia." Wikipedia. n.d. Accessed August 15, 2023. https://en.wikipedia.org/wiki/Apologia.

Augustine. *City of God*. n.d. Translated by Henry Bettenson. London: Penguin Classics, 2004.

Azar, Rima. "Opinion: Little Good Will Come from Adding Race to Driver's Licences." *Edmonton Journal*. November 9, 2022. https://edmontonjournal.com/opinion/columnists/opinion-little-good-will-come-from-adding-race-to-drivers-licences.

Barron, Robert, and Jordan Peterson. "Bishop Barron: Word on Fire." Jordan B. Peterson. July 13, 2019. YouTube video. https://www.youtube.com/watch?v=cXllaoNQmZY&t=2s.

Belzile, Germain, and Mark Milke. "Are Electric Vehicle Subsidies Efficient?" *Montreal Economic Institute*. June 2017.

Biggar, Nigel, James Orr, and Jordan Peterson. "Searching for God within Oxford and Cambridge | James Orr & Nigel Biggar | EP 194." Jordan B. Peterson. September 27, 2021. YouTube video. https://www.youtube.com/watch?v=RsmSBJMSRQk&t=13s.

"Big Stick Ideology." Wikipedia. n.d. Accessed December 8, 2023. https://en.wikipedia.org/wiki/Big_stick_ideology.

Black Lives Matter. "13 Guiding Principles." Black Lives Matter at School, n.d. https://www.blacklivesmatteratschool.com/13-guiding-principles.html.

Black Lives Matter. "Climate Justice Is Racial Justice." Black Lives Matter. August 30, 2021. https://blacklivesmatter.com/climate-justice-is-racial-justice/.

Boehmer, Tegan K., Lyudmyla Kompaniyets, Amy M. Lavery, Joy Hsu, Jean Y. Ko, Hussain Yusuf, Sebastian D. Romano, Adi V. Gundlapalli, Matthew E. Oster, and Aaron M. Harris. "Association Between COVID-19 and Myocarditis Using Hospital-Based Administrative Data—United States, March 2020–January 2021." *MMWR. Morbidity and Mortality Weekly Report* 70, no. 35 (2021): 1228–32. https://doi.org/10.15585/MMWR.MM7035E5.

Bourguignon, François, and Christian Morrison. "Inequality among World Citizens: 1820–1992." *American Economic Review* 92, no. 4 (August 2002): 727–44. https://doi.org/10.1257/00028280260344443.

Bryce, Robert. *Power Hungry: The Myths of "Green" Energy and the Real Fuels of the Future.* New York: PublicAffairs, 2011.

Busse, Jason W., Patrick Vankrunkelsven, Linan Zeng, Anja Fog Heen, Arnaud Merglen, Fiona Campbell, Lars-Petter Granan et al. "Medical Cannabis or Cannabinoids for Chronic Pain: A Clinical Practice Guideline." *BMJ* 374, no. 2040 (2021).

Cabinet Office of the Prime Minister. "Hungarian Government Based Its Family Policy on Five Pillars." Cabinet Office of the Prime Minister. September 23, 2021. https://2015-2022.miniszterelnok.hu/hungarian-government-based-its-family-policy-on-five-pillars/.

Canadian Institute for Health Information. "COVID-19 and Other Common Conditions: Comparing Hospital Costs." Canadian Institute for Health Information. 2021. https://www.cihi.ca/en/covid-19-and-other-common-conditions-comparing-hospital-costs.

Carolla, Adam, Dennis Prager, and Jordan Peterson. "No Safe Spaces? | Prager and Carolla | EP 190." Jordan B. Peterson. September 6, 2021. YouTube video. https://www.youtube.com/watch?v=dHXxtyUVTGU.

Centers for Disease Control and Prevention. "Understanding the Opioid Overdose Epidemic | Opioids." CDC. Last modified August 8, 2023. https://www.cdc.gov/opioids/basics/epidemic.html.

Chomsky, Noam, and Michel Foucault. *The Chomsky-Foucault Debate: On Human Nature.* New York: The New Press, 2006.

Cohen, Sheldon. "Perceived Stress in a Probability Sample of the United States." *The Social Psychology of Health* (1988): 31–67.

"Colorblindness." *Merriam-Webster*. n.d. Accessed August 17, 2023. https://www.merriam-webster.com/dictionary/colorblindness.

Cook, Gabriel I., Richard L. Marsh, and Jason L. Hicks. "Halo and Devil Effects Demonstrate Valenced-Based Influences on Source-Monitoring Decisions." *Consciousness and Cognition* 12, no. 2 (2003): 257–78.

Crenshaw, Dan, and Jordan Peterson. "Fortitude: American Resilience | Dan Crenshaw | EP 214." Jordan B. Peterson. January 3, 2022. YouTube video. https://www.youtube.com/watch?v=GnpHlc8O_sY.

Dayaratna, Kevin, Nicolas Loris, and David Kreutzer. "Consequences of Paris Protocol: Devastating Economic Costs, Essentially Zero Environmental Benefits." Heritage Foundation *Backgrounder*, no. 3080 (2016).

Delamotte, Philip Henry. *Crystal Palace General View from Water Temple*. Photograph. Smithsonian Libraries. 1854. https://commons.wikimedia.org/wiki/File:Crystal_Palace_General_view_from_Water_Temple.jpg.

"Demons (Dostoevsky Novel)." Wikipedia. n.d. Accessed August 26, 2023. https://en.wikipedia.org/wiki/Demons_(Dostoevsky_novel).

Department of Justice. "Justice Department Finds Yale Illegally Discriminates Against Asians and Whites in Undergraduate Admissions in Violation of Federal Civil-Rights Laws." August 13, 2020. https://www.justice.gov/opa/pr/justice-department-finds-yale-illegally-discriminates-against-asians-and-whites-undergraduate.

Department of the Environment. "Canada Gazette, Part 1, Volume 154, Number 51: Clean Fuel Regulations." Government of Canada. December 19, 2020. https://canadagazette.gc.ca/rp-pr/p1/2020/2020-12-19/html/reg2-eng.html.

Dodson, Frederick. *Levels of Energy*. North Charleston, SC: CreateSpace, 2010.

Dolgin, Elie. "The Tangled History of MRNA Vaccines." *Nature* 597, no. 7876 (2021): 318–24.

Dostoevsky, Fyodor. *Crime and Punishment*. 1866. Reprint, Oxford, UK: Oxford University Press, 2019.

———. *Demons*. 1872. Reprint, New York: Vintage Books, 1995.

———. *Notes from Underground*. 1864. Reprint, Munich, Germany: BookRix, 2019, Kindle.

———. *The Brothers Karamazov*. 1880. Reprint, London: Penguins Classics, 2003.

"Doublespeak." Wikipedia. n.d. Accessed August 15, 2023. https://en.wikipedia.org/wiki/Doublespeak.

"Doublethink." Wikipedia. n.d. Accessed August 15, 2023. https://en.wikipedia.org/wiki/Doublethink.

Douglass, Frederick. "A Plea for Freedom of Speech in Boston." Speech delivered at Boston's Music Hall, December 3, 1860. *Douglass' Monthly*, Vol. III, No. VIII, January 1861.

Dreher, Rod. *Live Not by Lies: A Manual for Christian Dissidents*. New York: Penguin, 2022.

Dreher, Rod, and Jordan Peterson. "Live Not by Lies | Rod Dreher | EP 268." Jordan B. Peterson. July 7, 2022. YouTube video. https://www.youtube.com/watch?v=i1JuWVeJS-E.

D'Souza, Mark. "The Ever-Expanding Goalposts of Euthanasia in Canada." *Toronto Sun*, July 18, 2022. https://torontosun.com/opinion/columnists/dsouza-the-ever-expanding-goalposts-of-euthanasia-in-canada.

Eastman, Max. *Reflections on the Failure of Socialism*. New York: The Devon-Adair Company, 1955.

Environmental Progress. "The Complete Case For Nuclear." Environmental Progress. 2021. https://web.archive.org/web/20210501041636/https://environmentalprogress.org/the-war-on-nuclear/.

"Equality vs. Equity: What Is The Difference?" *Merriam-Webster*. n.d. Accessed August 15, 2023. https://www.merriam-webster.com/grammar/equality-vs-equity-difference.

Ereaut, Gill, and Nat Segnit. *Warm Words: How Are We Telling the Climate Story and Can We Tell It Better?* Institute for Public Policy Research, 2006.

Falk, Armin, and Johannes Hermle. "Relationship of Gender Differences in Preferences to Economic Development and Gender Equality." *Science* 362, no: 6412 (2018): eaas9899.

"Fascio." Wikipedia. n.d. Accessed August 14, 2023. https://en.wikipedia.org/wiki/Fascio.

"Fascism." Wikipedia. n.d. Accessed August 14, 2023. https://en.wikipedia.org/wiki/Fascism.

FDA. "Dietary Supplements." FDA. December 21, 2021. https://www.fda.gov/consumers/consumer-updates/dietary-supplements.

Fisman, David N., Afia Amoako, and Ashleigh R. Tuite. "Impact of Population Mixing between Vaccinated and Unvaccinated Subpopulations on Infectious Disease Dynamics: Implications for SARS-CoV-2 Transmission." *CMAJ* 194, no. 16 (2022): E573–80.

Fleming, Kirsten. "AOC Wears 'Tax the Rich' Dress to Met Gala." *New York Post*, September 13, 2021. https://nypost.com/2021/09/13/aoc-wears-tax-the-rich-dress-to-met-gala/.

Flood, Alison. "Jordan Peterson 'Shocked' by Captain America Villain Red Skull Espousing '10 Rules for Life.'" *The Guardian*. April 8, 2021, sec. Books. https://www.theguardian.com/books/2021/apr/07/jordan-peterson-shocked-by-captain-america-villain-espousing-10-rules-for-life.

Frank, Joseph. *Dostoevsky: A Writer in His Time*. Princeton, NJ: Princeton University Press, 2010.

Frankl, Viktor E. *Man's Search for Meaning*. 1959. Reprint, Boston: Beacon Press, 2014.

Franklin, Benjamin. "On the Price of Corn and Management of the Poor." *Walker's Hibernian Magazine, or Compendium of Entertaining Knowledge, May 1785–Dec. 1811*, 1780, 266–67.

Freud, Sigmund. *Beyond the Pleasure Principle*. London: The International Psycho-Analytical Press, 1922.

Frontier Centre for Public Policy."The Greatest Canadian Supported User Fees." Frontier Centre for Public Policy. December 16, 2004. https://fcpp.org/2004/12/16/the-greatest-canadian-supported-user-fees/.

"Fyodor Dostoevsky." Wikipedia. n.d. Accessed August 19, 2023. https://en.wikipedia.org/wiki/Fyodor_Dostoevsky.

"Gaslighting." Wikipedia. n.d. Accessed August 17, 2023. https://en.wikipedia.org/wiki/Gaslighting.

"Gaslighting." *Merriam-Webster*. n.d. Accessed August 17, 2023. https://www.merriam-webster.com/dictionary/gaslighting.

Goethe, Johann Wolfgang von. *Goethe's Faust: Part One and Sections from Part Two*. 1832. Reprint, Garden City, NY: Doubleday, 1963.

Goldman, Emanuel. "How the Unvaccinated Threaten the Vaccinated for COVID-19: A Darwinian Perspective." *Proceedings of the National Academy of Sciences* 118, no. 39 (2021): e2114279118.

Goldstein, Lorrie. 2020a. "Trudeau Doubles down on 32 Years of Failed Climate Policies." *Toronto Sun*. September 26, 2020. https://torontosun.com/opinion/columnists/goldstein-trudeau-doubles-down-on-32-years-of-failed-climate-policies.

———. 2020b. "Do Electric Vehicle Subsidies Work? Don't Ask the Liberals." *Toronto Sun*. October 7, 2020. https://torontosun.com/opinion/columnists/goldstein-do-electric-vehicle-subsidies-work-dont-ask-the-liberals.

———. 2021a. "Trudeau's Carbon Tax to Increase 33% on April 1." *Toronto Sun*. March 17, 2021. https://torontosun.com/opinion/columnists/goldstein-trudeaus-carbon-tax-to-increase-33-on-april-1.

———. 2021b. "COVID Exposed the Folly of Our Approach to Climate Change." *Toronto Sun*. December 18, 2021. https://torontosun.com/opinion/columnists/goldstein-covid-19-exposed-the-folly-of-our-approach-to-climate-change.

Gonzalez, Mike. "Why Black Lives Matter Sides with Hamas against Israel." Heritage Foundation. May 27, 2021. https://www.heritage.org/middle-east/commentary/why-black-lives-matter-sides-hamas-against-israel.

Gordon, Julie, and Fergal Smith. "Canada's 'Tax the Rich' Plan Leaves Big Debt Risk Untouched." Reuters. October 18, 2021. https://www.reuters.com/business/canadas-tax-rich-plan-leaves-big-debt-risk-untouched-2021-10-18/.

Government of Hungary. "Hungarian Family Policy – The Hungarian Family Model." n.d. Accessed August 17, 2023. https://helsinki.mfa.gov.hu/assets/59/19/40/51495279420a1817043db761a69f20d1dd4e58ce.pdf.

Green, Kenneth P., Taylor Jackson, Ian Herzog, and Milagros Palacios. "Energy Costs and Canadian Households: How Much Are We Spending?" *Fraser Institute*, March 2016.

Griffin, Allie. "NOAA Director Shuts down CNN's Don Lemon for Linking Hurricane Ian to Climate Change." *New York Post*. September 28, 2022. https://nypost.com/2022/09/28/hurricane-expert-shuts-down-don-lemons-climate-change-comment/.

Haidt, Jonathan, and Craig Joseph. "Intuitive Ethics: How Innately Prepared Intuitions Generate Culturally Variable Virtues." *Daedalus* 133, no. 4 (2004): 55–66.

Haidt, Jonathan, and Jesse Graham. "When Morality Opposes Justice: Conservatives Have Moral Intuitions That Liberals May Not Recognize." *Social Justice Research* 20, no. 1 (2007): 98–116.

Haidt, Jonathan. "The Moral Roots of Liberals and Conservatives - Jonathan Haidt." TED-Ed. December 31, 2012. YouTube video. https://www.youtube.com/watch?v=8SOQduoLgRw&t=1s.

Haidt, Jonathan, and Joe Rogan. "The Joe Rogan Experience - #1221." *The Joe Rogan Experience*. January 7, 2019. Podcast, MP3 audio, 2:05:11. https://open.spotify.com/episode/40C1TzeSXuEnqQomY8ayQW?si=38a0633196574bd4.

Hallam, Mark. "Greta: Germany Making 'Mistake' by Ditching Nuclear for Coal." *Deutsche Welle*. November 10, 2022. https://www.dw.com/en/greta-thunberg-germany-making-mistake-by-ditching-nuclear-power-for-coal/a-63406732.

Hamid, Nafees, Clara Pretus, Scott Atran, Molly J. Crockett, Jeremy Ginges, Hammad Sheikh, Adolf Tobeña, et al. "Neuroimaging 'Will to Fight' for Sacred Values: An Empirical Case Study with Supporters of an Al Qaeda Associate." *Royal Society Open Science* 6, no. 6 (2019): 181585.

Hamilton-Wentworth District School Board. "Learn. Disrupt. Rebuild@HWDSB: Building a Community of Care Module 2 Understanding Identity and Intersectionality Lesson #12 Identity and Race, Part 1 (Grades 2-3)." 2021. https://www.hwdsb.on.ca/wp-content/uploads/2021/04/Lesson-12-Identity-and-Race-Part-1-PRIMARY-Grades-2-3.pdf.

Hasell, Joe, and Max Roser. *World Population Living in Extreme Poverty, World, 1820–2015*. Graph in "How Do We Know the History of Extreme Poverty?" Our World in Data, 2019. https://ourworldindata.org/extreme-history-methods.

Hawkins, David R. *Power vs. Force*. Carlsbad, CA: Hay House, Inc., 2014.

Hawkins, Stephen, Daniel Yudkin Míriam, and Juan-Torres Tim Dixon. "Hidden Tribes: A Study of America's Polarized Landscape." *More In Common*. 2018. https://www.immigrationresearch.org/system/files/Hidden_Tribes.pdf.

Henderson, Rob, and Jordan Peterson. "Sex and Dating Apps | Rob Henderson | EP 193." Jordan B. Peterson. September 20, 2021. YouTube video. https://www.youtube.com/watch?v=-6ZyQKiwMQw.

Heying, Heather, and Bret Weinstein. *A Hunter-Gatherer's Guide to the 21st Century: Evolution and the Challenges of Modern Life*. New York: Portfolio/Penguin, 2021.

Hickman, Caroline, Elizabeth Marks, Panu Pihkala, Susan Clayton, R. Eric Lewandowski, Elouise E. Mayall, Britt Wray, Catriona Mellor, and Lise van Susteren. "Climate Anxiety in Children and Young People and Their Beliefs about Government Responses to Climate Change: A Global Survey." *The Lancet Planetary Health* 5, no. 12 (2021): 863–73.

Hippisley-Cox, Julia, Martina Patone, Xue W. Mei, Defne Saatci, Sharon Dixon, Kamlesh Khunti, Francesco Zaccardi, et al. "Risk of Thrombocytopenia and

Thromboembolism after Covid-19 Vaccination and SARS-CoV-2 Positive Testing: Self-Controlled Case Series Study." *BMJ* 374 (2021): n1931.

Hirsh, Jacob B., Colin G. DeYoung, Xiaowen Xu, and Jordan B. Peterson. "Compassionate Liberals and Polite Conservatives: Associations of Agreeableness with Political Ideology and Moral Values." *Personality and Social Psychology Bulletin* 36, no. 5 (2010): 655–64.

Hirsh, Jacob B., Raymond A. Mar, and Jordan B. Peterson. "Psychological Entropy: A Framework for Understanding Uncertainty-Related Anxiety." *Psychological Review* 119, no. 2 (2012): 304–20.

Hirsh, Jacob B., Dominique Morisano, and Jordan B. Peterson. "Delay Discounting: Interactions between Personality and Cognitive Ability." *Journal of Research in Personality* 42, no. 6 (2008): 1646–50.

Hodal, Kate. "One in 200 People Is a Slave. Why?" *Guardian*. February 25, 2019. https://www.theguardian.com/news/2019/feb/25/modern-slavery-trafficking-persons-one-in-200.

Hopf, G. Michael. *Those Who Remain: A Postapocalyptic Novel.* Vol. 7. New York: Plume, 2016.

Hughes, Coleman, and Curt Jaimungal. "Coleman Hughes on #BLM, the Perilous Myth of Universal White Racism, and the Moral Landscape." Theories of Everything with Curt Jaimungal. July 10, 2020. YouTube video. https://www.youtube.com/watch?v=CAZogp2_pZ8.

Huxley, Aldous. *Brave New World.* London: Chatto & Windus, 1932.

"Ideology." *Merriam-Webster*. n.d. Accessed August 15, 2023. https://www.merriam-webster.com/dictionary/ideology.

Imtiaz, Sameer, Samantha Wells, Jürgen Rehm, Hayley A. Hamilton, Yeshambel T. Nigatu, Christine M. Wickens, Damian Jankowicz, and Tara Elton-Marshall. "Cannabis Use during the COVID-19 Pandemic in Canada: A Repeated Cross-Sectional Study." *Journal of Addiction Medicine* 15, no. 6 (2021): 484–90.

Institute for Energy Research. "The Mounting Solar Panel Waste Problem." Institute for Energy Research. September 12, 2018. https://www.instituteforenergyresearch.org/renewable/solar/the-mounting-solar-panel-waste-problem/.

IPCC. "Summary for Policymakers" In *Global Warming of 1.5° C. An IPCC Special Report on the Impacts of Global Warming of 1.5° C above Pre-Industrial Levels and Related Global Greenhouse Gas Emission Pathways, in the Context of Strengthening the*

Global Response to the Threat of Climate Change, Sustainable Development, and Efforts to Eradicate Poverty. Geneva, Switzerland: World Meteorological Organization, 2018.

"Ius Trium Liberorum." *Encyclopedia Britannica*. n.d. Accessed September 2, 2023. https://www.britannica.com/topic/ius-trium-liberorum.

Jarvis, Stephen, Olivier Deschenes, and Akshaya Jha. "The Private and External Costs of Germany's Nuclear Phase-Out." *NBER Working Paper*, no. 26598, 2019.

———. "The Private and External Costs of Germany's Nuclear Phase-Out." *Journal of the European Economic Association* 20, no. 3 (2022): 1311–46.

Jefferson, Thomas. "Letter to Joseph Milligan, April 6, 1816." *The Life and Selected Writings of Thomas Jefferson: Including the Autobiography, The Declaration of Independence & His Public and Private Letters*. 1858. Reprint, New York: Modern Library, 1998.

John Paul II. "Fides et Ratio." *Origins* 28, no 19 (1998).

jpatokal. "Camp Arbeit Macht Frei." Photograph. Wikipedia. n.d. Accessed August 17, 2023. https://commons.wikimedia.org/wiki/File:Camp_ArbeitMachtFrei.JPG.

Jung, Carl Gustav. *Collected Works of C.G. Jung, Volume 9 (Part 2): Aion: Researches into the Phenomenology of the Self.* Edited by Gerhard Adler and R. F. C. Hull. 2nd ed. Princeton, NJ: Princeton University Press, 1969.

Jung, Carl Gustav. *Flying Saucers: A Modern Myth of Things Seen in the Sky*. 1959. Reprint, Hove, UK: Psychology Press, 2002.

Kaczor, Christopher, and Matthew Petrusek. *Jordan Peterson, God, and Christianity: The Search for a Meaningful Life*. Park Ridge, IL: Word on Fire Institute, 2021.

Kafka, Franz. *The Trial*. 1925. Reprint, London: Penguin, 2015.

Kahan, Meldon, Anita Srivastava, and Sarah Clarke. "Cannabis Industry and Medical Cannabis Clinics Need Regulation." *Canadian Family Physician* 65, no. 12 (2019): 864–68.

Kanai, Ryota, Tom Feilden, Colin Firth, and Geraint Rees. "Political Orientations Are Correlated with Brain Structure in Young Adults." *Current Biology* 21, no. 8 (2011): 677–80.

Kaufman, Scott Barry, David Bryce Yaden, Elizabeth Hyde, and Eli Tsukayama. "The Light vs. Dark Triad of Personality: Contrasting Two Very Different Profiles of Human Nature." *Frontiers in Psychology* 10, no. 467 (2019).

Kendi, Ibram X. *How to Be an Antiracist*. New York: One World, 2019.

Kengor, Paul. *The Devil and Karl Marx: Communism's Long March of Death, Deception.* Gastonia, NC: Tan Books, 2020.

Kershner, Irvin, dir. *Star Wars: Episode V, The Empire Strikes Back*. United States: 20th Century-Fox, 1980.

Kharecha, Pushker A., and James E. Hansen. "Prevented Mortality and Greenhouse Gas Emissions from Historical and Projected Nuclear Power." *Environmental Science & Technology* 47, no. 9 (2013): 4889–95.

Kiefer, Peter, and Peter Savodnik. "Hollywood's New Rules." The Free Press. January 11, 2022. https://www.thefp.com/p/hollywoods-new-rules?utm_source=url.

Kierkegaard, Søren. *Concluding Unscientific Postscript to Philosophical Fragments*. Edited and translated by Howard V. Hong and Edna H. Hong. 1846. Reprint, Princeton, NJ: Princeton University Press, 1992.

King Jr., Martin Luther. "Nonviolence and Racial Justice." *Christian Century* 74, no.6 (1957): 165–67.

———. *Stride toward Freedom: The Montgomery Story*. 1958. Reprint, Surrey, England: Souvenir Press, 2011.

Kisin, Konstantin, and Jordan Peterson. "Konstantin Kisin and the Counter-Woke Revolution | EP 333." Jordan B. Peterson. February 20, 2023. YouTube video. https://www.youtube.com/watch?v=xnpUFLD_xlw.

Klotzbach, Philip J., Steven G Bowen, Roger Pielke Jr., and Michael Bell. "Continental US Hurricane Landfall Frequency and Associated Damage: Observations and Future Risks." *Bulletin of the American Meteorological Society* 99, no. 7 (2018): 1359–76.

Kopplin, Cristopher Siegfried, and Louisa Rosenthal. "The Positive Effects of Combined Breathing Techniques and Cold Exposure on Perceived Stress: A Randomised Trial." *Current Psychology* 42, no. 31 (2023): 27058–70. https://doi.org/10.1007/s12144-022-03739-y.

Kriegman, Zac. "The Post That Led to My Termination." Zac Kriegman (Substack). December 7, 2021. https://kriegman.substack.com/p/post-leading-to-termination-blm-falsehoods.

Krispenz, Ann, and Alex Bertrams. "Understanding Left-Wing Authoritarianism: Relations to the Dark Personality Traits, Altruism, and Social Justice Commitment." *Current Psychology*, March 20 (2023): 1–17. https://doi.org/10.1007/s12144-023-04463-x.

Kuehn, Bridget M. "WHO: More than 7 Million Air Pollution Deaths Each Year." *JAMA* 311, no. 15 (2014): 1486.

"Kulak." Wikipedia. n.d. Accessed August 15, 2023. https://en.wikipedia.org/wiki/Kulak.

Kurzweil, Ray. *The Singularity Is Near: When Humans Transcend Biology.* New York: Viking, 2005.

Lalupa. *Roman Statue of Atlas (2nd Century AD)*. Photograph. Wikipedia. n.d. Accessed August 17, 2023. https://commons.wikimedia.org/wiki/File:MAN_Atlante_fronte_1040572.JPG.

Latané, Bibb, and John M Darley. "Group Inhibition of Bystander Intervention in Emergencies." *Journal of Personality and Social Psychology* 10, no. 3 (1968): 215–21.

Lenin, Vladimir Il'ich. "April Theses." *Pravda*, April 20, 1917.

LifeSiteNews. "Hungary's Family Policy Is Widely Successful, Guaranteeing Prosperity for Those Desiring Children." LifeSiteNews. June 25, 2021. https://www.lifesitenews.com/news/hungarys-family-policy-is-widely-successful-guaranteeing-prosperity-for-those-desiring-children/.

Lomborg, Bjørn. 2016. "Impact of Current Climate Proposals." *Global Policy* 7, no. 1 (2016): 109–18.

———. 2020. *False Alarm: How Climate Change Panic Costs Us Trillions, Hurts the Poor, and Fails to Fix the Planet.* London: Hachette UK, 2020.

———. 2021a. "The Net-Zero Debate Turns Orwellian." *Forbes*. July 20, 2021. https://www.forbes.com/sites/bjornlomborg/2021/07/20/the-net-zero-debate-turns-orwellian/?sh=1b988eeb646e.

———. 2021b. "Allegra Stratton Is Right about Electric Cars." *The Telegraph*. August 4, 2021. https://www.telegraph.co.uk/news/2021/08/04/allegra-stratton-right-electric-cars/.

Lomborg, Bjørn, and Jordan Peterson. "Is Everything Better Than We Think? | Bjorn Lomborg | EP 163." Jordan B. Peterson. April 26, 2021. YouTube video. https://www.youtube.com/watch?v=vDNSnMTem98&t=1s.

Lopez Bernal, Jamie, Nick Andrews, Charlotte Gower, Eileen Gallagher, Ruth Simmons, Simon Thelwall, Julia Stowe, et al. "Effectiveness of Covid-19 Vaccines against the B. 1.617. 2 (Delta) Variant." *New England Journal of Medicine* 385, no. 7 (2021): 585–94.

Lucas, George, dir. *Star Wars: Episode III, Revenge of the Sith*. United States: 20th Century Fox, 2005.

Maddeaux, Sabrina. "Sabrina Maddeaux: How China Is Using These Olympics to Perfect Their 'Wolf Warrior' Tactics." National Post. July 30, 2021. https://nationalpost.com/sports/olympics/sabrina-maddeaux-how-china-is-using-these-olympics-to-perfect-their-wolf-warrior-tactics.

Mahjar-Barducci, Anna. "Russia's New 'Conservative' Ideology to Counter Liberalism." MEMRI. January 11, 2022. https://www.memri.org/reports/russias-new-conservative-ideology-counter-liberalism.

Malas, Mahmoud B., Isaac N. Naazie, Nadin Elsayed, Asma Mathlouthi, Rebecca Marmor, and Bryan Clary. "Thromboembolism Risk of COVID-19 Is High and Associated with a Higher Risk of Mortality: A Systematic Review and Meta-Analysis." *EClinicalMedicine* 29 (2020): 100639.

Marasco, Giovanni, Cesare Cremon, Maria Raffaella Barbaro, Giulia Cacciari, Francesca Falangone, Anna Kagramanova, Dmitry Bordin, et al. "Post COVID-19 Irritable Bowel Syndrome." *Gut* 72, no. 3 (2023): 484–92.

Markandya, Anil, and Paul Wilkinson. "Electricity Generation and Health." *The Lancet* 370, no. 9591 (September 2007): 979–90. https://doi.org/10.1016/s0140-6736(07)61253-7.

Marx, Karl. *Critique of Hegel's Philosophy of Right*. 1844. Reprint, Cambridge, UK: Cambridge University Press, 1970.

Marx, Karl, and Friedrich Engels. *The Communist Manifesto*. 1848. Reprint, London: Penguin UK, 2004.

McLanahan, Sara, Laura Tach, and Daniel Schneider. "The Causal Effects of Father Absence." *Annual Review of Sociology* 39 (2013): 399–427.

Međedović, Janko, and Boban Petrović. "The Dark Tetrad." *Journal of Individual Differences* 36, no. 4 (2015): 228-236.

Mendez, Mario F. "A Neurology of the Conservative-Liberal Dimension of Political Ideology." *Journal of Neuropsychiatry and Clinical Neurosciences* 29, no. 2 (2017): 86–94.

Miconi, Diana, Gabrielle Geenen, Rochelle L Frounfelker, Anna Levinsson, and Cécile Rousseau. "Meaning in Life, Future Orientation and Support for Violent Radicalization among Canadian College Students during the COVID-19 Pandemic." *Frontiers in Psychiatry* 13 (2022): 765908.

"Microaggression." *Merriam-Webster*. n.d. Accessed August 17, 2023. https://www.merriam-webster.com/dictionary/microaggression.

Mill, John Stuart. *On Liberty*. 1859. Reprint, Clark, NJ: The Lawbook Exchange, Ltd, 2002.

Milton, John. 1667. *Paradise Lost.* Reprint, Indianapolis, IN: Hackett Publishing, 2005.

Ministry of Education. "Mathematics." Government of Ontario. 2021. https://www.dcp.edu.gov.on.ca/en/curriculum/secondary-mathematics/courses/mth1w/course-intro.

Moir, Mackenzie, and Bacchus Barua. "Comparing Performance of Universal Health Care Countries, 2022." Fraser Institute, 2022.

Murphy, Robert, and Jordan Peterson. "Is Property Theft? | Dr Robert Murphy | EP 189." Jordan B. Peterson. August 30, 2021. YouTube video. https://www.youtube.com/watch?v=_OtZ49i-yyk.

Naglieri, David, dir. *Liberating a Continent: John Paul II and the Fall of Communism.* United States: Public Broadcasting Service, 2018.

National Institutes of Health. "Q&A: COVID-19, Vaccines, and Myocarditis." National Institutes of Health. July 1, 2022. https://covid19.nih.gov/news-and-stories/covid-19-vaccines-myocarditis.

New World Encyclopedia contributors. "Nikolai Chernyshevsky." New World Encyclopedia. October 12, 2011. https://www.newworldencyclopedia.org/entry/Nikolai_Chernyshevsky.

"Newspeak." Wikipedia. n.d. Accessed August 17, 2023. https://en.wikipedia.org/wiki/Newspeak.

Nietzsche, Friedrich. *Beyond Good and Evil.* 1886. Reprint, Seattle: AmazonClassics, 2017.

———. The Gay Science: With a Prelude in Rhymes and an Appendix of Songs. Translated by Walter Kaufmann. 1882. Reprint, New York: Vintage Books, 1974.

———. *The Twilight of the Idols.* 1889. Reprint, Oxford, UK: Oxford Paperbacks, 2008.

———. *Thus Spake Zarathustra.* 1885. Reprint, New York: Dover Publications, 1999.

"Nihilism." Wikipedia. n.d. Accessed August 14, 2023. https://en.wikipedia.org/wiki/Nihilism.

Nordhaus, William. "Projections and Uncertainties about Climate Change in an Era of Minimal Climate Policies." *American Economic Journal: Economic Policy* 10, no, 3 (2018): 333–60.

Nuclear Energy Institute. "Nuclear Waste." Nuclear Energy Institute. 2019. https://nei.org/fundamentals/nuclear-waste.

Oakley, Barbara, Ariel Knafo, Guruprasad Madhavan, and David Sloan Wilson, eds. *Pathological Altruism.* Oxford, UK: Oxford University Press, 2011.

Odozor, Chioma U., Thomas Kannampallil, K. Roles, C. Burk, B. C. Warner, H. Alaverdyan, D. B. Clifford, J. F. Piccirillo, and S. Haroutounian. "Post-Acute Sensory Neurological Sequelae in Patients with SARS-CoV-2 Infection: The COVID-PN Observational Cohort Study." *Pain* 163, no. 12 (2022): 2398-2410. https://doi.org/10.1097/j.pain.0000000000002639.

Ok, Ekin, Yi Qian, Brendan Strejcek, and Karl Aquino. "Signaling Virtuous Victimhood as Indicators of Dark Triad Personalities." *Journal of Personality and Social Psychology* 120, no. 6 (2021): 1634–61.

O'Neill, Jesse, and Julia Marsh. "BLM Leader Hawk Newsome Threatens 'Riots, Fire, Bloodshed' in NYC If Eric Adams Gets Tough on Crime." *New York Post*. November 11, 2021. https://nypost.com/2021/11/11/blm-leader-hawk-newsome-threatens-riots-after-sit-down-with-eric-adams/.

Orr, James, Arif Ahmed, and Jordan Peterson. "Free Speech and Cambridge | James Orr & Arif Ahmed | EP 218." Jordan B. Peterson. January 17, 2022. YouTube video. https://www.youtube.com/watch?v=9wjw3udMNBc.

Orwell, George. *1984*. London: Secker & Warburg, 1949

———. *Animal Farm*. London: Secker & Warburg, 1945.

———."Mein Kampf." *New English Weekly*, March 1940.

———. "Politics and the English Language." *Horizon*, April 1946.

———."Review: *The Road to Serfdom* by F.A. Hayek / *The Mirror of the Past* by K. Zilliacus." *Observer*, April 9, 1944.

"Overton Window." Wikipedia. n.d. Accessed December 16, 2023. https://en.wikipedia.org/wiki/Overton_window.

Pageau, Jonathan. "What Is the Supreme Good? | Jonathan Pageau." Alliance for Responsible Citizenship. November 1, 2023. YouTube video. https://www.youtube.com/watch?v=Fsmqhu8-L1E&t=923s.

Park, Yeonmi, and Jordan Peterson. "Tyranny, Slavery and Columbia U | Yeonmi Park | EP 172." Jordan B. Peterson. May 31, 2021. YouTube video. https://www.youtube.com/watch?v=8yqa-SdJtT4.

Park, Yeonmi, and Maryanne Vollers. *In Order to Live: A North Korean Girl's Journey to Freedom*. London: Penguin, 2016.

Parsley, Kirk. "The Most Overlooked Factor in Health and Longevity." TheIHMC. November 29, 2016. YouTube video. https://www.youtube.com/watch?v=dn-GACHPr1nM&t=3062s.

"Performative Contradiction." Wikipedia. n.d. Accessed August 17, 2023. https://en.wikipedia.org/wiki/Performative_contradiction.

Peters, Russell. "Russell Peters - Somebody Gonna Get Hurt Real Bad." Just For Laughs. March 18, 2016. YouTube video. https://www.youtube.com/watch?v=Adz4l5qEpD4.

Peters, Russell, Jordan Peterson, and Mikhaila Peterson. "How We're Breeding Narcissists | Russell Peters & Jordan Peterson." Life's Like That . . . . January 10, 2022. YouTube video. https://www.youtube.com/watch?v=YxuFWt4-HdQ.

Peterson, Jordan. 2017a. "2017 Personality 07: Carl Jung and the Lion King (Part 1)." Jordan B. Peterson. January 31, 2017. YouTube video. https://www.youtube.com/watch?v=3iLiKMUiyTI&t=32s.

———. 2017b. "2017 Personality 18: Biology & Traits: Openness/Intelligence/Creativity I." YouTube video. Jordan B. Peterson. April 18, 2017. https://www.youtube.com/watch?v=D7Kn5p7TP_Y&t=5393s.

———. 2017c. "Lecture: Biblical Series II: Genesis 1: Chaos & Order." Jordan B. Peterson. May 27, 2017. YouTube video. https://www.youtube.com/watch?v=hdrLQ7DpiWs&t=3s.

———. 2017d. "Lecture: Biblical Series VII: Walking with God: Noah and the Flood." Jordan B. Peterson. July 18, 2017. YouTube video. https://www.youtube.com/watch?v=6gFjB9FTN58&t=118s.

———. 2017e. "Lecture: Biblical Series XII: The Great Sacrifice: Abraham and Isaac." Jordan B. Peterson. August 19, 2017. YouTube video. https://www.youtube.com/watch?v=-yUP40gwht0&t=20s.

———. 2018. *12 Rules for Life: An Antidote to Chaos*. Toronto: Random House Canada, 2018.

———. 2019a. "Lecture: Who Dares Say He Believes in God?" Jordan B. Peterson. June 8, 2019. YouTube video. https://www.youtube.com/watch?v=MnUfXYGtT5Q.

———. 2019b. "Equity: When the Left Goes Too Far." Jordan B. Peterson, May 15, 2019. https://www.jordanbpeterson.com/political-correctness/equity-when-the-left-goes-too-far/.

———. 2021. "Jordan Peterson - Lecture on Free Speech, 10/19/21 Bucknell Program for American Leadership." Bucknell University. November 1, 2021. YouTube video. https://www.youtube.com/watch?v=GlW5A4EoWtQ.

Peterson, Jordan B., and Maja Djikic. "You Can Neither Remember nor Forget What You Do Not Understand." In *Justice and the Politics of Memory*, 85–118. Abingdon, UK: Routledge, 2017.

Peterson, Jordan, and Christie Blatchford. "Jordan Peterson on the #Metoo Moment." *National Post*. March 24, 2018. YouTube video. https://www.youtube.com/watch?v=g8GSlP2yCD8.

Peterson, Jordan, and Andrew Doyle. "Free Speech and the Satirical Activist | Andrew Doyle | EP 178." Jordan B. Peterson. June 21, 2021. YouTube video. https://www.youtube.com/watch?v=aoH1g5GYhPw.

Peterson, Jordan, and Michael Franzese. "Breaking Good | Michael Franzese | EP 302." Jordan B Peterson. November 3, 2022. YouTube video. https://www.youtube.com/watch?v=RzKM-VwriK0.

Peterson, Jordan, Christopher Kaczor, and Matthew Petrusek. "Jordan Peterson, God, & Christianity | Kaczor & Petrusek | EP 212." Jordan B. Peterson. December 27, 2021. YouTube video. https://www.youtube.com/watch?v=m9Njk8vpToQ.

Peterson, Jordan, and Andrew Lo. "The Future of Capitalism | Q&A With MIT Students." Jordan B. Peterson. May 12, 2022. YouTube video. https://www.youtube.com/watch?v=4De8xhcknGE&t=1245s.

Peterson, Jordan, and Douglas Murray. "Radical Ideology and the Nihilistic Void | Douglas Murray | EP 152." Jordan B. Peterson. January 25, 2021. YouTube video. https://www.youtube.com/watch?v=g_RrYz85E1A.

Peterson, Jordan, and Jonathan Pageau. "Beyond Order: Montreal Lecture | Jonathan Pageau | EP 262." Jordan B. Peterson. June 16, 2022. YouTube video. https://www.youtube.com/watch?v=iPcILp35oU4.

———. "The Perfect Mode of Being | Jonathan Pageau | EP 156." Jordan B. Peterson. February 14, 2021. YouTube video. https://www.youtube.com/watch?v=2rAqVmZwqZM.

Peterson, Jordan, and Marian Tupy. "10 Global Trends Every Person Should Know | Marian Tupy | EP 165." Jordan B. Peterson. May 21, 2021. YouTube video. https://www.youtube.com/watch?v=VIANLddo-ec&t=2882s.

Peterson, Jordan, and Bret Weinstein. "Jordan Peterson Is Back! - Bret Weinstein's DarkHorse Podcast." Bret Weinstein. March 8, 2021. YouTube video. https://www.youtube.com/watch?v=O55mvoZbz4Y&t=3744s.

Peterson, Jordan, and Jocko Willink. "Literacy and Strength | Jocko Willink | EP 160." Jordan B. Peterson. April 5, 2021. YouTube video. https://www.youtube.com/watch?v=HA4Bkybx1ps&t=2s.

Peterson, Jordan, and Slavoj Zizek. "Jordan Peterson & Slavoj Zizek- 'Happiness: Capitalism vs. Marxism.'" Truthspeak. April 20, 2019. YouTube video. https://www.youtube.com/watch?v=pT1vutd4Gnk.

Pew Research Center. "Progressive Left: Very Liberal, Highly Educated and Majority White; Most Say U.S. Institutions Need to Be Completely Rebuilt Because of Racial Bias." In *Beyond Red vs. Blue: The Political Typology*. Pew Research Center. November 9, 2021. https://www.pewresearch.org/politics/2021/11/09/progressive-left/.

Plato. *The Republic*. n.d. Wiley Online Library, n.d.

Pokrovsky, B. *Mock Execution Ritual 1849*. Drawing. Runivers. 1849. https://commons.wikimedia.org/wiki/File:B_pokrovsky_kazn_1849.jpg.

Pooley, Gale, and Marian L. Tupy. "The Simon Abundance Index 2022." HumanProgress.Org. April 22, 2022. https://www.humanprogress.org/the-simon-abundance-index-2022/.

Postmedia News. "Dropping Ds and Fs for California Students Gets Failing Grade by Some." *Toronto Sun*. December 10, 2021. https://torontosun.com/news/world/dropping-d-and-f-grades-for-california-students-gets-failing-mark-by-some.

"Postmodernism." Wikipedia. n.d. Accessed August 15, 2023. https://en.wikipedia.org/wiki/Postmodernism.

Poussin, Nicolas. *Golden Calf*. Image of a painting. One Peter 5. 1633. https://onepeterfive.com/wp-content/uploads/2019/09/golden-calf.jpg.

Prestigiacomo, Amanda. "Report: Royal Air Force Stops Hiring White Men To Keep With Diversity Quotas, Female Head Of Recruiting Quits In Protest." Daily Wire. August 18, 2022. https://www.dailywire.com/news/report-royal-air-force-stops-hiring-white-men-to-keep-with-diversity-quotas-female-head-of-recruiting-quits-in-protest.

Pretus, Clara, Nafees Hamid, Hammad Sheikh, Ángel Gómez, Jeremy Ginges, Adolf Tobeña, Richard Davis, Oscar Vilarroya, and Scott Atran. "Ventromedial and Dorsolateral Prefrontal Interactions Underlie Will to Fight and Die for a Cause." *Social Cognitive and Affective Neuroscience* 14, no. 6 (2019): 569–77.

"Psychological Projection." Wikipedia. n.d. Accessed August 18, 2023. https://en.wikipedia.org/wiki/Psychological_projection.

Rand, Ayn. *Atlas Shrugged*. London: Penguin, 1957.

Ravallion, Martin. *The Economics of Poverty: History, Measurement, and Policy*. Oxford, UK: Oxford University Press, 2016.

Raymond, Eric S. "Kafkatrap." Wikipedia. n.d. Accessed August 17, 2023.

"Reaction Formation." Wikipedia. n.d. Accessed August 17, 2023. https://en.wikipedia.org/wiki/Reaction_formation.

Rector, Robert. "Married to the Welfare State." Heritage Foundation. February 10, 2015. https://www.heritage.org/welfare/commentary/married-the-welfare-state.

Reuters Fact Check. "Fact Check-COVID-19 Vaccines Did Not Skip Animal Trials Because of Animal Deaths." Reuters. June 1, 2021. https://www.reuters.com/article/factcheck-covid-vaccine-animal-idUSL2N2NJ1IK/.

Riordan, Daniel Vincent. "Mimetic Theory and the Evolutionary Paradox of Schizophrenia: The Archetypal Scapegoat Hypothesis." *Medical Hypotheses* 108 (2017): 101–7.

———. "The Scapegoat Mechanism in Human Evolution: An Analysis of René Girard's Hypothesis on the Process of Hominization." *Biological Theory* 16, no. 4 (2021): 242–56.

Ritchie, Hannah. "What Was the Death Toll from Chernobyl and Fukushima?." Our World in Data. July 24, 2017. https://ourworldindata.org/what-was-the-death-toll-from-chernobyl-and-fukushima.

Ritchie, Hannah and Pablo Rosado. *Death Rates per Unit of Electricity Production*. Graph in "Nuclear Energy." Our World in Data, July 10, 2020. https://ourworldindata.org/nuclear-energy.

Robbins, Tony. "Date with Destiny." Convention, Fort Lauderdale, 2016.

Roberts, Amanda, Jim Rogers, Rachael Mason, Aloysius Niroshan Siriwardena, Todd Hogue, Gregory Adam Whitley, and Graham R Law. "Alcohol and Other Substance Use during the COVID-19 Pandemic: A Systematic Review." *Drug and Alcohol Dependence* 229 (2021): 109150.

Rogan, Joe, and Jordan Peterson. "#958 – Jordan Peterson." *The Joe Rogan Experience*. May 10, 2017. Podcast, MP3 audio, 2:57:34. https://open.spotify.com/episode/5194p3rIfeyMGbo8YKGMJK?si=873278c593744f60.

Rogan, Joe, Jordan Peterson, and Bret Weinstein. "Joe Rogan Experience #1006 - Jordan Peterson & Bret Weinstein." The Joe Rogan Experience. September 1, 2017. YouTube video. https://www.youtube.com/watch?v=6G59zsjM2UI&t=95s.

Rogmann, Jens J. "Notes on Piaget & Inhelder's Formal Operational Stage as a 'Messianic Stage'" (Research Report, updated 2021). Hamburg, Germany: University of Hamburg, Faculty of Education, Department of Educational Psychology.

Roser, Max, and Esteban Ortiz-Ospina. *Distribution of Population between Different Poverty Thresholds, World, 1981 to 2017*. Graph in "Global Extreme Poverty." Retrieved March 3, 2021. Archived March 3, 2022, at the Wayback Machine. https://web.archive.org/web/20220303145148/https://ourworldindata.org/extreme-poverty.

Roser, Max, and Esteban Ortiz-Ospina. "Global Extreme Poverty." Created 2013. Updated 2019a. Archived March 3, 2022, at the Wayback Machine. https://web.archive.org/web/20220303145148/https://ourworldindata.org/extreme-poverty.

Roser, Max, and Esteban Ortiz-Ospina. *Share of the World Population Living in Absolute Poverty, 1820–2015*. Graph in "Global Extreme Poverty." Updated 2019b. Archived March 3, 2022, at the Wayback Machine. https://web.archive.org/web/20220303145148/https://ourworldindata.org/extreme-poverty.

Rousseau, Jean-Jacques. *Émile, or, on Education: Includes Emile and Sophie, or, the Solitaries*. Edited by Christopher Kelly. Translated by Allan Bloom. 1762. Reprint, Lebanon, NH: University Press of New England, 2010.

Routledge, Clay, Andrew A. Abeyta, and Christina Roylance. "We Are Not Alone: The Meaning Motive, Religiosity, and Belief in Extraterrestrial Intelligence." *Motivation and Emotion* 41 (2017): 135–46.

Routledge, Clay, and Taylor A. FioRito. "Why Meaning in Life Matters for Societal Flourishing." *Frontiers in Psychology* 11 (2021): 3925. https://doi.org/10.3389/fpsyg.2020.601899.

Routledge, Clay, and Jordan Peterson. "Death, Meaning, and the Power of the Invisible World | Clay Routledge | EP 199." Jordan B. Peterson. November 1, 2021. YouTube video. https://www.youtube.com/watch?v=3yV0b-NhKTY&t=18s.

Rubio, Marco, and Chip Roy. "Woke Warfighters: How Political Ideology Is Weakening America's Military." *GOP Report*, November 2022. https://roy.house.gov/sites/evo-subsites/roy.house.gov/files/evo-media-document/woke-warfighters-report-compressed.pdf.

Rushdie, Salman. "Democracy Is No Polite Tea Party." *Los Angeles Times*. February 7, 2005. https://www.latimes.com/archives/la-xpm-2005-feb-07-oe-rushdie7-story.html.

Saad, Gad. *The Parasitic Mind: How Infectious Ideas Are Killing Common Sense*. Washington, DC: Regnery Publishing, 2020.

Saad, Gad, and Joe Rogan. 2022. "#1816 – Gad Saad." *The Joe Rogan Experience*. May 11, 2022. Podcast, MP3 audio, 3:11:47. https://open.spotify.com/episode/6rDI1et-n04E0qJM0qfG3p5?si=rEpsru-sQFWjBJkw8arMeg.

Saad, Lydia. "Black Americans Want Police to Retain Local Presence." Gallup. August 5, 2020. https://news.gallup.com/poll/316571/black-americans-police-retain-local-presence.aspx.

Sahakian, Teny. "North Korean Defector Says 'Even North Korea Was Not This Nuts' after Attending Ivy League School." Fox News, June 2021. https://www.foxnews.com/us/north-korean-defector-ivy-league-nuts.

Sovacool, Benjamin K., Rasmus Andersen, Steven Sorensen, Kenneth Sorensen, Victor Tienda, Arturas Vainorius, Oliver Marc Schirach, and Frans Bjørn-Thygesen. "Balancing Safety with Sustainability: Assessing the Risk of Accidents for Modern Low-Carbon Energy Systems." *Journal of Cleaner Production* 112, no. 5 (January 2016): 3952–65. https://doi.org/10.1016/j.jclepro.2015.07.059.

Scanlan, James P. "The Case against Rational Egoism in Dostoevsky's 'Notes from Underground.'" *Journal of the History of Ideas* 60, no 3 (1999): 549–67.

"Shadow (Psychology)." Wikipedia. n.d. Accessed August 17, 2023. https://en.wikipedia.org/wiki/Shadow_(psychology).

Shakhnazarova, Nika. "Tax Filings Reveal How BLM Co-Founder Spent Charity Funds." *New York Post*. May 17, 2022. https://nypost.com/2022/05/17/inside-blm-co-founder-patrisse-cullors-questionable-tax-filings/.

Shapiro, Ben. 2021a. *The Authoritarian Moment: How the Left Weaponized America's Institutions against Dissent*. New York: Broadside Books, 2021.

———. 2021b. "How To Defeat Critical Race Theory | Ep. 1280." The Ben Shapiro Show. June 21, 2021. YouTube video. https://www.youtube.com/watch?v=A6sg-u4KKzE.

———. 2021c. "The Decline And Fall Of The United States | Ep. 1334." The Ben Shapiro Show. September 9, 2021. YouTube video. https://www.youtube.com/watch?v=CsoatCbeAqQ.

Shapiro, Ben, and Joe Rogan. "Joe Rogan Experience #1276 - Ben Shapiro." The Joe Rogan Experience. April 3, 2019. YouTube video. https://www.youtube.com/watch?v=sCD9zjf_YRU.

Sharpsteen, Ben, Hamilton Luske, Bill Roberts, Norman Ferguson, Jack Kinney, Wilfred Jackson, and Thornton Hee, dirs. *Pinocchio*. 1940, United States: RKO Radio Pictures.

Shellenberger, Michael. 2019. "Why Wind Turbines Threaten Endangered Species with Extinction." *Forbes*. June 26, 2019. https://www.forbes.com/sites/michaelshellenberger/2019/06/26/why-wind-turbines-threaten-endangered-species-with-extinction/?sh=3b0fdd7564b4.

———. 2020. *Apocalypse Never: Why Environmental Alarmism Hurts Us*. New York: Harper, 2020.

———. 2021a. *San Fransicko: Why Progressives Ruin Cities*. New York: Harper, 2021.

———. 2021b. "Dark Side to Solar? More Reports Tie Panel Production to Toxic Pollution." *Forbes*. June 21, 2021. https://www.forbes.com/sites/michaelshellenberger/2021/06/21/why-everything-they-said-about-solar---including-that-its-clean-and-cheap---was-wrong/?sh=6e8f029f5fe5.

Shellenberger, Michael, and Jordan Peterson. "Apocalypse Never? | Michael Shellenberger | EP 197." Jordan B. Peterson. October 18, 2021. YouTube video. https://www.youtube.com/watch?v=aLxZF_EWaLE.

Solzhenitsyn, Aleksandr. 1974. *The Gulag Archipelago 1918–56*. London: Collins/Fontana, 1974.

———. 1974. "Live Not By Lies." Reprint. *Index on Censorship* 33 (2004): 203-207.

———. 1974. "Live Not By Lies." Translated by Yermolai Solzhenitsyn. 1974. Reprint, The Aleksandr Solzhenitsyn Center, 2006. https://www.solzhenitsyncenter.org/live-not-by-lies.

———. 1983. "Aleksandr Solzhenitsyn's 'Men Have Forgotten God' Speech." *National Review*. July 22, 1983. https://www.nationalreview.com/2018/12/aleksandr-solzhenitsyn-men-have-forgotten-god-speech/.

Sowell, Thomas. 2002. *The Quest for Cosmic Justice*. New York: Free Press, 2002.

———. 2004. "War on Poverty Revisited by Thomas Sowell." *Capitalism Magazine*. August 17, 2004. https://www.capitalismmagazine.com/2004/08/war-on-poverty-revisited/.

———. 2018. "Thomas Sowell on the Myths of Economic Inequality." Hoover Institution. December 3, 2018. YouTube video. https://www.youtube.com/watch?v=mS5WYp5xmvI.

———. 2019. *Discrimination and Disparities*. London: Hachette UK, 2019.

———. n.d. "Thomas Sowell Quotes." BrainyQuote.Com. Accessed August 26, 2023b. https://www.brainyquote.com/quotes/thomas_sowell_440803.

Spratt, David, and Ian Dunlop. "Existential Climate-Related Security Risk: A Scenario Approach." *National Centre for Climate Restoration (Breakthrough)*, May 2019.

Steger, Michael F, Patricia Frazier, Shigehiro Oishi, and Matthew Kaler. "The Meaning in Life Questionnaire: Assessing the Presence of and Search for Meaning in Life." *Journal of Counseling Psychology* 53, no. 1 (2006): 80–93.

Stoet, Gijsbert, and David C Geary. "The Gender-Equality Paradox in Science, Technology, Engineering, and Mathematics Education." *Psychological Science* 29, no. 4 (2018): 581–93.

"Straw Man." Wikipedia. n.d. Accessed December 16, 2023. https://en.wikipedia.org/wiki/Straw_man.

"Struggle Session." Wikipedia. n.d. Accessed August 15, 2023. https://en.wikipedia.org/wiki/Struggle_session.

Subramanian, Anuradhaa, Krishnarajah Nirantharakumar, Sarah Hughes, Puja Myles, Tim Williams, Krishna M Gokhale, Tom Taverner, et al. "Symptoms and Risk Factors for Long COVID in Non-Hospitalized Adults." *Nature Medicine* 28, no. 8 (2022): 1706–14.

Sudre, Carole H., Benjamin Murray, Thomas Varsavsky, Mark S. Graham, Rose S. Penfold, Ruth C. Bowyer, Joan Capdevila Pujol, et al. "Attributes and Predictors of Long COVID." *Nature Medicine* 27, no. 4 (2021): 626–31.

Taleb, Nassim Nicholas. *Antifragile: Things That Gain from Disorder*. Vol. 3. New York: Random House, 2012.

"Thoughtcrime." Wikipedia. n.d. Accessed August 17, 2023. https://en.wikipedia.org/wiki/Thoughtcrime.

Tsampasian, Vasiliki, Hussein Elghazaly, Rahul Chattopadhyay, Maciej Debski, Thin Kyi Phyu Naing, Pankaj Garg, Allan Clark, Eleana Ntatsaki, and Vassilios S. Vassiliou. "Risk Factors Associated with Post-COVID-19 Condition: A Systematic Review and Meta-Analysis." *JAMA Internal Medicine* 183, no. 6 (2023): 566-580. https://doi.org/10.1001/jamainternmed.2023.0750.

Tupy, Marian. "'Climate Activism Is a Religion' - Marian Tupy." Triggernometry. October 19, 2022. YouTube video. https://www.youtube.com/watch?v=n1Ph2eCoi8M&t=2518s.

Turgenev, Ivan. *Fathers and Sons*. 1862. Reprint, Oxford, UK: Oxford Paperbacks, 2008.

Turner, Ted, and Barbara Pyle, dirs. *Captain Planet and the Planeteers*. 1990; United States: TBS.

Tzu, Lao. *Tao Te Ching*. Translated by James Legge. Scotts Valley, CA: CreateSpace, 2017.

UN News. 2012. "Global Partnership Key to Achieving Millennium Development Goals by 2015 – UN Report." UN News. July 2, 2012. https://news.un.org/en/story/2012/07/414572.

UN Press. "Chernobyl: The True Scale of the Accident." United Nations. September 6, 2005. https://press.un.org/en/2005/dev2539.doc.htm.

United States Nuclear Regulatory Commission. "Backgrounder on the Three Mile Island Accident." United States Nuclear Regulatory Commission. April 2022. https://www.nrc.gov/reading-rm/doc-collections/fact-sheets/3mile-isle.html.

UNSCEAR. "Sources of Ionizing Radiation: UNSCEAR 2008 Report, Volume 1." UNSCEAR, 2008. https://www.unscear.org/unscear/en/publications/2008_1.html.

Van Maren, Jonathon. "Family Policy: Investing in Hungary's Future." The American Conservative. May 14, 2021. https://www.theamericanconservative.com/family-policy-investing-in-hungarys-future/.

Verbeke, Rein, Ine Lentacker, Stefaan C. De Smedt, and Heleen Dewitte. "The Dawn of MRNA Vaccines: The COVID-19 Case." *Journal of Controlled Release* 333 (2021): 511–20.

Vervaeke, John, Christopher Mastropietro, and Filip Miscevic. *Zombies in Western Culture: A Twenty-First Century Crisis*. Cambridge, UK: Open Book Publishers, 2017.

"Victimhood." *Merriam-Webster*. n.d. Accessed August 15, 2023. https://www.merriam-webster.com/dictionary/victimhood.

Victims of Communism Memorial Foundation. "U.S. Attitudes Toward Socialism, Communism, and Collectivism." YouGov, October 2020.

Voss, Chris, and Tahl Raz. *Never Split the Difference: Negotiating as If Your Life Depended on It*. New York: Random House, 2016.

Watts, Jonathan S. *When a Billion Chinese Jump: How China Will Save Mankind—or Destroy It*. New York: Simon and Schuster, 2010.

Weiner, David, dir. *Brave New World.* 2020; United States: Peacock.

Weinstein, Bret, Heather Heying, and Jordan Peterson. "Evolution and the Challenges of Modern Life | Bret Weinstein and Heather Heying | EP 216." Jordan B. Peterson. January 10, 2022. YouTube video. https://www.youtube.com/watch?v=jKh0n i7HlNw.

Weiss, Bari, and Jordan Peterson. "Journalist or Heretic? | Bari Weiss | EP 175." Jordan B. Peterson. June 10, 2021. YouTube video. https://www.youtube.com/watch?v= tFTA9MJZ4KY&t=7842s.

West, Thomas G. "Poverty and Welfare in the American Founding." Heritage Foundation *First Principles*, no. 53 (2015). http://report.heritage.org/fp53.

"What Is to Be Done? (Novel)." Wikipedia. n.d. Accessed August 14, 2023. https://en.wikipedia.org/wiki/What_Is_to_Be_Done% 3F_(novel).

"White Guilt." Dictionary.Com. n.d. Accessed August 15, 2023. https://www.dictionary .com/browse/white-guilt.

Wilford, Denette. "Left-Wing Extremism and Psychopathic Tendencies Go Hand in Hand: Study." *Toronto Sun*. June 1, 2023. https://torontosun.com/news/world/left-wing-extremism-and-psychopathic-tendencies-go-hand-in-hand-study.

Wilson Center. "Doctrine of Hamas." Wilson Center. October 20, 2023. https://www.wilsoncenter.org/article/doctrine-hamas.

"Wolf Warrior Diplomacy." Wikipedia. n.d. Accessed August 17, 2023. https://en.wikipedia.org/wiki/Wolf_warrior_diplomacy.

Woollacott, Emma. "Electric Cars: What Will Happen to All the Dead Batteries?." BBC News. April 27, 2021. https://www.bbc.co.uk/news/business-56574779.

worker. *Lenin Fist*. Image. Openclipart. July 11, 2011. https://openclipart.org/detail/150853/lenin-fist#google_vignette.

World Bank. "PovcalNet." World Bank, February 2019. Archived March 3, 2022, at the Wayback Machine. https://web.archive.org/web/20220303173031mp_/http://iresearch.worldbank.org/PovcalNet/.

WHO. "Depression." WHO. n.d. Accessed August 12, 2023. https://www.who.int/health-topics/depression#tab=tab_1.

Wulfsohn, Joseph. "NYT Magazine Reporter Suggests Destroying Property 'Is Not Violence.'" Fox News, June 3, 2020. https://www.foxnews.com/media/nyt-magazine-nikole-hannah-jones-destroying-property-not-violence.

Xie, Yan, and Ziyad Al-Aly. "Risks and Burdens of Incident Diabetes in Long COVID: A Cohort Study." *The Lancet Diabetes & Endocrinology* 10, no. 5 (2022): 311–21.

Xie, Yan, Evan Xu, and Ziyad Al-Aly. "Risks of Mental Health Outcomes in People with Covid-19: Cohort Study." *BMJ* 376 (2022). https://doi.org/10.1136/bmj-2021-068993.

Xie, Yan, Evan Xu, Benjamin Bowe, and Ziyad Al-Aly. "Long-Term Cardiovascular Outcomes of COVID-19." *Nature Medicine* 28, no 3 (2022): 583–90.

York Region District School Board. "Part 2: The Strategy; Dismantling Anti-Black Racism Strategy: Creating Anti-Racist and Black-Affirming Learning and Working Environments." 2021. https://www2.yrdsb.ca/sites/default/files/2021-03/ABR-STRATEGY-Part2.pdf.

Yusuf, Hamza, and Jordan Peterson. "What We Can All Learn from Islam & the Quran | Hamza Yusuf | EP 255." Jordan B. Peterson. May 23, 2022. YouTube video. https://www.youtube.com/watch?v=x7ZlXD7COMU&t=41s.

Zeng, Ginger Qinghong, Xue-Zhen Xiao, Yang Wang, and Chun-Yu Tse. "Belief in Biological Origin of Race (Racial Essentialism) Increases Sensitivities to Cultural Category Changes Measured by ERP Mismatch Negativity (MMN)." *Scientific Reports* 12, no. 1 (2022): 4400.

ENDNOTES

1 Humans are not only consumers but also producers. The Simon Abundance Index aims to quantify the relationship between population growth and resource abundance. For example, every 1 percent increase in the population corresponds to an increase in personal resource abundance of 2.69 percent and increase in population resource abundance of 5.8 percent (Pooley and Tupy 2022).

2 There is no consensus-based definition of the radical left. The closest approximation I have thus far derived is those who believe in equal outcome over equal opportunity and who believe that people who disagree with them should be silenced.

3 The concept of an indefinable and incomprehensible ultimate principle is a theme in both Western and Eastern traditions. In the Bible, God instructs Moses not to look directly at him in the burning bush (Exodus 33:20–23). Similarly, the Tao Te Ching says, "The Tao that can be trodden is not the enduring and unchanging Tao. The name that can be named is not the enduring and unchanging name" (Lao Tzu 2017).

4 Perhaps Raskolnikov inspired Dexter in the hit 2006–2013 TV series by the same name. The premise is exactly the same. Both characters have a code for which murders are justifiable. I would disagree with how relatively psychologically stable Dexter appears, as I'm sure Dostoevsky would, but it made for an incredible show!

5 The word *fascism* is derived from the Italian word *fascio*, which means bundle of rods. It came to symbolize strength through unity ("Fascio" n.d.). Fascism's origins are, oddly enough, from Marxist philosopher Giovanni Gentile ("Fascism" n.d.).

6 Karl Marx's famous quote, that religion is the opioid of the masses, seems laughable these days ([1844] 1970). Opioids are the opioids of the masses.

7 Tony Robbins formally lists six core human needs—besides certainty and uncertainty/variety, the rest are significance, love/connection, growth, and contribution (Robbins 2016).

8 The Abraham Accords are a series of agreements between Israel and multiple Muslim countries whereby Israel's sovereignty is recognized, and there are now bilateral normalized relations and trade deals. This is after decades of Arab-Israeli conflict. These agreements were brokered by the US under Trump, with his son-in-law, Jared Kushner, playing a key role ("Abraham Accords" n.d.)

9 Moreover, alcohol and marijuana use levels skyrocketed during the pandemic (Roberts et al. 2021; Imtiaz et al. 2021). These are further indicators of decreased societal vibration.

10 How much meaning do you have in your life, and how much are you searching for it? Take the Meaning in Life Questionnaire. It was derived and validated by psychologist Michael Steger and his team (Steger et al. 2006).

11 Ice hockey is probably Canada's only domain not accompanied by our renowned humility; instead, we are full of bravado!

12 In his duel with his former mentor after Anakin falls to the dark side, Anakin exclaims, "If you're not with me, then you're my enemy." Obi-Wan Kenobi, replies, "Only a Sith deals in absolutes" (Lucas 2005).

13 You can only have two of the following three for your healthcare system—free, fast, and high quality. Pick your two. Politicians like to sell us on the idea of all three, which is completely unrealistic.

14 In Maoist struggle sessions, "'class enemies' were publicly humiliated, accused, beaten, and tortured . . . Children were manipulated into exposing their teachers and even parents. Scripts were prearranged by Maoists to incite crowd support. The aim was to instill a crusading spirit among the crowd to promote Maoist thought reform" ("Struggle Session" n.d.). North Korean escapee Yeonmi Park gives us a more modern example, as she escaped in 2007. She describes regular self-criticism meetings, which were essentially public confessions, held by the state to keep account of everyone's activities. These were organized around student and work units. Students would report to their class friends and workers to their offices. When it was your turn to stand up in front of the group, Park says you might start

with something like "This week, I was too spoiled and not thankful enough for my benevolent Dear Leader's eternal and unconditional love." To this Park would add, "I had not worked diligently enough to fulfill the mission that the party ordered us to do, or did not study hard enough, or did not love my comrades enough . . . Since then, our Dear Leader has forgiven me because of his benevolent, gracious leadership. I thank him, and I will do better next week." After your confession, it was time to criticize others (Park and Vollers 2016).

15 For more detail, see my opinion editorial "The ever-expanding goalposts of euthanasia in Canada," *Toronto Sun*, July 18, 2022.

16 Article 13 of the original 1988 Hamas Charter states, "Initiatives, and so-called peaceful solutions and international conferences, are in contradiction to the principles of the Islamic Resistance Movement" (Wilson Center 2023). The spiritual and ideological anti-Western, anti-establishment convergence evident here is eerily familiar.

17 The 1619 Project is a group that wants people to believe that America's history started in 1619 when the first slave arrived, rather than in 1776 with the Declaration of Independence.

18 In Genesis, God puts a mark on Cain in part so people know he's a pariah (Genesis 4:9–15).

19 Kafkatrap is a term coined by Eric Raymond in 2010. In Franz Kafka's *The Trial*, a man is accused of crimes that are never specified ([1925] 2015). Raymond's use of the term indicates that denial serves as evidence of guilt (Raymond n.d.).

20 In *Captain America* Volume 9 #28, arch enemy Red Skull, who is an actual Nazi, gives his view on "10 rules for life" and "chaos and order," thinly veiled allusions to Peterson's book *12 Rules for Life: an Antidote to Chaos* (Flood 2021).

21 See "Jordan Peterson debate on the gender pay gap, campus protests and postmodernism" (YouTube) for an example in which an ideologue simply cannot engage in real dialogue. In particular, see whether you can find the point where, for a moment, she is knocked out of her ideology. For that one moment, Peterson can speak with the real person. In a more formal debate on the topic of political correctness, ("Political correctness: a force for good? A Munk Debate," YouTube), Peterson's opponents liberally use ad hominem attacks (for example, "he's a mean White man"), instead of tackling his arguments. As expected, their lexicon is filled with emotion and flowery language.

22 The classical definition of racism is treating you as superior or inferior based on your race; that your racial characteristics define you (racial essentialism).

23 Because the frontier must always be just a little out of reach, if you think you're starting to get on board with diversity-equity-inclusivity, look for it to be superseded shortly by an even more elitist trinitarian slogan, ESG, which stands for environmental, social, and corporate governance.

24 Black Lives Matters co-founder Patrisse Cullors is under investigation for the purchase of a nearly $6 million house. She found this triggering and traumatic, and claims that these allegations are rooted in racism and sexism (O'Neill and Marsh 2021). In total, more than $37 million was spent on grants, real estate, and private flights (Shakhnazarova 2022). She has since resigned due to this controversy. The concern is that she used her proclaimed victimhood to secure donations, then used some of those funds for personal gains.

25 Jordan Peterson has a multidimensional approach to the definition of poverty. If you have an intimate relationship, a functional family, friends, a job/career, hobbies, some degree of civic engagement, mental and physical self-care, and overall sobriety, even if you aren't materially wealthy, how can you be considered poor? (J. Peterson and Lo 2022)

26 Sadism has since been discovered as a distinct psychological dimension, making it a dark tetrad (Međedović and Petrović 2015).

27 Atlas in Greek mythology is a titan who holds up the world.

28 For more detail, see my opinion editorial "Government, OMA deal is a Trojan horse," *Toronto Sun*, June 15, 2017.

29 However, in response to the German energy crisis in light of the war in Ukraine, Thunberg says, "I feel it's a mistake to close [German nuclear power plants] and focus on coal" (Hallam 2022). I really respect that she is able to see and articulate this nuance as she's been challenged over time.

30 Vaccine hesitancy is a technical term developed within the scientific community for those who weren't necessarily opposed to pre-pandemic vaccines but were skeptical of those developed for COVID-19.

31 There is a suggestion in a psychological study that the presence of meaning correlates well with life satisfaction, love, and joy, while guarding against depression and neuroticism. Meanwhile, the search for meaning correlates well with depres-

sion, neuroticism, sadness, and fear. It's almost as if the more meaning you have in life, the higher you vibrate in the levels of energy scale (Steger et al. 2006).

32 Note that the inquisitor is using Christianity as an ideology. He is a true Pharisee, using the idea of Jesus to further his own power. When Jesus actually returns, his faulty belief system comes crumbling down, so he has to sentence Jesus to death or risk exposing his fraud. For subscribers to replacement religions, when truth comes knocking, it is unbelievably difficult to open the door.

33 I define meta-solution as singular approaches that solve a set of problems.

34 Government promotion of societal fertility goes at least as far back as the Roman Empire. *Jus trium liberorum* was a Roman law granting special rights to fathers of at least three children ("Ius Trium Liberorum" n.d.).

35 Neville Chamberlain was the prime minster of the UK, who made famous the words "peace in our time" when cutting a deal with Hitler.

36 Ben Shapiro coined this term as a parlance taught at American universities and spoken only by those who have attended it, or adopted by those who aspire to membership in the new ruling class (Shapiro 2021a).

37 If you are really up for a challenge, try getting an opinion editorial published, or even writing a book. The process is not for the faint of heart, but it has done wonders for collecting and refining my own beliefs.

Printed in the USA
CPSIA information can be obtained
at www.ICGtesting.com
JSHW022109150824
68219JS00005B/289

9 781636 983837